LOOKING
AT LAW
SCHOOL

LOOKING AT LAW SCHOOL

A Student Guide from the
Society of American Law Teachers

THIRD REVISED EDITION

EDITED BY
Stephen Gillers

WITH A PREFACE BY
William J. Brennan, Jr.
Associate Justice
United States Supreme Court

A MERIDIAN BOOK

MERIDIAN
Published by the Penguin Group
Penguin Books USA Inc., 375 Hudson Street, New York, New York 10014, U.S.A.
Penguin Books Ltd, 27 Wrights Lane, London W8 5TZ, England
Penguin Books Australia Ltd, Ringwood, Victoria, Australia
Penguin Books Canada Ltd, 2801 John Street, Markham, Ontario, Canada L3R 1B4
Penguin Books (N.Z.) Ltd, 182-190 Wairau Road, Auckland 10, New Zealand

Penguin Books Ltd, Registered Offices: Harmondsworth, Middlesex, England

First published by Meridian, an imprint of Penguin Books USA Inc.

First Meridian Printing, October, 1977
First Meridian Printing (Third Revised Edition), August, 1990
10 9 8 7 6 5 4

REGISTERED TRADEMARK—MARCA REGISTRADA

LIBRARY OF CONGRESS CATALOGING IN PUBLICATION DATA
Main entry under title:

Looking at law school.

    1. Law—Study and teaching—United States. 2. Law students—United States.
3. Law schools—United States. I. Gillers, Stephen, 1943–   . II. Society of American
Law Teachers.
KF283.L66   1984   340'.07'1173   84-9897
ISBN 0-452-01049-7

Printed in the United States of America
Set in Times Roman
Designed by Julian Hamer

Contents

PART ONE

Deciding to Go to Law School

PART TWO

The Law School Experience

PART THREE

First-year and Required Courses

PART FOUR

Special Courses
and Course Selection

LOOKING
AT LAW
SCHOOL

Preface

William J. Brennan, Jr.
ASSOCIATE JUSTICE
UNITED STATES SUPREME COURT

Legal education has come a long way from the time before 1784, when would-be lawyers learned their profession by clerking and "reading the law" under the tutelage of an established lawyer. In 1784 a more formalized method came into existence in Litchfield, Connecticut, when Tapping Reeve opened the nation's first school of law. The school was a success from the start and by the time the one-room school house closed its doors, forty-nine years later, some one thousand students had passed through its fourteen-month curriculum. They were a distinguished group, including six who became cabinet officers, a Vice-President, over one hundred members of Congress, fourteen state governors, three Justices of the United States Supreme Court, and thirty-four members of the highest courts in their respective states. It has been said that "perhaps there has never been a professional school in America that produced more graduates of public distinction than Litchfield."

Now competent law schools proliferate throughout the country and *Looking at Law School* is in its third edition. Thousands aspire each year to be admitted to law school to formalize their training for the law. This book is an invaluable guide to what law school is all about.

Readers may ask, "Why should I select law for a career?" There are several reasons, but one that particularly comes to mind. Only by preserving, enriching, and strengthening the Rule of Law can this nation continue to be the world's foremost commonwealth respecting and furthering the dignity of every human being in it.

Law schools have a major role in the job of thinking through just what it is, to achieve our goals, we must inculcate about the Rule of Law and the Bill of Rights.

Surely we want to achieve some understanding of the text of the first ten amendments. But law schools have a major responsibility for teaching the precarious quality of those words—by pointing out, for example, that the bare words of the Bill of Rights of the Soviet Constitution seem perhaps even more generous than our own. If the goal of freedom for every individual is to be realized, the contemporary world requires a breadth of outlook and a degree of sensitivity unlike any required in the previous history of mankind. We therefore must also teach something about the conflicts in values that often make the Bill of Rights much harder to apply than to recite.

The new and still changing role of the United States in world affairs is a fact of life in our society, and we must be prepared to meet the responsibility it entails. To do so we must, in addition to the more obvious aspects of international relations, become more sensitive to the many diverse cultures that reflect the myriad manifestations of the human spirit. With the multiplication of new nations, those varying sets of beliefs and values and instinctive habits of behavior become more critical, and an understanding of them becomes central to the development of constructive attitudes and wise policy. No culture is static, least of all our own. To understand ourselves we must be able to understand both how we differ in outlook and value systems from other peoples, and how our own complex network of social, economic, political, and intellectual factors evolved from the interaction of forces within our society and forces acting from without.

Law school training can (and most law schools do) provide a concept of law that is both realistic and compassionate, both durable and flexible. Part of the educational job is to create a realization that law is not an end in itself, nor does it provide ends. It is preeminently a means to serve man's ends—both mediate and ultimate. The day is past when the law erected the Constitution into a barrier against social and economic reform, and at the same time watered down the guarantees of human rights and liberties into mere admonitions against government. Today constitutional interpretation leaves the people wide latitude to experiment with

social and economic reforms that further social justice. In the area
of human rights and liberties, courts are giving constitutional restraints on government more generous sweep to prevent oppression of the human spirit and erosion of human dignity.

Perhaps in no period of human history has the Rule of Law
loomed larger as the essential stabilizer of the complex organism
that society has become. In but a few decades, since the end of
World War II, the world and this nation have witnessed a remarkable transformation. The unity of the human family is becoming
more distinct on the horizon of human events. The gradual civilization of all people instead of the former civilization of only the
elite, the rise of mass education and mass media of communication, the formation of new thought structures due to scientific
advances and social evolution—all these phenomena hasten that
day. Our own nation has shrunk its distances to hours; its population is becoming primarily urban and suburban and religiously
pluralistic; its technology has spurred an economy capable of fan-
tastic prodigies of production; and we have become leader of a
world with a host of new countries that are ready to follow but also
quick to reject the path that we take. Our political, industrial,
agricultural, and cultural differences cannot stop the process which
is making us a more united nation.

Our society is committed to the constitutional idea of libertarian
dignity protected through law. Crises at hand and in prospect are
creating, and will create, more and more threats to the achievement of that ideal. It has become the business of all of us—not just
the responsibility of lawyers and judges—to protect fundamental
constitutional rights threatened today in ways not possibly envis-
aged by the Framers. And it is also the business of all of us to
teach respect for the responsibilities without which the rights are
meaningless. We are all destined to labor earnestly in the endeavor
to reconcile the complex realities of our time with the necessary
principles of a free people.

It is gratifying to see that the legal profession is ever more
conscious that the law cannot be isolated from the other social
sciences or be understood without them. The developing law,
rightly viewed as an increasingly effective tool of social engineering, draws more and more from other disciplines—each of which is
achieving greater perfection in the study of that part of the human

condition pertinent to its investigation of our complex social organism. This is essential if law is to be kept abreast of the changing mores of our society and brought into agreement with society's advancing insights and emerging needs. So lawyers more than ever are turning their minds to the knowledge and experience of other disciplines and, in particular, to those disciplines that investigate and report on the functioning and nature of society.

Lawyers and educators together ought then to be able effectively to teach that the genius of our Constitution resides not in any static meaning it may have had in a world that is dead and gone, but in its applicability and adaptability to current needs and problems. We need only remember the rapid changes of our lifetime when alarm is expressed that constitutional change is coming too fast and going too far. For in today's world what our constitutional fundamentals once meant to the wisdom of other times cannot be the full measure of their meaning to us and the vision of our time.

If we can reformulate the Rule of Law along these lines, then it offers us something that can and should be taught.

Introduction

Norman Dorsen

NEW YORK UNIVERSITY

When the first edition of this book appeared in 1977, it was already long overdue. Generations of students—in a world where a generation is three years—had endured the intimidating, if exhilarating, experience of studying to become lawyers. They had done so without an authoritative guide to law school—to opportunities and pitfalls, to courses and overall curriculum, and to ethical and emotional problems that are often ignored or misunderstood. The Society of American Law Teachers filled this gap by publishing a book that advised law students, and those considering law school, on how to cope with the perplexities and stresses of legal education.

Now a third edition of the book appears. The twin earthquakes of Vietnam and Watergate, which rocked all Americans and particularly the young, have faded from public consciousness. At the same time the unprecedented humanism of the Supreme Court under Earl Warren has been replaced by a cautious and conservative view of the Constitution as interpreted by the current majority of the Court. The ebullient social concern that once dominated the thinking of many students has been succeeded, among many, by cynicism and materialism. Law professors are rethinking legal education; many new ideas are afloat. Readers of this book will profit from the ferment reflected in its pages.

Above all, this is a practical book. At the outset Stephen Gillers forces readers to consider the possibility that law school may not be right for them. Common conceptions of the work and lives of lawyers are frequently wrong—lawyers are usually neither stars nor deep thinkers in the manner portrayed by the media. Lawyers almost always pursue the agenda of others, the clients. Sometimes the work is interesting, sometimes dull; sometimes it is very well paid, more often it is not; sometimes there are the satisfactions of public service, usually these are absent. At a time when the legal profession continues to show signs of overcrowding, each person should ponder carefully whether a life in the law is indeed the right choice.

If the decision is to go forward, there are the inevitable questions of which law school to attend, and how to pay for it. The essays by Gerald Wilson and John Kramer provide a fund of information on these topics.

The second part of this book will, I believe, strike the nonlawyer with particular force. Everyone has heard of the dehumanizing tendencies of law school, of the strains and assaults on self-image and self-respect. Dr. Bernard Diamond, a psychiatrist who served for many years on the faculty of the University of California Law School at Berkeley, explores the psychological problems of law students. Diamond contrasts the challenge and opportunities of law schools with the soaring tension level induced by competition for grades and prestigious employment. It is not surprising that more and more law schools provide counseling and psychotherapeutic services to students; it is surprising (and heartening) that Diamond considers law students to be a "well-adjusted group who adapt remarkably well to what at times is an almost intolerable stress."

Stress may be greatest for female students, gay and lesbian students, and members of racial minorities. Students in these groups will profit from the essays by Carole Goldberg-Ambrose, Rhonda R. Rivera and Robert L. Eblin, and Charles Lawrence, all of whom display uncommon insight and empathy in discussing these issues.

Sylvia Law sets her sights at a more general level. In what is the most frankly political chapter in the book, she focuses on the disparities of wealth and power in American society. These goals motivate people to go to law school and also present a central challenge to our social and legal arrangements. Professor Law analyzes different approaches to law—formalism, realism, and Critical

Legal Studies—and tries to show how they affect legal education and a proper understanding of the law. She concludes that the legal profession and legal education often mystify rather than illuminate the understanding of social relations and increase rather than decrease perceptions of personal insecurity.

The heart of the book is Part Three, which concentrates on the first year of law school. Here we find descriptions and analyses of the six principal first-year courses, along with an overview of the first-year curriculum. In addition, there is a splendid chapter by James Boyd White on legal writing, its relation to substance and to self; he shows by precept and example that the stereotypical lawyer's prose—convoluted, verbose, and pompous—is neither inevitable nor effective in achieving the purposes of the written word.

The final part views legal education from broader perspectives. Robert Gorman provides guidance to students in planning a three-year course program; Geoffrey Hazard examines legal ethics, a subject of intellectual fascination and moral complexity; Gary Bellow examines the most important innovation in legal education in recent decades: clinical studies, which is emerging as a full partner in the pedagogical process; and Anita Allen discusses the vital role, often unrecognized or unacknowledged, that legal philosophy plays in the intellectual life of American law schools.

Some aspects of legal education are not easily pigeonholed but nevertheless profoundly affect the experience of students. Three of these are the pervasive uncertainty of the law, the place of the classroom in the learning process, and graded examinations.

One of America's greatest judges, Benjamin Cardozo, commented on the uncertainty:

> I was much troubled in spirit, in my first years on the bench, to find how trackless was the ocean on which I had embarked. I sought for certainty. I was oppressed and disheartened when I found that the quest for it was futile. I was trying to reach land, the solid land of fixed and settled rules, the paradise of a justice that would declare itself by tokens plainer and more commanding than its pale and glimmering reflections in my own vacillating mind and conscience.

Judge Cardozo sought certainty. Most law students also seek certainty. But they will not find it. They will be unhappy about that, and often they will resent professors who expose the futility of the search. But this process is healthy; it helps the student to recognize that the law is unstable because it is always changing, and it is always changing because society changes. According to Roscoe Pound, the dean of Harvard Law School for many years, a typical rule of law lasts but one generation. This doesn't mean law students shouldn't learn and assimilate rules; it means that simultaneously one must also appreciate that the rule is moving, sometimes visibly and sometimes more like a submerged glacier.

An important side effect of recognizing uncertainty in the law is that students are encouraged to seek the reasons for it and to understand when stability is to be preferred and when movement. This complex subject is known to lawyers as the doctrine of *stare decisis*, which does not merely encompass, as is often imagined, its literal meaning—"let the decision stand"—but rather refers to both movement and stability in the law. When and why one is to be preferred is ordinarily not taught in a systematic way in law school, but it is one of the most important parts of a sophisticated legal education.

I turn now to the classroom, the focal point of a legal education. Much important learning takes place outside the class—in solitary study, in small discussion groups, and, after the first year, in work on law journals and other extracurricular activities. But the classroom is where most learning is conveyed: factual and doctrinal analysis, legal theory, linguistic facility, and the rudiments of tactics.

The instructor bears a major responsibility for making the classroom work right. He or she must be knowledgeable, prepared, stimulating, and fair. All of us fall short to some degree in meeting these standards, but if an instructor falls significantly below the line, students are cheated. Professors therefore should be evaluated. But I suggest that students should be tentative in their judgments, especially at the outset. Sometimes professors are popular because they "lay out the law" clearly but without regard for complexities. Others are entertaining but without substantive depth and eventually that will wear thin. Instructors who present the law in a more subtle, even if initially less accessible, way are often better teachers because they penetrate problems more deeply and encourage thorough class preparation and hard thinking. In the long run the elusive professor may best enhance a student's ability to understand and analyze difficult problems.

At the same time a student must cooperate if the classroom experience is to work. Preparation is essential; it is almost impossible to learn more than superficially if assigned reading is not completed before class. In addition, the student must participate. By this I do not refer merely to a student's oral participation when intermittently called on or as a volunteer. Such participation is valuable to the student, and it helps to assure a stimulating, lively class for the benefit of all. But more important is a student's "silent participation"—thinking hard in class when a question is asked and answered. Is the question unclear or tangential, or the answer wrong or incomplete? What alternative responses are possible? What new questions does the answer raise? How does the assigned reading fit it? Earlier reading and discussion? The degree to which you think along with class discussion is the degree to which you are participating. Silent participation is a crucial part of learning because it means that your mind is in gear and your ideas engaged by the minds of other students. You are simultaneously testing yourself and stretching your capacities.

Let us also consider the consequences of a failure to prepare for class. A telling analogy is the difference between a well-schooled student of music and someone who is unaware of the implications and subtleties of theme, counterpoint, rhythm, and meter. The latter will "enjoy the music," but the former will have far greater understanding of what she is hearing. Someone reading a novel that refers to the Bible or to Greek myths and who is unaware of these sources may enjoy the story but surely will not appreciate its richness or nuance. Similarly, a law student who reads an assignment and has reflected on it will understand what is happening in class far more clearly. It is not easy to understand a problem if you haven't read or don't remember a point made in an assigned opinion, and often you won't even know you do not understand.

The third subject that I will discuss here is examinations. Examinations are a threat, an opportunity, and a part of the learning process. Few people like to be judged. No one likes to appear before an examining committee or to be tested under the rigorous conditions of law school. But written examinations exist in almost all law schools, and grades are important, especially first-year grades.

Some law professors would probably abolish examinations, thinking that they do not test very much and create anxiety out of proportion to their benefit. I agree that grades have frequently been abused by inappropriate tests and are overrated in the job market in comparison with other forms of student evaluation. Relevant qualities of character and mind are ignored by the automatic use of grades as a basis for appraising an individual.

But I do not think that examinations should be abolished; they are useful in several respects. First, they tell people how they are doing: those who are doing well that they are on the right track; those in the middle of the class that they should work harder or adjust their study habits; and those at the bottom that they ought to rethink their situation and even consider whether law is right for them. Former Dean Robert Pitofsky of Georgetown Law School has put the point strongly: "Any judge, practicing lawyer, or even client knows that some people are better lawyers than others, and it would be absurd for law schools to participate in an attempt to conceal that fact."

A second value of examinations is the preparation they require; this is an important part of the learning process. Assimilating the material from an entire course and forcing yourself to work under tense conditions, the way lawyers often work, is a powerful educational experience. Even the process of anticipating the kind of examination that will be given—"psyching out" the professor—is analogous to assessments that litigators and negotiators regularly make of judges or adversaries.

Finally, grades in law school lead to opportunities for a first job. People at the top of their class, no matter how improvised their background, can be clerks to judges, "honor" participants in government agencies, associates at respected law firms—largely on the basis of performance. To quote Robert Pitofsky again:

> Take away grades and this "social elevator" in American society will largely disappear. Opportunities will then come more easily do young people with rich parents or powerful uncles—a system that hardly seems an improvement.

This does not mean that Professor Pitofsky or I think that grades are the *only* reliable predictor of which students will become the better lawyers. Nor does it mean that the form and reliability of examinations cannot be improved. Nothing of the sort. But examinations that are intelligently prepared and scrupulously graded do perform several positive functions in legal education.

Anyone who enters law school now will not only embark on a new career—he or she will also enter a field in which there is ferment and excitement. Justice Oliver Wendell Holmes said many years ago that "a man may live greatly in the law as well as elsewhere; that there as well as elsewhere his thought may find its unity in an infinite perspective."

One academic recently asserted that "legal education and legal scholarship is at a standstill," and others have assailed legal education at a time, paradoxically, when law schools are having great success in attracting and training students. I think these criticisms are largely wrong. There is much to improve in the way we train lawyers, but there has also been much progress and new thinking. Student quality has never been higher. Teaching and research are more varied than ever. Even the most demanding law student will have plenty of intellectual challenge.

Attending law school can be a heady business. In an astonishingly brief period a neophyte can be transformed into a professional, often with offers of lucrative jobs or prestigious judicial clerkships as preludes to careers combining fortune, security, public influence, and even fame. While social mobility is among the attractions of the profession, a consequence is fierce competitiveness among law students. This striving is widely deplored, but it is inevitable; there are hungry law students, like hungry ball players, and energy and desire are important to results.

But competition can get out of hand and impair personal relationships. It can also lead students to ignore, in a quest for conventional success, ethical norms that should guide every decent person. Power and status are not everything.

You must keep hold of yourself, not just try to get ahead, not just try to be better than the next person, and not let the Watergate notion—that nothing counts but winning—pervade your attitudes and objectives. Competition is healthy, and achievement is admirable as well as satisfying. But also important are your values, the relationships you develop with others, and personal integrity.

PART ONE

Deciding to Go to Law School

CHAPTER 1

Making the Decision to Go to Law School

Stephen Gillers
NEW YORK UNIVERSITY

You think law school's for you? Join the crowd.

In 1950, there were about 220,000 lawyers in the United States. By 1960, that number had jumped to 285,000, then to 355,000 ten years later, to 542,000 in 1980, and to more than 800,000 today. The American Bar Association predicts an American lawyer population of 930,000 in 1995. At this rate the profession will top one million by the end of the century.

The nation's population is also growing, but not as fast. In 1960, there were 627 Americans for each lawyer. The ratio was 572 to 1 ten years later, and 418 to 1 in 1980. Today there are 310 Americans per lawyer. A ratio of 279 to 1 is predicted for 1995.

As you might expect, the number of people entering law school and the number of law schools have also increased. In 1963, nearly 21,000 students entered the first year at 135 accredited law schools. A dozen years later, 39,000 students entered 163 accredited law schools. In 1988, 175 accredited law schools received nearly 43,000 new students. The number of first law degrees awarded by accredited schools nearly quadrupled in the quarter century from 1964 to 1989, jumping from about 9,600 to 35,700.

How do we explain the astonishing popularity of law? What are the reasons to choose legal training and then, predictably but not necessarily, a career in law? What are the reasons not to do so? What in your view do lawyers actually do? Where did you get your ideas?

Like most law school applicants or new law students, you proba-

3

bly have a favorable image of legal work. It may have been drawn from the press and popular culture. Or perhaps a relative or family friend is a lawyer, enjoys the work, and tells interesting stories about it. Maybe your interest in law school was sparked because prelaw or other advisers told you that skills you revealed in college or on a job would make you a good lawyer. The income, status, and prominence that lawyers enjoy—and the attention the law itself receives—are further lures to many. So is the expectation that it is possible through law to foster change that will make the world more just and fair.

I do not presume to tell whether a particular reason for attending law school is "good" or "bad." But many law students and law school aspirants partly misconceive what it means to be a lawyer—to spend a life doing the work of a lawyer. Still others may lack a firm concept of the work. This chapter, among others in the book, is directed at that gap.

Unless a close relative or friend is a lawyer or one has worked in a law office for some time—and perhaps not even then—how is a law student or law school applicant likely to have acquired a sense of what lawyers do, of what he or she will do as a lawyer? Two sources of information are our culture and the classroom.

Let us distinguish here between work and role, between what lawyers "do" and what lawyers "are." Popular presentations of lawyers encompass mainly their roles—he fought for justice, she made the government act honorably, he saved an innocent man, she closed down a large industrial polluter—and portray their work—what they do day-to-day—only incidentally. Presentations of the work, when it occurs in books, on stage, in films, on television, or in the press, whether presented as fiction or fact, are dramatic. They emphasize the glamour and ignore the routine. It has become a cliché to say that Perry Mason is atypical, in fact apocryphal. But Perry Mason is too easy to write off. We did not give up all our illusions the day we stopped believing in Santa Claus and the Tooth Fairy. Neither does our recognition that Perry Mason is fantasy mean we have become hard-nosed realists about the legal profession. Every tense TV trial scene, every play or movie, such as *Jagged Edge, The Verdict, Kramer vs. Kramer, Witness for the Prosecution, The Caine Mutiny,* and *Twelve Angry Men*; every book or newspaper account of a momentous trial, such as those of John Hinckley, Jr., Claus von Bulow, Oliver North, Bernhard Goetz, Julius and Ethel Rosenberg, Jean Harris, Sacco and Vanzetti, Wayne Williams, or Dr. Spock; every trial lawyer's selected memories of his life in court, such as Louis Nizer's *My Life in Court*, Edward Bennett Williams's *One Man's Freedom*, Alan Dershowitz's *The Best Defense*, Gerry Spence's *Gunning for Justice*, F. Lee Bailey's *The Defense Never Rests*; every TV series about the adventures of lawyers (*L.A. Law, The Storefront Lawyers, The Associates, the Defenders*) or law students (*The Paper Chase*) creates an image of lawyers and their work that must impress anyone not familiar with the more routine daily tasks of practicing lawyers.

The focus of the press's interest in law is primarily on the decisions of courts, especially the U.S. Supreme Court. In our society many critical decisions of governance are made by courts, and by the Supreme Court especially. Supreme Court and lower-court opinions are repeatedly issued on such controversial issues as school prayer, abortion, capital punishment, free speech, affirmative action, the environment, the right to die, busing, sex discrimination, and police practices. These decisions, covering the front pages of newspapers and announced on national television, promote the view that the institutions of the law are at the frontier of social progress, that they are therefore exciting places to be, and that those at the helms of these institutions—lawyers—must do exciting work.

This attention to glamorous lawyers, to famous trials, and to controversial court decisions may mislead an unsuspecting observer about the work of a lawyer. Ignored are the uneventful, daily labors of uncelebrated lawyers pursuing the mundane goals of anonymous clients through the intellectually unchallenging, often perfunctory skills with which most lawyers earn a living most of the time. The media is understandably unconcerned with the ordinary. The lawyer, even the law itself, is pursued and presented as a "star."

The conception of the lawyer as star, unrealistic as it may be, is a strong and persistent one, even among lawyers themselves. Think about whether part of your own attraction to law school and a legal career is not influenced by this flashy, if remote, image. How will you feel if most of your work is routine and of consequence to few but your clients? These realizations will give you more realistic expectations of where your choice may lead.

Another popular conception of lawyers is of the lawyer as intellectual, as a thinker, a person whose professional life is spent dealing in ideas. Law students are encouraged in this view by the nature of legal education. The law school classroom, traditional or clinical, is a place of ideas and, properly so, a place that celebrates the life of the mind and rewards intellectual achievement. Lawyers and law teachers often say that in law school a student is taught to "think like a lawyer."

The law teacher proposes to question the legal rule—the statute, constitutional construction, court decision—to test its implications and examine whether it follows from the reasons advanced. Drawing from work in philosophy, economics, the social and natural sciences, even literary criticism, attendant always to reason and disdainful of sloppy thinking, law teachers and law students discuss, sometimes heatedly, how through law and legal institutions society ought to treat particular cases. Academic insularity affords law students and law faculty the chance to engage in free-roaming criticism.

Although the image of lawyer as critical thinker is not as remote as the one of lawyer as star, it is likewise not representative of what most lawyers do most of the time. In the law school classroom there is the luxury to contemplate the intellectual universe and the leisure to call upon the learning of other disciplines in search of the most nearly perfect rule. The practicing lawyer rarely enjoys that excitement. The rule is the rule. Whether representing a client in litigation, preparing a contract, drafting a trust instrument, or handling a house closing, the practicing lawyer works on the assumption that the law is not about to change. The classroom's intellectual freedom yields to the exigencies of servicing clients.

Doesn't the informed application of fixed rules also draw on the lawyer's intellectual powers? It can for some, but usually in a way, and to an extent, far less rigorous than encountered in the classroom. For many others, legal practice will be largely mechanical, requiring little in the way of intellectual activity. Some may be pleased at this, preferring to make a living with (and doing better at) skills that depend more on personality than intellect, such as negotiating or seeking business. Others may be disappointed. You may not now be able to predict your own response, but you should know what to expect.

This is a good place to take note of another facet of lawyers' work, even the work of stars and thinkers. It is derivative work; it builds on or responds to the actions or wishes of others. Most star lawyers, for example, achieve that status because of the identity of their clients (rich, famous, controversial) or the nature of the subject on which they work (civil rights, consumer protection, free speech). Rarely is it anything special about the lawyers—his personality, her brilliance—that commands the public's interest. Other than Daniel Webster and Clarence Darrow, how many lawyers in American history can you name who are posthumously remembered for their legal brilliance or advocacy skills?

The work of the intellectual lawyer is derivative in another way. He or she generally builds on the learning of thinkers in other fields and tries to use this knowledge in the articulation and application of legal rules. This is, to be sure, important work. Professor Charles Fried, a former U.S. Solicitor General who teaches at Harvard Law School, has written that the philosopher's abstractions would be of little use unless lawyers enabled us to bring them to bear on the concrete events of daily life. In this view the lawyer's task is to apply the learning of others (philosophers, economists, social scientists), just as a doctor applies the learning of research biologists. The learning, however, is not the lawyer's. His or her specialty is the application. Lately a good many law teachers and some lawyers have sought expertise in a second discipline—and an increasing number of scholars from other fields are attending or teaching at law schools—leading to a group of men and women educated not only in the means of applying a rule but also in its experiential or theoretical justification.

In an even more apparent way, the professional life of the ordinary practitioner is derivative. He or she is paid to pursue the goals of a client, whether a large company or a welfare recipient. The lawyer usually deals in means—how to use the law to achieve the client's goals—not in ends, not in selecting the goals themselves or, often, not even in the broad strategies to reach them. Of course, lawyers have the opportunity to influence a client's choice of goals, depending on the parties and their relationship. But the final decision belongs to the client. The lawyer's job is to do the job.

Financial security is a reason that may lead students to pick a legal career. For the most part lawyers earn a good living compared to people in other callings. Financial security should not be the only reason to study law, of course; there must be other attractions, but it is certainly something to consider.

Becoming a lawyer is an unlikely route to great wealth, however. Lawyers sell their time or the time of other lawyers they employ and supervise. Even at high hourly rates there are only so many productive hours in a week or year. Lawyers rarely earn as much as prominent doctors and substantially less than successful stockbrokers, investment bankers, or business executives. Indeed, some lawyers eventually find their way into business, as principals or investors, in search of monetary rewards many times greater than accrue in practice.

True, law graduates probably earn more in their first jobs than friends in other fields. In 1990, starting lawyers at some large New York City firms earned more than $80,000, though they worked hard for it. (This is up about $30,000 from the starting salary only five years earlier.) New lawyers in other large cities get comparable salaries. But there are few of these prestigious jobs nationwide, compared with the 40,000 new lawyers annually, and they tend to go to graduates of the twenty top schools or to the best students at less prestigious ones. Nevertheless, the more numerous jobs a tier or two down (and even ones below that) are also attractive, compared to the opportunities available to graduates in other fields.

A discussion of jobs and income must touch on three current trends that might affect both. First is the stunning increase in the number of lawyers. Jobs and clients are not increasing as quickly as the lawyer population. This means more competition among lawyers. (I recall a *New Yorker* cartoon showing a woman speaking to a man at a cocktail party. She is saying: "What do you mean, how do I know you're a lawyer? Everyone's a lawyer.") Nobody knows exactly how this surge in the number of lawyers will dislocate members of the profession—young lawyers or established ones, specialists and generalists—or affect the nation. It is an astonishing trend, one that you need to consider in deciding whether to pursue a legal career. At the very least the trend means that more lawyers than ever before will be competing for the same client dollar. (One lesson may be that if you do go to law school, you should consider specializing in a particularly uncrowded area of the law.)

A second trend is the rise of legal paraprofessionals, a field virtually nonexistent two decades ago. In one study lawyers were asked how many of their work tasks could be performed by a paraprofessional under their supervision. Many of the respondents, including lawyers doing highly sophisticated work at large firms, acknowledged that half or more of their tasks could be handled by a supervised paraprofessional. The rise in the number of paralegal workers is a reflection of this acknowledgment. It may suggest that much work now performed by lawyers, especially subordinates or lawyers who work on routine matters, will increasingly be done, less expensively but as effectively, by others. There is even discussion about allowing paralegals to take a less rigorous bar examination and be licensed to provide routine legal services on their own. As with the large increase in the number of lawyers, the competitive effect of such developments cannot be determined, but it may be significant.

A final trend is the rise of computers. In the last dozen years lawyers have benefited from this new technology. At the very least, word processing and artificial memory increase capacity for speed and volume. (Legal advertising has in turn given lawyers means to drum up the volume.) This, in turn, has led to lower prices for routine legal services and the rise of national and regional legal clinics. What effect will these developments have on the number of legal jobs? It might reduce them, or it might lead to new clients and new work that would not otherwise have been performed. In either event computerized legal services present little cerebral challenge to lawyers themselves, further eroding the intellectual pretensions of legal work. More speculative, but of potentially vast consequence, is the effort, already begun, to program computers to simulate legal reasoning. Although we cannot know where this effort will lead, it is happening today. It is not science fiction.

Status and prestige and the chance for membership in a learned profession are also motives for entering law school, not unlike the monetary one. Lawyers, despite criticism, do enjoy substantial respect and deference. Newly admitted members of the bar may experience their heightened position almost palpably the first few times they have occasion to introduce themselves as attorneys. As with money, it would be foolish to act solely on this incentive, but it is an incentive. Again, as with money, you should be mindful of the dilution in status that may accompany disproportionate growth on the "supply" side.

What about the fact that a lawyer's job is to help others—help protect their property or their liberty, help assert their rights, help get what is legally theirs? This is surely a worthy motive and one that must be encouraged. At the individual level, lawyers have the satisfaction of knowing that they can use their special learning to make life easier for their clients. On a grander scale, law students might anticipate that they will be able to use their knowledge to achieve social justice through broad structural reform.

American lawyers, unlike lawyers in nearly every other nation, are able to translate client representations into judicial decisions that force major (even massive) changes in our social and political institutions and affect the lives of thousands, even millions, including future generations. Think of the Supreme Court's decisions outlawing school segregation, recognizing a right to privacy that includes a right to choose abortion, granting criminal suspects a panoply of the due process rights, making it harder to impose the death penalty, and guaranteeing the right to speak freely even when others find the speaker's message repulsive. American courts have the power of judicial review, which enables them to invalidate decisions of other branches of government and makes cases like these possible. But remember that each of these cases required a lawyer willing to argue it. Lawyers act, judges react. One result of this aspect of the American judicial system is the growth of the public-interest-law movement which, although still relatively young (its modern roots go back less than forty years), has won much influence and attention. Public-interest lawyers practice in the areas of civil liberties and civil rights, consumer protection, environmental law, and sex and race discrimination, among others.

Whether a lawyer is trying to establish a constitutional principle that, if successful, will affect tens of thousands, or is simply representing a poor person in his or her fight with a city agency, the common denominator can be the personal satisfaction the lawyer may reap from the chance to help others. There is, however, a caveat here as well, an especially important one because the essays accompanying law school applications often identify, I think honestly, the chance to do justice by helping others as a strong reason for the student's choice of a legal career. Unfortunately for many, that chance might be hard to come by. To appreciate why, it is important to understand how and to whom legal services are provided.

Overwhelmingly, clients get legal help by buying it. Knowledge is a product lawyers sell. The client is generally free to choose the lawyer he or she wants, and the lawyer is generally free to accept or reject the client. The primary limitation on the amount of a lawyer's fee is competition from other lawyers. President Carter once got headlines by noting that under this system of laissez-faire distribution, 90 percent of the lawyers serve 10 percent of the people. Whether or not his percentages were accurate, the distribution of legal services is heavily skewed in favor of a small number of clients for two reasons.

First, a good deal of what lawyers are trained to do for people is help them protect or acquire property. Such standard legal skills as the formation of corporations, writing trust agreements, registering securities, merging companies, negotiating and preparing contracts, and giving tax advice all have as their goal the maximization of wealth. Law schools teach and law students want to learn these skills because they are desired by people with substantial property, or claims to it. These are people who are best able to pay for legal talent. Demand begets supply. But these clients are not likely to be the ones most law school applicants have in mind when they write about the chance to work for justice.

Second, where needier members of the society do require a lawyer—to fight the department of welfare, to protect constitutional rights, to resist an eviction, to get a divorce, to defend themselves against criminal charges, or to mount a class action against official policies—they will often be unable to afford one. If they are going to be represented at all, someone else must pay. Lawyers can work for free, of course, which in effect means the lawyer "pays" by absorbing the uncompensated time, and many lawyers are generous in giving free help. But unless a lawyer has independent wealth, he or she cannot do free work only. And many lawyers will give no time to the problems of the unrepresented. When a prestigious commission suggested that every American lawyer be required to do about fifty hours of free work each year for people in need, the idea was emphatically rejected by lawyers throughout the country.

In our society sources of funding enable lawyers to get paid to work for people who cannot afford them. In criminal cases the government will pay lawyers to do this job because the Constitution requires that indigent criminal defendants get free counsel. In civil cases the government sometimes pays lawyers to work for the poor and near poor, although the Constitution does not require it. To a lesser extent, foundations and other private contributors also provide money. But all these funds together are a small fraction of the tens of billions of dollars paying clients annually spend on American lawyers. Furthermore, the level of funding is always in doubt, as can be seen in the periodic battles over the continuation of the Legal Services Corporation. To understand how low the funding is, consider that even though there is one American lawyer for every 300 people in the United States, legal-services lawyers struggle to maintain a ratio of one poverty lawyer for every 5,000 people living below the poverty level.

What does this mean to the new lawyer who was in part impelled to enter the profession by a professed desire to give human service, to help? It means, at the very least, that the chance is small that he or she will be able to get a governmentally or privately funded job that will make it possible to work for the needy or to confront large issues of social injustice. If he or she gets such a job, there may be no assurance of future funding, and the salary will be half or a third of what classmates working for paying clients receive. As the new lawyer gets older and has added financial responsibilities, the widening income gap may prove unacceptable. Even at the start of a career, repayment of school loans may make a legal-aid or public-interest job impossible.

You might suppose that, whomever you represent, at the very least you can work for justice in the context of each particular representation. To some extent this is true. A lawyer can always advise a client that a particular tactic is unfair or that a particular goal is morally questionable, even if both are entirely legal. But the ultimate decision about what goals to pursue and whether a particular overall strategy will be used belongs to the client, not the lawyer. Indeed, many clients do not expect or want their lawyers to talk to them about fairness, and lawyers may refrain from doing so for fear that their clients will not consider them sufficiently "tough."

Aren't lawyers free to reject clients whose ends or tactics they find unpalatable? Yes, and sometimes—but not always—a lawyer may even be able to withdraw from an existing relationship with a client because it has become apparent that the lawyer's values and the client's values are at odds. But lawyers are in business to earn a living. There is a limit to how many clients a lawyer can turn away and remain in practice. And if the lawyer is an employee of a firm or works for a corporate or governmental body, freedom to refuse to do what the boss asks will be even more severely restricted.

Does this mean that if a lawyer accepts a representation, he or she may sometimes have to use tactics or pursue goals the lawyer believes are repugnant? The answer is yes, provided the tactics or ends are legal. As a lawyer, your ultimate obligation is not necessarily to do justice, bring out the truth, or ensure fairness. Your job under current ethics rules will be to achieve the client's legal goals to the best of your ability. Once you take the case it is often of no moment that you view particular goals or tactics as unfair or improper.

If this duty startles you, so much the better that it is stated here. Nor should you believe that all agree that this is the best way for members of the legal profession to behave. There is much dissent, but not enough to change the rules. When the same commission that urged lawyers be required to work fifty free hours a year also suggested that lawyers have some duty to ensure that their clients act fairly, American lawyers dismissed the proposal by a lopsided margin.

Two final reasons many students cite for attending law school are that it will provide good training in rational thinking—a useful quality even if one does not go on to law practice—and that it is a logical route to a career in public office, as shown by the large number of public officials who are lawyers. Each of these reasons is valid, though in my view neither suffices as an exclusive reason to seek a legal education.

Something further should be said about the first reason. Law school does indeed teach students to think rigorously and to avoid sloppy reasoning. The usefulness of this quality can hardly be exaggerated. Law school, however, is not the only place to learn about clear thinking. If we limit our list to postgraduate education choices, I think we would have to include schooling in any of the natural sciences, historiography, philosophy, mathematics, business, and economics, to name a few other areas of study. But even if you have aptitude and interest in any of these other fields, you might object that job prospects in most of them are dimmer than in law or that salaries are not as high. Perhaps so, but to me that means you must then think hard about whether the nature of the work you will likely do as a lawyer, rather than these differences, is the reason for choosing law (as it should be); and how you will adjust if the rapid increase in the population of the profession severely reduces job prospects for, or income expectations of, new graduates.

The nature of the work you can do as a lawyer may certainly justify the choice of a legal career. There may be much excitement in it, moments of intense intellectual challenge and achievement, and opportunities to cause beneficial change of a degree and kind few other professionals can effect, all while earning a good living. You will have to be dedicated and work hard to be among the relatively few lawyers who achieve this. Perhaps you are willing to take that chance. Perhaps what you know of the professional lives of even ordinary lawyers will cause you to proceed, regardless. Perhaps, finally, you will conclude that whatever the drawbacks of legal work, they are substantially fewer than those in other careers for which you are suited. These choices are, and should be, very personal.

CHAPTER 2

Selecting a Law School

Gerald Lee Wilson
DUKE UNIVERSITY

Selecting a law school, like most of life's important decisions, is a process that is too important to be determined by the flip of a coin. There seems, as well, to be an "embarrassment of riches" when it comes to the number of people willing to give advice on the matter and the amount of resource material available. So how does a person select the "best" or "right" law school?

The applicant should begin the process by taking advantage of available printed and people resources. Probably the best resource in the former category is the *PreLaw Handbook* published annually by the Association of American Law Schools and the Law School Admission Council. In many cases the best people resource can be a college or university prelaw adviser. The rise of prelaw advising to the position of a subprofession in the last decade or so has come as a direct result of the increasingly competitive nature of law school admissions. In many undergraduate institutions the prelaw adviser(s) and members of his or her staff can serve as information sources, coaches, confidants, and strategists, as well as writers of recommendations.

The next step in the selection process is that of organizing the factors to be considered in making the decision in some sort of logical order with designated priorities. For almost everyone there are at least three major factors as well as a host of other considerations, which may be major to some applicants, minor to others, or possibly can serve as "tiebreakers" in the final stages of the process. The major factors, shorn of sophistication and put in

15

question form are: Where can I get in? What are the job opportunities when I graduate? and How much will it cost? Other factors to be examined include location, size, reputation of the law school, offerings and atmosphere, and, legitimately, a person's "gut reaction" to a particular school.

The first question, "Where can I get in?" is one that can best be answered by comparing the credentials of the applicant with the admissions profile of recent entering classes of the law schools in which the applicant has an initial interest. Conventional wisdom would suggest that the applicant follow the same procedure that he or she probably followed in applying to college. That is, the student should set up *three* categories of schools and apply to an appropriate number of schools in each category. The categories selected are, of course, relative and determined by both the credentials and the particular desires of the individual applicant. The first category, the "long-shot" schools, is the one in which the student lists those schools that he or she would most like to attend, but which seem to be the most difficult in terms of gaining admission. The second category, the "possible schools," is comprised of those schools the applicant would be perfectly happy to attend and on the basis of available information present at least a "fifty-fifty" chance of admission. The third category represents the "safe schools," those that are not the applicant's first or even second choice but are acceptable and do offer the opportunity for an individual to receive a quality legal education.

The implicit assumption in this suggested approach is that the "numbers"—Undergraduate Grade Point Average (UGPA) and Law School Admissions Test Score (LSAT)—are the crucial factors in determining admissibility to law schools. This is, in fact, true for virtually all law schools and, indeed, in a number of cases (especially state law schools) the "numbers" seem to be the only factors considered. In considering the UGPA as an admissions factor, from the applicant's point of view, the guiding principle was clearly stated by a law school admissions officer to a group of undergraduates. He said simply: "a student should not mortgage his or her undergraduate career for the sake of law school." This is true in the dual sense that the UGPA should represent performance in demanding courses as well as selection of a curriculum that provides a good broad background. In general, it does not matter what major a student chooses or what specific courses he or she takes if these courses enhance a student's ability to think critically and communicate effectively both in oral and written form. The student, of course, could benefit from some study of history, political science, English, economics, philosophy, and the like. A final course that many believe crucial for law study is one in basic accounting procedures.

These comments refer to what the UGPA should mean to the applicant. What does the UGPA mean to the law school admissions committee? If the numbers are right, many admissions committees will attempt to assess the strength of the applicant's total curriculum and the difficulty of individual courses insofar as such an assessment can be made. Many committees seem to be willing to take into account an upward progression in the UGPA. This is especially helpful to that applicant who was miscast as a premed during his or her freshman year or who experienced difficulties adjusting to college.

The LSAT, officially defined as "a half-day standardized test . . . designed to measure skills essential for success in law school . . . ," represents the other half of the "numbers" factor. The words *other half* of the factor were deliberately chosen because this score is generally given equal weight with the UGPA by admissions committees. Students can and should prepare for this test, although the specific manner of preparation is very much an individual matter. Some students have found materials published by law services quite adequate. Others purchase commercial test preparation booklets and, increasingly, it seems students are enrolling in commercial preparatory courses. To repeat, students should make some preparations for the test.

In sum, the "numbers" are the major factors in the admissions process, but fortunately, in most cases, they are not the *only* factors. To put it another way, the "numbers" get the applicant into the ball game; once in the ball game other factors can help determine whether the applicant makes a winning score. Curiously enough, although the numbers increasingly seem to dominate in determining admissions decisions, other nonquantifiable factors seem also to be taking on increasing importance. These other factors include essays, recommendations, and college activities.

The essays, those torturous creatures centered around the question "Why do you want to go to law school?" or the request "Tell us about yourself" are getting more than a casual reading by members of admissions committees at many law schools, and in close calls may tip the balance. The schools that request these essays are attempting both to appraise the writing ability of the applicant and to judge his or her motivation for legal studies. Obviously, these statements should be carefully written with attention given to neatness, use of correct grammar and syntax, and, of course, proper spelling.

What to say depends on the individual writer. It is doubtful that a particularly original "Why I want to go to law school" essay can be written by anyone. But the point is not to be original but rather personal. Because this is the applicant's only chance to present something other than objective data, the essay should be one that reveals clearly the individual personality of the applicant. The applicant in preparing the essay should carefully avoid the twin temptations of explaining how through the legal profession he or she hopes to reform Western Civilization and of writing in an artificial style that may be imitative of an eighteenth-century novel, or worse yet, a government document. Hopefully the essay will be interesting enough to make the readers *want* to read all of it. Further, if the writer has a sense of humor, it might be worthwhile to let a little of that show. In many cases, the length of the essay will be specified. If it is not, then the applicant should set a limit of approximately two double-spaced typed pages.

If an autobiographical statement is requested, the applicant should at all costs avoid a mere factual, chronological outline of his or her life, such as "I was born on April 22, 1969, at Baptist Hospital in Winston-Salem and attended R. J. Reynolds High School where I was a hall monitor." The most effective autobiographical statement is a thoughtful, impressionistic explanation of the crucial events that have shaped the applicant into the person he or she is. Experiences such as foreign study, producing a play, or significant employment should be highlighted. If certain books, events, or people have been influential in the applicant's life, comment on these will probably be of more value than a list of high school or college activities. The essay should include at least a paragraph about the applicant's intellectual development, explaining both growth and change. Extensive research projects or other major individual accomplishments such as publication should certainly be included.

Not only is the essay the best place for the applicant to sell himself or herself and emphasize his or her best qualities, it is also often the one place where any explanations concerning the objective credentials can be made. For example, if the applicant presents high grades and low LSAT scores, but has a history of poor performance on standardized tests, that should be discussed. If the applicant's first few semesters in college were weaker ones academically because he or she was miscast as a premed, this also should be mentioned. When there is something to be explained, however, it is probably best to give a simple, cogent explanation and let the committee draw the appropriate conclusions.

Perhaps the most misunderstood part of the application is the recommendations. Campus lore seems to run the gamut from "recommendations don't really mean anything" to "if so-and-so recommends you, you'll get in." The truth of the matter may well lie somewhere in between. Undoubtedly, the most valuable letters of recommendation are those that come from the academic community and more especially those that come from instructors who have actually taught the applicant. These letters are most helpful if they are both analytical and specific, appraising the applicant's performance in the course, and, on that basis, estimating his or her likely performance as a law student and practicing attorney. Positive, incisive letters are of far more value than glowing, general ones.

Recommendations from the applicant's prelaw adviser can be helpful if the prelaw adviser knows the applicant, has access to the applicant's total record, and is familiar with the law school. Oftentimes the prelaw adviser can point out things on the student's overall academic record of which an individual instructor may not have knowledge. Further, if the undergraduate institution has a track record at a particular law school, the prelaw adviser can compare the application with other students who have attended that law school. In brief, if the applicant has worked closely with the prelaw adviser, he or she will be able to do more than just fill out a citizenship clearance form, and this "more" can often be helpful to the applicant.

In general, with one notable exception, letters from outside the academic community carry little weight with admissions committees.

This exception refers to recommendations from employers in cases where an applicant has had a job that carried considerable responsibility or where something significant was accomplished. The employer recommendation is of special significance for the applicant who has taken some time off prior to entrance into law school. One word of caution: If the applicant has worked for a member of Congress or some well-known figure, he or she may be tempted to have that person write a recommendation on the assumption that the "name" alone will carry a great deal of weight. In fact, admissions committees can be "turned off" by so-called names. In most cases, the applicant would probably be better off if he or she had an administrative assistant or the person who directly supervised the applicant's work write the letter of recommendation.

These comments on recommendations and the mention of "names" provide as good an opportunity as any to mention the matter of "pull." Many applicants know someone who has offered to help and indicated that he or she "knows someone" on the admissions committee. No one can deny that in some cases, probably a very small number, this approach works. However, the best way to regard such offers of help is to remember that definition of *pull*, which calls it "what everybody thinks he or she has until he tries to use it." In sum, if someone offers to help, let him or her, but don't count on its effectiveness.

The final nonquantifiable factor making up the applicant's total credentials is the list of activities in which the student was involved. Here again, mythology abounds. On the one hand, admissions committees like to see that an applicant has done something other than "nerd out" in the library, but, on the other hand, they cannot judge the value of any specific activity or the intensity of the commitment to that activity on the part of the student. Rather than flooding the committee with a long list of activities (which can raise the question of when the applicant found time to study) it is probably best to list only those that were most important to the individual, reveal something of his or her personality and interests, and help paint a total picture of the applicant. The applicant should, of course, highlight those activities in which he or she assumed major responsiblity or had a leadership role. A good list of activities in combination with a high UGPA and good LSAT scores can be impressive, but activities alone cannot substitute for the other two elements.

The applicant should also realize that the actual mailing in of all of the application materials should not complete the process on his or her part. Follow-up should take the form of careful monitoring and, if necessary, "gentle pestering." Within a reasonable time after the application materials have been mailed, the applicant should contact each school to which he or she has applied to make sure that the application is complete. Many schools do not automatically notify the applicant of the status of the file. "Gentle pestering" can be effective in those instances where the applicant falls into the marginal category of being neither an automatic accept nor an automatic reject. If the applicant finds himself or herself on a waiting list or in some other purgatorial category, then the act of "gentle pestering" or "friendly persuasion" can sometimes pay dividends. The applicant should not hesitate to enlist the aid of his or her prelaw adviser in this campaign and should, if appropriate, send further grades, additional letters of recommendation, and perhaps more essays. Although personal interviews with someone at the law school are, in most cases, not encouraged, the applicant should at least inquire as to whether or not such an interview would be helpful in his or her specific case. In close cases, following this sort of game plan may make the difference.

One last word before leaving the "Where can I get in?" question. Every applicant, *no matter how high his or her academic average and LSAT scores and how strong other credentials may be*, should apply to as many schools as feasible and to a broad range of schools in terms of admissions requirements.

The reverse side of the "Where can I get in?" question is, "What are the job opportunities for me when I get out (with a degree)?" Part of the answer to this question is unknowable in advance, part is uncontrollable, and part depends on the individual's own initiative. The unknown part has to do with the individual's rank in class, which is, for better or worse, a real key in getting a job. The uncontrollable part is the condition of the job market at the time the individual graduates. The individual's own initiative and hustle form that part which is definitely under his or her control. In examining material provided by the law school the applicant should study carefully the information on job placement and should not be hesitant about asking hard questions. Such questions include: Does the law school have a full-time placement officer? What percentage of the class obtains jobs within a reasonable time after receiving their degrees? What types of jobs do they get? Where are these jobs? How many agencies and firms recruit at the law school? Does the law school placement office offer continuing help if job changes are necessary or desired later on? Although a good placement office and officer may exist at a law school, the applicant should remember that no placement office can get a person a job; the office can help, but in the end, the student is the one who gets the job.

Frequently in this chapter such words as *large, small, state, national,* and the like will be used when referring to law schools. Perhaps the best way of defining these terms is to point to some specific examples. In terms of size, Harvard, whose total enrollment in a recent year was 1,782, with an entering class of 551, is an example of a large school. Duke and Cornell, with total enrollments of about 550 each and entering classes of about 180, are examples of medium-size schools. Small schools include Washington and Lee and the University of New Mexico, whose total enrollments of 364 and 338, respectively, include entering classes of 133 and 113.

A further distinction that can be of importance to an applicant is that between a "public" and a "private" school, especially with reference to admissions standards and tuition costs. Because public schools are subsidized by taxpayers, they generally enroll a higher percentage of state residents and charge them less tuition than nonresidents. Private institutions, on the other hand, view applications with little reference to geography and charge the same tuition to all students.

A final distinction worth noting is that between "national" and "state" or "local" law schools. In some cases, because of the constituency they serve, state or local schools may, in their academic program, place more emphasis on state or local law and practice. This distinction is also significant in terms of admissions standards and placement possibilities. National law schools actively seek applicants from throughout the nation and generally have broader placement connections. State or local schools draw primarily from their locality and usually concentrate their placement efforts in the area they serve.

When any of the above distinctions are important to an applicant, he or she should check on each school, because names can be misleading. For example, William and Mary is a state school and New York University is private. Further, many state schools such as the universities of Virginia and Michigan are also considered to be national schools.

When most applicants wrestle with the questions, "Should I go to my state law school or a private one in the state or region in which I intend to practice?" or "Should I go to a national school far away?" they are really asking (financial considerations aside for the moment) the job opportunity question. Probably the best rule-of-thumb answer to this question is that a student should go to the best school he or she can get in; if the best is no better or not significantly better than the one in the state or region in which the student intends to practice, then go with the school in that state or region. Having said that, the applicant should remember that all schools, including many of the great national ones, may have their best placement connections in the geographical region in which they are located. However, if the school has enough national visibility, getting a job out of the region in which the school is located is not a major problem.

The third major question to be asked by the applicant in selecting a law school, "How much will it cost?" is, unfortunately, increasingly becoming the bottom line for many applicants. No matter how attractive school X may be and how admissible the applicant is, financial considerations have to be faced squarely. First, the applicant needs to assess how much he or she already owes if he or she has been on financial aid as an undergraduate. Second, using information provided by the law schools under consideration, the applicant should set up a budget that includes both law school expenses and personal expenses. Most people don't realize how much they spend in a day or a year. The applicant should examine how much he or she really spends for coffee, books, movies, auto insurance, and the like. After establishing a realistic budget, the applicant should add up these expenses and compare them with available resources. To be safe, a 10 percent inflation factor should be added to these estimated expenses. Because most law schools discourage work for pay the first year, or encourage only a limited amount, the applicant should have adequate funds available for entry into the first year.

In brief, the applicant should ask if school X is really worth it. The applicant should also remember that the amount of debt he or she may incur as a result of attending school X may limit job options available after graduation. For example, if a graduate is heavily in debt, he or she may not be able to afford to take a social service or public defender's job, but have to look to higher paying private law firms. Fortunately, some law schools have instituted "Loan Forgiveness Programs" to encourage students to consider low paying public service jobs. Applicants should contact individual law schools for further information.

Because law school is expensive, the question "Can I really afford school X?" is a critical one. Because law school is an investment, the question "Can I afford *not* to attend school X?" must also be considered.

Though the questions of admissibility, opportunity, and affordability comprise the major factors in selecting a law school, there are a number of other factors to be considered which can take on the role of tiebreakers or, in toto, can have the same impact on the selection process as the major factors. Though these are "soft" factors in that in many cases they are nonquantifiable, they merit careful exploration.

The first category of questions to be asked concerns the program and total atmosphere of the law school. A word of caution is in order for avid catalog readers. Because most applicants are among the uninitiated in the terminology of the law and the content of the courses listed in the law school's bulletin, he or she should read the curricular and course offerings very carefully. This caution should extend to examination of special programs or emphases also. Because a law school education is basically one that focuses on the general practice of law, and specialization most often occurs after graduation from law school, it may be unwise to choose a given law school solely on the basis of a specialized curriculum or program. Oftentimes, such special areas are contingent on the presence of one or a small number of faculty members who might leave the school to go elsewhere or retire. The point is that an applicant, in selecting a law school, should never sacrifice overall quality for a specialized program.

The factor that is the greatest single one in determining the quality of a law school is the faculty. Applicants should find out as much about the faculty as possible. What is the general reputation of the faculty? Are they recognized experts in their fields? What members of the faculty are near retirement? Is the faculty noted for having good teachers? What are their teaching styles? Are they accessible to students outside of class? Do they have extensive outside commitments?

Next in importance to the faculty in determining both the quality of the school and its desirability for the individual applicant is the question of the character of the student body. As one law school professor has put it, "in law school, half of what a student learns comes from other students both in the formal setting of the classroom and informal interchange outside the classroom." Size of the student body can often be important to the applicant. He or she should ask if, in the case of large law schools, the class is sectioned and, if it is, does this sectioning prove to be effective in making the law school experience a more personal one? It is not only important to note the objective credentials of the entering class, but applicants will also want to find out where and what type of undergraduate institutions the members of the class come from. What are the major feeder schools? In some cases the applicant may feel more comfortable with students who come from under-graduate institutions similar to his or her own; in other cases, an applicant may welcome a different experience. This is also true in a geographic sense. Some students may prefer to be with law students who come, for the most part, from his or her region of the country; others may prefer geographic diversity. To what extent are women and members of minority groups recruited and enrolled is a question of significance for many applicants. Because the average age of entering classes seems to be going up and law schools generally react favorably to applications from people who are older, many applicants may want to know how many of the students fall into different age groups. Finally, the applicant may well want to know how competitive the students are. Although no law school can truly be described as "laid back," some schools are noted as being highly competitive, whereas others seem to be a bit more relaxed and possess more of a cooperative spirit. The individual has to decide which atmosphere will provide him or her with the best educational experience.

The final set of factors under the general rubric of atmosphere are the "books and bricks" questions. Though the size of the library is important, the more important question is the adequacy of the library resources. If a law school is part of a university, then questions about the availability and accessibility of the total university library system should be asked. The applicant should also look at the "bricks." Are the physical facilities adequate? What plans are there for expansion if expansion seems necessary? Additional questions in this category would include questions about housing for students, sports, and other nonacademic facilities.

Another factor of concern to many students is the school's location with reference to things other than job opportunities. Some students prefer schools located in large metropolitan areas; others seek a more bucolic atmosphere. Some students come alive in cold crisp air, others find that their minds freeze and their spirits fall when the temperature goes below seventy degrees. Some like the given life-style of a region; others find certain regional life-styles not to be their cup of tea. Some find law school more tolerable if they have ACC basketball available; others feel better if snow-skiing is no more than an hour away. Though location in these terms should never be the major deciding factor, it may be a useful tiebreaker.

The final two factors to be considered in selecting a law school involve perception and process. The perception factor centers around the perceived reputation and prestige of a law school. Lists of rankings are the easiest and most readily available sources of information, but, alas, in actuality, often reflect the prejudices of those participating in the ranking procedures more than the real quality of the law schools. Yet, such ranking lists can be useful in serving as a starting point in the determination of the reputation and prestige of law schools. The individual applicant should read carefully as much material as possible, talk to a wide variety of people who are familiar with legal education, and then make his or her own judgments. After all, there is no "best" law school in the country in an objective sense. The "best" school is the one that best meets the individual applicant's own needs and personal goals.

The applicant to law school is a rational person who probably prides himself or herself on the ability to weigh carefully all the evidence and then make a logical decision, bringing the full force of reason to bear on the process of selecting a law school. But on the theory that "the whole is greater than the sum of its parts," you should remember that even after a careful reasoning process, it may be important to make the final selection on the basis of a "gut reaction." You should trust your instincts as well as your reason. Before the final decision is made, ask such questions as "Does the school feel right for me?" and "Will I be proud to hold a degree from that school?" In this connection, if at all possible, visit the schools you are seriously considering. Selecting a law school sight unseen is a bit like selecting a spouse sight unseen: on paper everything may seem right, but the "chemistry" may not be there. Although many law schools do not encourage visits for admission purposes, all would agree on the value of a visit before making a final choice.

This chapter has suggested a number of factors to be considered in selecting a law school, but in the end, both the process and the choice belong to the individual. Even if the same questions are asked by individual applicants and similar answers result, the weight each answer carries as a decision-making factor will vary from applicant to applicant. The only given for all applicants, it seems, is the time and money spent on the process. Opportunity most often comes to the prepared.

CHAPTER 3

Financing a Legal Education

John R. Kramer
TULANE UNIVERSITY

Law school is an expensive undertaking. But you've got to have it. You cannot afford not to go to law school. However great the cost of attending—and it is going to be steep, even at the seventy-four ABA-accredited public law schools—the investment you make for three years should be recouped in full by no later than four years after you graduate and, in many instances, sooner. You will continue to receive dividends at an accelerating rate over the forty to fifty years you practice. You will enjoy access to social power and prestige as well as, hopefully, the legal work you perform. Any investment counselor would advise you to put your money into such a proposition. Quickly.

The High Cost of Learning

You have to be aware of the financial hurdles. They exist, although they readily can be overcome with careful planning. In the 1970s, the cliché was that the second most sizable financial investment an individual would ever make, after buying a home, would be the purchase of a car. By the early 1980s, however, the cost of professional education, especially legal and medical education, had easily displaced the cost of a car, except perhaps for a luxury car such as a Mercedes-Benz. By the 1990s, even the Mercedes-Benz has succumbed. Only a Rolls-Royce or Lamborghini stands ahead of legal education (and, of course, medical education) as the most expensive capital asset, other than a home, that an individual can purchase. By the year 2000, a prospective law student might even find a two-bedroom condominium (outside of New York and Los Angeles) cheap by comparison.

Law school tuition has continued to outpace the cost of living by a wide margin. During the decade 1977–78 to 1987–88, the average tuition paid by students at private law schools ballooned by 183 percent.[1] The Consumer Price Index only rose by 86 percent over the same time frame.[2] For the 1988–89 academic year, the average tuition in the 100 accredited private law schools surveyed by the American Bar Association was $9,652.[3] That figure had increased by an average of 10.7 percent a year since 1978–79, but only 9 percent a year since 1983–84. For in-state residents at the 74 accredited public law schools in the survey, the comparable figure was $2,608 (up 10.5 percent a year since 1978–79 and 9.4 percent a year since 1983–84), while nonresidents paid $6,017 on the average (rising at 11.2 percent a year for the ten-year period, but only 9.4 percent a year for five years).[4] To be an in-state resident you may only have to live in a particular state for one year. That is the only bargain in legal education.

The 1988–89 average estimate of living (room, board, supplies, transportation, and miscellaneous personal expenses) and book expenses for a single student living away from home was $7,820.[5] Accordingly, combining tuition and living expenses, the average full cost of attendance figures for law students at private and public (resident and nonresident) institutions in 1988–89 were $17,472, $10,428, and $13,837, respectively. If the general inflation level for the next seven academic years averages 5 percent (a reasonable projection in light of past history), while law school tuition figures continue to climb at the same rate as during the last decade (also probable), the full-cost-of-attendance figures in 1995–96 would be $30,667, $16,250, and $23,654, respectively. Even if tuition increases were held to an annual 9 percent, the average private school cost of attendance in 1995–96 would still be $29,648.

The average student starting at a private law school in the fall of 1990 could, therefore, expect to pay almost $67,000 in order to obtain a degree by the time he or she graduated in 1993. For a law

graduate in the year 2000, that figure could exceed $118,000.
The following tables tell the tale.

AVERAGE TUITION

	Private School	Public School (Resident)	Public School (Nonresident)
1988–89 (act.)	$ 9,652	$2,608	$ 6,017
1995–96 (proj.)	19,663	5,246	12,650
1999–2000 (proj.)	29,529	7,822	19,343

AVERAGE COST OF ATTENDANCE
Tuition, Room, Board, Books, Supplies, Transportation, and Miscellaneous Expenses

	Private School	Public School (Resident)	Public School (Nonresident)
1988–89 (act.)	$17,472	$10,428	$13,837
1995–1996 (proj.)	30,667	16,250	23,654
1999–2000 (proj.)	42,904	21,197	32,718

These figures only represent averages. People who are five feet tall can drown in a river that has an average depth of three feet when they encounter a six-foot depression. It is advisable to beware of the extreme situation. In 1988–89, 43 law schools (25 percent of all schools) had tuitions in excess of $10,000, with three exceeding $14,000, eight between $13,000 and $14,000, and eight more between $12,000 and $13,000.[6] Should these price tags increase in the next twelve years at a rate comparable to that during the preceding twelve, tuition levels at some schools that are now in the $14,000–15,000 range could approach $50,000 by the year 2000. Similarly, the $7,820 cost-of-living figure reflects the average in a range between $3,020 and $20,170, with 24 schools estimating the cost to be in excess of $10,000 (and even that only covers nine months of the year).[7]

Thus, at the most expensive private school in the country, the cost of attending as of the fall 1988 was already slightly in excess of $24,500 a year, room and board included, which could balloon to as much as $44,000 a year by 1995 or $67,500 a year by 2000. On a three-year basis a student starting out in the most expensive school in the fall of 1995 might well have to pay as much as $144,000 to earn a degree as of 1998.

The Virtually Nonexistent Cost of Not Earning a Living Because of Going to Law School

Normally there is an additional, substantial cost that must be taken into account when contemplating graduate or professional education —the lost economic opportunity for full-time employment during the years while attending school. That cost is less and less troublesome for prospective law students. While there are no absolutely reliable figures on the average starting salaries for graduates with a bachelor's degree, there is some evidence that the 1989 crop earned between $20,000 and $22,000 on the average.[8] Assuming an annual 5 percent increase in that figure, graduates in 1990 might earn $22,000 in 1990–91 or a total of $63,450 from September 1990 through May 1993. That is, on the surface, a formidable sum to forgo.

In the past several years, however, work has become an increasingly lucrative pursuit for students enrolled in law school, particularly after the first nine months of their first year. Law firms want law students to clerk for them both winter and summer as a dry run for selecting future associates. Law firm work is also amazingly compensatory even as it drains students' energies and diverts their attention from academic challenges. As the following table indicates, even the laziest of students, as long as he or she works at all, can bring in, as of 1989–90, a minimum of $20,300 over the 33 months he or she is in school, $68,250 at the outside. Those sums are sufficient at the top end to make lost economic opportunity no longer worth worrying about. No gap at all would exist over the 1990–1993 period on the assumption of a 5 percent annual wage increase during that time.

EARNINGS POTENTIAL OF LAW STUDENTS

Second and Third Year, Fall and Spring

Hours × Weeks Worked

$/Hr.	15 × 20	20 × 20	15 × 30	20 × 30
6	1,800	2,400	2,700	3,600
9	2,700	3,600	4,050	5,400
12	3,600	4,800	5,400	7,200
15	4,500	6,000	6,750	9,000
20	6,000	8,000	9,000	12,000
30	9,000	12,000	13,500	18,000

First and Second Year, Summer

Weeks Worked

$/Wk	10	12	15
600	6,000	7,200	9,000
700	7,000	8,400	10,500
800	8,000	9,600	12,000
900	9,000	10,800	13,500
1,000	10,000	12,000	15,000
1,200	12,000	14,400	18,000
1,500	15,000	18,000	22,500
1,750	17,500	21,000	26,250

Overall Earnings During Law School

	Min. effort, min. pay	Min. effort, max. pay	Max. effort, min. pay	Max. effort, max. pay
First Year, Summer	6,000	12,000	12,000	15,000
Second Year, Fall and Spring	2,700	3,600	5,400	9,000
Second Year, Summer	8,000	17,500	15,000	26,250
Third Year, Fall and Spring	3,600	9,000	9,000	18,000
Totals	20,300	42,100	41,400	68,250

Earnings Ranges in School

First Calendar Year	0
(Sept.–Dec.)	
Second Calendar Year	7,350–19,500
(Jan.–Dec.)	
Third Calendar Year	11,150–39,750
(Jan. Dec.)	
Fourth Calendar Year	<u>1,800–9,000</u>
(Jan.–May)	
Total	20,300–68,250

Where lost earnings for three years were once a deterrent to applying to law school, they no longer are. The most income that might be forgone over three years is $43,000, which, after subtracting approximately $3,300 for Social Security taxes and $7,100 for federal income taxes, adds only about $33,000 to the most expensive private law school cost of attendance during the same period (1990–93) of $67,000.[9]

A college graduate applying rudimentary economics to thinking about attending law school in the fall of 1990 would thus confront as the highest (average) cost $100,000, representing average private law school tuition and cost of attendance for three years plus the greatest lost economic opportunity. Given a law student's earning potential, $67,000 would be more like the worst case.

It no longer makes sense to stay out of school for a year (for example, 1990–91) in order to save money to pay tuition and living costs. The sum that might be put aside would fall $2,500 short of covering the average private-school tuition. The $22,050 salary would have to be reduced by approximately $4,400 in Social Security and income taxes and further by $10,450 for a moderate twelve-month consumption budget,[10] leaving $7,200 or less to apply to tuition. With average private-school tuition in 1990–91 projected to be $11,830, the effort would have been futile. You would still have to borrow to go to a public law school, which would cost approximately $11,800, including all costs of attendance. Ironically you would have exchanged paying average private-school tuition in 1990–91 ($11,830) for paying it in 1992–94 ($16,050), a deadweight loss of $4,220, to be coupled with the sacrifice of one year of a salary as a lawyer that should be well in excess of $40,000.

To repeat: You cannot afford not to go to law school. Not if you can count and realize that working instead of going to school could set you back well over $37,000. Deferred gratification in this case would be counterproductive.

The Rewards of Investing in Law School

Even if there is little lost economic opportunity, going to law school is still not cheap. Who would want to invest in a product as expensive as legal education? By virtue of the act of applying, more than 80,000 college graduates in the course of 1988–89 had clearly determined that there must be a favorable benefit-cost ratio. Without calculating the precise nature of the pecuniary benefits, they instinctively realized that going to law school ultimately would return much more than the $5,533 a year (the lowest combination of living costs and tuition) to $24,475 a year (the highest) it cost then.

That intuition is accurate. Although data on the earnings of attorneys tend to be shaky on a nationwide basis, the graduating class of 1988 reported its average starting salary as $39,159, or 9.3 percent higher than in 1987, with attorneys entering private practice reporting between $28,475 for firms with fewer than ten attorneys and $58,936 for firms with more than 100.[11] Working for business and industry led to salaries whose median was $33,626, while government pay had a median of $26,906. Public interest work resulted in a median of $23,856.

That is 1987 data. Every indication is that the salary surge of recent years has continued unabated. A 1988 law firm average starting salary for 700 firms was computed at $40,000.[12] The top New York starting salary for the fall of 1989 jumped from $76,000 to $82,000, including bonuses.[13] The top rate three years before had been $65,000. If the economic conditions of practice were to hold steady through 1993, a law student graduating that spring might well be offered an average of $53,000, peaking at well over $100,000 and close to $105,000 in New York City. At $53,000, the average starting salary for a law school graduate would be approximately $27,500 a year more than what a bachelor of arts degree holder would earn in 1993–94, while an individual beginning in New York would earn as much as $80,000 or more. That gap would increase with each successive year during the first several years of practice by a minimum of $1,000 to $2,000 and a maximum of $10,000 to $15,000.

Thus an applicant to a public law school contemplating paying an average of approximately $38,000 over three years for tuition and living expenses in addition to forgoing from $20,000 to $35,000 in lost wages could reasonably expect to recoup the entire investment of from $58,000 to $73,000 through salary differentials over anywhere from one to slightly less than three years. A person seeking admission to a private law school would have to wait somewhat longer to recover the investment. Average private-school tuition and living expenses of $67,000, combined with $20,000 to $35,000 in lost economic opportunity, would take from slightly over one to less than four years to recoup. At the maximum, for the most expensive private school costing $95,000 from 1990 to 1993, with lost salary between $20,000 and $35,000, a job in New York City would retrieve the investment inside of eighteen months, although an average earner might require four and a half years after beginning to work to recover the entire sum. While these estimates are somewhat rough, since they do not account for taxes or discount the value of future income or consider the potential added cost of financing education through debt, they suggest the returns legitimately to be anticipated from becoming an attorney.

An investment that will pay for itself in a year or even four (a 25% rate of return) is remarkable, particularly if that investment will continue to provide greater and greater fiscal dividends at an accelerating rate for forty to fifty years after initial recoupment and unmeasurable psychic dividends. Given this potential, the J.D. degree is probably a better investment than any stock listed on any stock exchange, unless the company discovers gold or the graduating law student chooses public interest or local government work.

The question, then, is not whether the investment is worth it. The real issue is whether a college graduate can afford the hefty down payment and, particularly, where he or she can find the resources to underwrite it.

Who Pays for Law School?

The cost of going to law school can be secured from four sources: parents, through savings and current income; the law schools themselves, through redistributed tuition revenues, endowment, or gifts obtained from businesses, foundations, and alumni; federal and state taxpayers, through governmental financial-assistance programs and subsidies; and you, through self-help by work and borrowing.

Parents

Parents remain a major factor, not by virtue of law but by virtue of loyalty and generosity. For many years the basic assumption underlying the financing of higher education has been that parents would use savings and current earnings to pay for their children's educations. This assumption becomes less valid once a child has graduated from college. Parents who have sacrificed to pay for a child's undergraduate education may be increasingly less willing to pay for graduate or professional school and more inclined to demand that their child cover some of the costs, particularly when the child's earning potential is as substantial as that of a young lawyer.

The changing assumption about parental responsibility for financing education appears even more reasonable when one considers the age of law students. The percentage of law school applicants who were over age 25 was 41.4 percent in 1988–89, with 19.4 percent over age 31.[14] These students could hardly turn to their parents for the money necessary to finance their legal education.

The Higher Education Amendments of 1986 at last acknowledged the legitimacy of the student's need for relief. Under the 1986 amendments, graduate or professional students are recognized per se as independent of their parents for purposes of computing need for federal aid, provided either they are 24 years old by December 31 of the year they enter law school or are under 24 years old but not claimed as tax dependents in the first calendar year for which the federal aid was awarded (the year in which the student is seeking admission to law school).[15]

Parents of law students are no longer under a formulaic mandate to contribute, except when the parents decide that a $2,000-plus tax exemption is more important than facilitating their child's access to as much as $11,500 in government-guaranteed loans. As long as the exemption is not claimed, each law student is presumed to bear the full burden of the costs of legal education.

Whether or not actual parental contributions will decline as a result of this change is uncertain. Parents remain free to help their children attend law school. Such contributions reduce the amount the students would otherwise have to obtain. Indeed the Conference Report on the 1986 amendments contained a warning by the managers that "it is the intention of the conferees" that aid officers carefully evaluate students from high-income families enrolled in high-cost programs "to determine if a parental contribution is warranted."[16]

The exact level of current parental contributions is not known. It has been estimated to be at least $400 million and perhaps as much as $500 million—an average of $3500 to $4000 per student. This contribution level puts the family nearly on a level with the federal government with regard to the subsidy provided students for their legal education. The reality, however, is that the average figure is irrelevant. Most students are given either more than $10,000 or nothing at all. The legal transfer of funding responsibility from the generation of the parents to the generation of the students may encourage some parents to abandon a previously accepted responsibility. To the extent that the roles are reversed and students assume the obligation to find money for legal education themselves, the traditional social contract governing education will have been turned upside down. That change places a greater burden on the remaining sources of support for a student's legal education.

Law Schools

All education is subsidized to some extent by the institutions that provide it. In law schools, subsidies come either by way of earnings from the endowment or through annual gifts or, most commonly, pursuant to a scheme of internal redistribution of wealth that alchemizes as much as 10 to 15 percent of tuition into scholarship aid. In 1988–89 these grant/scholarship resources amounted to

$103.5 million but covered only 11.8 percent of all tuitions and fees.[17] They were primarily derived (37 percent) from tuition rebates, which, unfortunately, are translated into tuition increases applicable to all students. Endowments supported only 22 percent of law school–awarded scholarships.

While scholarships ease the financial strain for some students, the relief is relatively minor. The average dollar level of scholarships is $3,000.[18] Only 28.5 percent of all students receive them. The inadequacy of scholarships as a source of funding to attend law school is likely to continue, particularly as the dollar-volume increase in fellowships continues to lag well behind the dollar-volume increase in tuition. From 1983–84 to 1988–89, gross tuition and fees for all schools went up $323.5 million, from $556.3 million to $879.3 million.[19] Law school scholarships rose by $44.9 million over the same period,[20] stretching over only 14 percent of the tuition boost. Law schools can dig only so deeply into their own pockets or those of their students as a method of financing legal education.

Some law schools have loan programs of their own. These amounted to $13.5 million in 1988–89,[21] down from $16.1 million in 1984–85.[22] Many offer students paying jobs outside of work study; $10.4 million went for this purpose in 1988–89.[23]

State Government

State government contributes heavily to legal education through appropriations for public law schools. The $7,044 differential between the average public law school tuition and the average private law school tuition in 1988–89 was the result of state subsidies. The cost of attending law school for all enrollees would rise as much as $315 million if the state subsidies were removed. This support, of course, is selective—only students attending public law schools benefit.

States do fund modest loan programs, but these programs will become increasingly more modest with the federal income tax cap on the issuance of tax-exempt bonds to underwrite student loans. The level of state loans in 1988–89 was $3.1 million, down $17.7 million from 1985–86.[24]

Federal Government

Without the intervention of the federal government in the 1970s, legal education as we know it today would not exist. Law schools, which serve the needs of clients who are predominantly corporations or wealthy individuals, are essentially socialized institutions. If public, they are dependent for their survival on the state that funds them (only Alaska, Nevada, and Rhode Island do not have publicly supported law schools) as well as on federal loans. If private, they have become heavily dependent upon the subsidized loan programs offered by the federal government.

This dependence on federal loans is relatively recent. The Guaranteed Student Loan (GSL), now the Stafford Loan program, was created in 1965. Law students did not begin to use Stafford (then GSL) loans to a significant extent until after 1978, when the Middle Income Student Support Act removed some income eligibility limitations. As of 1988–89, law students had $390 million in Stafford loans ($285 million for students at private law schools, $105 million for those in public law schools), which accounted for 44.3 percent of the $879.8 million in tuition and fees at the nation's 174 law schools ($726.8 million at private institutions, $152.9 at public institutions).[25] In addition, law students used $38 million in National Direct Student loans (now Perkins loans)[26] and $100 million in Supplemental Loans for Students (SLS)[27] for a grand total of $529 million in federally derived loans, enough to pay for 60.1% of all tuition and fees.

While the percentage of private school tuition and fees accounted for by loans is below the peak of 68% it reached in 1981–82,[28] law students are, pound for pound, the most vigorous federal loan program users. In 1988–89, they represented only slightly over 9% of all of the students enrolled full-time in graduate and professional education and less than 1 percent of all of the students involved in higher education, but they consumed slightly under 5% of all the Stafford and SLS loans awarded that year.[29] Similarly, they obtained 4% of the Perkins loans.

All told, including Stafford, SLS, and Perkins loans ($529 million) as well as Federal work-study monies ($8.7 million),[30] Graduate and Professional Opportunity program fellowships ($1.9 million),[31] and Council on Legal Education Opportunity fellowships (\$.9 million),[32] both targeted to minorities, federal aid to legal education in 1988–89 amounted to \$540.5 million.

Although some of this \$540.5 million went for room and board as well as tuition because its use is unrestricted after receipt, the great bulk is nonetheless properly linked to tuition. The entire enterprise of legal education in 1988–89 cost in the vicinity of slightly over \$1.8 billion, including housing and feeding the students. The federal government contributed 30% of that sum. This level of federally related support demonstrates the degree of reliance upon federal aid of the 120,694 full-time and part-time students seeking J.D. degrees.[33] The disproportionately high level also reflects the unusual alertness of the law student population to the existence of the federal programs, their aggressiveness in utilizing them, and, of course, the high cost of attending law school compared to other forms of higher education.

The Hows of Federal Aid

If the other sources of support discussed above (parents, law schools, and states) and the self-help approach considered below prove insufficient, the federal government may be able to fill the gap between the resources available to you and your cost of attending the law school of your choice. By far the largest federal sustenance comes in the form of the trio of loan programs—Stafford, SLS, and Perkins—whose terms are contrasted in the following chart.[34]

Stafford Loan (used to be Guaranteed Student Loan or GSL)	Supplemental Loan for Students (SLS)	Perkins Loan (used to be National Direct Student Loans or NDSL)
(1) *Income Eligibility* Almost all law students will be independent and thus should qualify for full amount after application of full financial need test.	No limitation but must apply for Stafford (GSL) before being eligible for SLS.	Same as Stafford, although each law school usually further assesses relative need in order fairly to distribute its limited allotment, determined by its parent university.

Stafford Loan (used to be Guaranteed Student Loan or GSL)	Supplemental Loan for Students (SLS)	Perkins Loan (used to be National Direct Student Loans or NDSL)
(2) *Other Eligibility Characteristics* Enrolled on at least half-time basis (as defined by school) in accredited law school. Citizen or permanent resident of the United States. Maintaining satisfactory progress as defined by school. Registered for draft if required to do so with form filled in reciting compliance or lack of need for such compliance (e.g., if female). Not in default on any loan at school attended.	Same as Stafford plus requirement of credit worthiness if only part-time student.	Same as Stafford.
(3) *Annual loan maximum* $7500	$4,000	$5,000, but few law students get that amount because of allotment limits.
(4) *Cumulative maximum* $54,750, which includes undergraduate Staffords.	$20,000	$18,000, which includes undergraduate Perkins.

Stafford Loan (used to be Guaranteed Student Loan or GSL)	Supplemental Loan for Students (SLS)	Perkins Loan (used to be National Direct Student Loans or NDSL)

(5) *Interest rate*

After July 1, 1988, 8 percent for first four years (after start of repayment, that is, until 4½ years after graduation), with 10 percent for the remainder of repayment. If 91-day Treasury bill rate plus 3.25 percent is less than 10 percent, the difference is credited against principal balance. The repayment rate will remain at 8 percent throughout repayment for anyone who first took out a Stafford loan after September 13, 1983, but before July 1, 1988, and at 9 percent throughout repayment, if the first loan was between January 1, 1981, and September 13, 1983.

After July 1, 1987, set each year at the bond equivalent rate for 52-week Treasury bills (at final auction prior to June 1) plus 3.25 percent, with 12 percent maximum.

5 percent if loan after October 1, 1981.

(6) *In-school payment*

None required.

Due 60 days after loan, but principal and interest may be deferred and capitalized.

None required.

Stafford Loan (used to be Guaranteed Student Loan or GSL)	Supplemental Loan for Students (SLS)	Perkins Loan (used to be National Direct Student Loans or NDSL)
(7) *Grace period prior to repayment* Six months after graduation.	60 days after graduation.	Nine months after graduation.
(8) *Out-of-school payment duration*		

Ten years maximum for each loan, subject to consolidation of all such loans if they exceed a total of $5,000 at a weighted average interest rate, but in no event less than 9 percent, with term of 12 years for loans of from $5,000 to $9,999; 15 years for loans from $10,000 to $19,999; 20 years for loans from $20,000 to $44,999; and 25 years for loans of $45,000 or more. Graduated/income sensitive repayment schedules up to lender.

Stafford	SLS	Perkins
(9) *Minimum repayment* $50 a month.	$30 a month.	$30 a month.
(10) *Origination fee* Five percent— $375 maximum	None.	None.
(11) *Deferment* Less than full-time student; whenever unemployed for 24 months; parental leave for up to 6 months; 2 months for preschool mothers entering work force and earning less than $1 over minimum wage.	Same as Stafford.	Parental leave and preschool mothers as in Stafford.

Stafford Loan (used to be Guaranteed Student Loan or GSL)	Supplemental Loan for Students (SLS)	Perkins Loan (used to be National Direct Student Loans or NDSL)
(12) *Insurance premium* Limited to 3 percent of loan (variable but up to 1 percent per year in schools plus eleven months). None in 1989–90.	Same as Stafford (variable, but up to 1 percent per year during lesser of life of loan or 60 months). None in 1989–90.	Not applicable.

The Blessings and Problems of Loan Financing

When coupled with aid from one of the other sources of funding, the modified federal loan programs (Stafford and SLS) have enabled nearly every admitted applicant to attend law school since 1987. Some of the problems that rendered the program difficult to use before then have been resolved either by congressional amendment or the intervention of the Law School Admission Council and its Law Access Program, although there remain some issues with respect to eligibility, the dollar value of loans, and, most significant of all, the manageability of loan repayment.

Eligibility

Eligibility used to be a serious issue because parental income was counted in determining a student's resources unless the student could meet a stringent showing of independence. Your parents' income often was sufficient to end your eligibility for any loan. With the expanded concept of independence in the 1986 amendments, under which all law students will be automatically independent and thus need not account for parental income unless they are claimed as tax dependents, most students pass needs analysis with very little impact on their ability to borrow the maximum sums available under law (as long as those sums do not exceed the cost of attendance).

The school (or schools) to which you apply will dictate which type of approved needs-analysis forms you must fill out to ascertain your need for federal aid to enable you to pay the full cost of a law education. The usual services are the Graduate and Professional School Finance Aid Service (GAPSFAS) and the College Scholarship Financial Aid Form (FAF). These are complex forms that require considerable time and concentration to fill out because of the complexity of the governing federal rules or "uniform Congressional methodology" that is applied to analyze the data to ascertain how large a loan you are entitled to.

The only tricky eligibility question remaining involves the treatment of sums you earn in the year prior to entry into law school. The critical factor in determining how much of the $11,500 in Stafford and SLS loans you can obtain is your "expected family contribution," which is subtracted from the cost of attendance at the school you have selected to calculate your loan potential.[35] Under the 1986 amendments, "expected family contribution" is to be calculated by reference to your adjusted gross income for the calendar year preceding the academic year in which you apply for a loan.[36] That income is then adjusted for income, Social Security, state and local taxes, as well as $600 per month maximum maintenance allowance for each month you are not enrolled in law school before a portion of the remainder is subtracted from cost of attendance.[37]

For example, a student who took a year off between college and law school and earned $20,000 in a state with a 5% income tax would be deemed to have approximately $8,108 in available taxable income, which would be assessed at 70 percent ($5,676) and deducted from the estimated cost of attendance at law school in order to ascertain the need for a loan. Such a student would have to attend a school costing at least $17,176 in tuition and living costs in order to be eligible for the full $11,500 in Staffords and SLS.

Because many entering law students take more than one year off prior to returning to school, a full calendar year's worth of past earnings would be attributed to them, and the level of loans for which they would be eligible could be sharply limited, particularly at public or low-cost private law schools.

The solution currently in effect permits financial-aid administrators at schools to use their professional judgment to decide that the proper base year for measuring available income should be the projected year (e.g., 1990 for academic year 1990–91) and not the prior calendar year (1989), which would relieve the expected family contribution of income no longer being earned.

Size of Loans

The 1986 amendments also changed some of the repayment terms. Law students, under the specific terms of SLS, need not repay any part of their federally subsidized loans while in law school. All SLS interest payments can, if the lender is willing, be capitalized quarterly and added to the principal amount of the loan.[38] Although that makes the SLS more palatable to students, capitalization substantially increases the sum that ultimately must be repaid. A loan of $4,000 each year over three years at an interest rate of 9 percent with quarterly capitalization of interest and a sixty-day grace period prior to repayment results in a debt of $14,590—not $12,000.

As for the dollar value of loans, the 1986 boost in loan limits, accompanied by the rise in the cumulative limits of Stafford loans and SLSs to $54,750 and $20,000, respectively, places almost all public law schools within the reach of applicants. Although as of 1988–89, the loans covered only 66 percent of the cost of attending the average private law school and only 47 percent of the price tag on the most expensive, many private schools still did not exceed $11,500 as of 1988–89, while the more expensive schools usually have an abundance of high-paying law firms dangling term-time work in front of their students as well as more scholarship funds to bridge the gap.

That $11,500 in loans may have been adequate in 1988–89 does not suggest that the overall increase in Stafford and SLS limits from $8,000 in 1976 to $11,500 in 1986 was reasonable, given the pace of inflation during the same period. From 1976 to 1986, the consumer price index nearly doubled, while the higher-education price index went up at least as much.[39]

The failure of the Stafford and SLS loan limits to keep pace with inflation has not yet interfered with access to legal education because of the various private-loan mechanisms that have developed that offer even more. The existing inflation gap will, however, only widen with each passing year and each inflationary increase in tuition, room, and board. Congress is not likely to boost loan limits by much in the near future, given concerns about the deficit and the number of loan defaults. More supplemental private loans of the kind described below in "Self Help: Nonfederal Loans," p. 53, will continue to be vital.

Manageability of Debt Burden

The more substantial and legitimate objection to increased loan limits, whether those limits be raised to $11,500 or $25,000, stems from concern about jeopardizing students' capacity to manage debt. The most serious problems created and enhanced by the rising cost of a legal education, and the emphasis it puts on borrowing after the other sources of funding have been exhausted, will not occur when you are in law school but thereafter. A heavy debt burden may result in either unbearable pressure to seek out a job in one of the highest-paying large law firms, failure to save, or outright default. Some young and even middle-aged attorneys may well find their debt burdens impossible to handle. Debt burdens could—and the emphasis has to be on the word *could*—significantly affect career choices, family formation, and capital investment.

The problem is that the true range of debt burden law school graduates confront remains uncertain. There is no good evidence, because few have the time or the money or, indeed, the incentive to collect the data. We have no aggregate nationwide data from LSAC. The ABA annual questionnaire does not request any such information on students, only on gross annual loans within a school. In the absence of data we can only make assumptions and hypothesize various debt levels in order to assess manageability. For example, $20,000 to $25,000 might be a reasonable average range for most graduates in the next several years, based on projections from old data and the advent of the expanded Stafford loan plus LAL; $37,090 is the fully capitalized debt a student would accumulate by taking out the full Stafford and SLS amounts while in law school but having no debt prior to that. The outer limits of cumulative debt for graduates in the next few years would be $50,000 and $60,000, even if they borrowed to complete college. After 1992 or thereabouts, however, the $60,000 figure could readily be breached.

After a three-year hiatus Congress revived loan consolidation in 1986.[40] Large debts can once again be consolidated, this time at a weighted-average interest rate, but in no event at less than 9 percent. A 20-year repayment term is available for consolidation loans between $20,000 and $45,000; a 25-year repayment term is available for loans above $45,000. Congress further provided that the consolidating lender should establish repayment terms that would ease repayment and avoid default, including graduated or income-sensitive repayment schedules.[41]

These provisions make debt burdens more manageable and permit individuals to attend expensive law schools and repay their debts without serious difficulty in their early professional years when their earnings are invariably lower. The new provisions, however well intended, may not achieve their objective. The following table is based on the new consolidation rules and an assumed 9 percent interest rate.

PAYMENT

Amount Borrowed	Monthly Flat	Monthly Consolidated	Annual Salary	Consolidated Payment as % Salary (Gross Income)	Consolidated Payment as % Disposable Income
$25,000	224.94	187.50	25,000	9.0	11.3
			35,000	6.4	8.6
			40,000	5.6	7.9
			60,000	3.75	5.3
			80,000	2.8	4.0
$37,090	333.71	278.17	25,000	13.4	16.8
			35,000	9.5	12.7
			40,000	8.3	11.7
			60,000	5.6	7.9
			80,000	4.2	6.0

Amount Borrowed	Monthly Flat	Monthly Consolidated	Annual Salary	Consolidated Payment as % Salary (Gross Income)	Consolidated Payment as % Disposable Income
$50,000	419.60	375.00	25,000	18.0	22.6
			35,000	12.9	17.1
			40,000	11.3	15.8
			60,000	7.4	10.6
			80,000	5.6	8.0
$60,000	503.52	450.00	25,000	21.6	27.1
			35,000	15.4	20.6
			40,000	13.5	19.0
			60,000	9.0	12.7
			80,000	6.8	9.6

The table shows that at the maximum debt level for law students entering law school in 1993 (approximately $60,000), a graduate earning at the projected median starting salary for the student's year of graduation ($53,000 in 1993) would have to make debt repayments amounting to approximately 14 percent of disposable income and slightly above 10 percent of gross income. A single student earning $60,000 would have approximately $3,540 a month left after taxes, prior to making the debt repayment. With educational debts deducted, $3,100 would remain. While this would hardly permit a high style of living in major urban areas, it would be a quite comfortable level of post-tax, post-debt repayment discretionary income. But what if the student earned less than $53,000? The amount of after-tax discretionary income would seriously shrink should the starting salary be less than the expected median, which by definition would be the case for half of the total number of students.

The resolution of today's debt burden manageability depends, like everything else, on the circumstances. Students who go to schools in the average cost of attendance range should be able, with a reasonable work effort, to hold their gross loan requirements to the capitalized Stafford–SLS maximum of $37,090. At that level of debt and with the 20-year graduated repayment option, debt burden would command only 6 percent of the projected $53,000 national average beginning salary for the fall of 1993, assuming an average interest rate of 9 percent, or slightly more than 3 percent of the gross starting high salary in New York City.

The problem that will continue to plague graduating students will involve the ability of those who earn less than the national average salary to finance much in excess of $35,000 to $40,000. That means that debt may overwhelm individuals in the smallest of firms or who choose to work in the public interest sector or for any level of government, federal, state, or local.

Two other factors require mention. Exercising the consolidation option and stretching out repayment for twenty-five years exacts a hidden penalty. What was a $50,000 debt in a lump sum is $72,800 over ten years and becomes $125,800 when repaid over twenty-five years—2.5 times larger its original amount. If repaid at a 10% interest rate, it would grow to $136,300, or 2.7 times.

Because of the effect of inflation, however, the total amount of dollars exacted by the penalty may overstate the actual burden on the graduate. If two thirds of the debt's repayment could be postponed until the last ten years of the twenty-five-year period and inflation averaged 5% annually, dollars repaid at the end of the period would have a real value of about thirty cents in current dollars, and dollars repaid after fifteen years would have a value of less than forty-five cents. Time would be responsible for paying back over 50 percent of the entire debt, almost paralleling the increase in the debt brought about by extended repayment.

There are only a few possible ways out of the high-debt bind. First, law school applicants could choose to go to public or the less expensive private schools, thereby reducing the tuition-related portion of their borrowing and keeping their loans well below the federal maximum. Second, law students could reduce borrowing by relying more heavily on their parents, applying for larger grants-in-aid from the schools, which, if awarded, automatically inflate the amounts that others will need to borrow, or stepping up their in-school and vacation-time work effort, which may entail a significant cost to their legal education.

Even then there is some hope in the form of the provision of fiscal incentives for students to pursue public-interest careers, with the funding coming from an allocation of tuition resources, which must be replenished by taxing the existing and next wave of students.

The most significant subsidies offered in recent years include loan forgiveness or what the National Association for Public Interest Law (NAPIL) prefers to call LARPs (loan assistance repayment programs), since most do not forgive but only help for several years.[42]

Forgiveness of loans based on work in the public sector or public-interest activity was proposed by law schools and rejected by Congress in 1979. A number of law schools have taken the initiative to shape and implement relatively modest private programs. Under such programs a qualifying graduate either receives an interest-free loan from the school to pay off some portion of existing federal loans, a small stipend, or a deferral of loans owed to the school. Over time some of the new and old debt will be forgiven. In order to be eligible, a graduate usually must earn below a specified sum, often including adjusted earnings of a spouse, and work either for public (federal, state, or local) employers or institutional employers that are tax-exempt under section 501(c)(3) of the Internal Revenue Code. Graduates in clerkship posts are often excluded.

LARPs are hardly universal. The latest NAPIL count is that 22 ABA-accredited schools have them, which leaves 152 others out in the cold, although NAPIL suggests that 30 additional law schools "are considering" them.[43] The existing programs all cover public-interest jobs, most government service. Only four (Harvard, Penn, Tulane, and Yale) offer direct payments for student loans from the outset, while the rest merely lend students more money to enable them to meet their debts. Many have tight income ceilings. NAPIL's 1989 LARP census revealed only 350 law school graduates benefiting at the time (presumably more are now), with funds disbursed per school, mainly in the form of loans, ranging from $6,000 to $538,000.[44] In 1989 Yale transcended LARP by engaging in general income redistribution unrelated to public-interest work that could help some graduates earning as much as $50,000 if $60,000 in debt were at stake or $45,000 with $50,000 in debt (a more likely figure).[45]

LARPs are mildly beneficial (there is no evidence demonstrating that they induce any previously uncommitted student to forsake Wall Street for the low-rent district) and by no means cheap. Most schools do not have the resources available to offer such aid.

Unless you go to a law school that offers a LARP, or your

parents help you out, or you get a generous scholarship, or you work effort is extraordinary, small-firm, public-interest, or government jobs may not be in your future if you borrow to go to law school.

Self-help: Work

Obviously the most direct of the four ways of financing a law school education is to pay for it yourself. To do that you either have to be well-to-do by virtue of inheritance, accumulate substantial savings from past summer jobs and year-round labor, or borrow from private sources without federal subsidy or guarantees, relying only on the value of your degree and your ability as an attorney to pay off your loans. If your own portfolio can support not only your tuition but also your room and board, congratulations. Few can clear that financial hurdle. The odds against anyone bankrolling enough money through summer savings to meet even the first year's cost of attendance are essentially insuperable. Deferring admission for a year in order to earn and save is, as we already noticed, an economic mistake. The lesson is clear: Learn and pay either right away (through work) or thereafter (by repaying loans).

Work during the years in law school and non-federal loans are the primary vehicles for self-help. The most accordionlike resource for financing a legal education, other than nonmandatory parental contributions, is student earnings. Current earning possibilities over the three years of law school, as the table on page 32 illustrates, range from $20,300 to $68,250. Even after deducting Social Security taxes, income taxes, and summer living expenses, work can yield a sum that is two thirds as large as the proceeds from loans. The work opportunities offered by the law schools themselves, which generally involve either reshelving library books or performing research for professors, are carefully monitored to avoid interference with the learning process. Law-firm hours, on the other hand, are not monitored and compete with the classroom. ABA rules require that a full-time student devote substantially all of his or her working hours to the study of law, interpreted to mean that no student may work in excess of twenty hours per week and still be viewed as full-time.[46] The ABA rules are most honored in their breach. The incentives for those of the 100,000 full-time students who can become law-firm clerks to do so are obvious.

The real contribution of law firms to legal education stems from the salaries they pay law students. The prospect of highly paid law-firm work is what attracts many applicants to law school in the first place. Furthermore, high salaries make tuition payment possible. Law firms can do more to make law school affordable by hiring students than by giving relatively insubstantial donations directly to the school. A firm that donates $10,000 a year to a law school to support a scholarship in the firm's name will reduce tuition costs for one student. The altruistic benefit of that gift does not compare with the benefits that a number of students (and the firm) receive when a firm employs a flotilla of student law clerks.

Of course, a student can earn even more than the table indicates if the student selects a law school with an evening or part-time division (there are sixty-four of them)[47] so as to utilize the entire day to pay for school. But the fourth year in school inevitably results in slightly higher tuition (for the credits in that final year) and the loss of a full year's earning capacity as an attorney. Also, combining work and study in a twelve- to sixteen-hour-a-day package makes it hard to participate in the social and cultural life of law school, curtails family time and is physically exhausting. Work helps. Work hurts. The benefits and costs have to be balanced by each individual.

Self-help: Non-federal Loans

The combined federal loan limits for law students do not represent the actual limit on what students can borrow. Students facing high costs of attendance can obtain substantial additional loan money with non-usurious, even reasonable interest rates and repayment terms from private sources. Unfortunately, however, such borrowing only compounds the debt-manageability problem analyzed above. Since the mid-1980s a number of private sources have developed loan programs targeted to professional and graduate education, with some aimed solely at law students.

The Law Access Loan Program (LAL) offered through LSAC enables a student to borrow as much as $12,500 a year (not to mention a bar examination loan of up to $3,000 after the student has graduated), or $37,500 in the aggregate. No one can borrow more than the cost of attendance at their law school. To be eligible for the loan the student must be credit-ready with no prior defaults of bankruptcy or present debt overburden. LAL requires the student borrower to pay a quarterly floating interest rate based upon the ninety-one-day Treasury bill rate plus 3.25 percent to be repaid over fifteen years. Interest payments can be deferred and capitalized annually while in school. There is a guaranty fee of either 6 percent (if the borrower decides to pay interest on a quarterly basis) or 8 percent (if the interest is capitalized) plus an origination fee of .25 percent of the total loan, which is deducted from the proceeds. Debt repayment is eased in the early stages of practice by a nine-month grace period. Deferments and forbearance of principal are possible.

LSAC is not the only supplier in the private loan market. Its previous loan program, which it abandoned in 1989, has been maintained at the $12,500 level by Norwest Bank. The loan is labelled LSL. The main differences are that it requires a credit application (LAL doesn't), has no origination fee (LAL's is .25 percent), has insurance ranging from 6 percent with a cosigner and interest paid quarterly to 8.875 percent with no cosigner (LAL requires no cosigner and is either at 6 or 8 percent), charges interest based on the ninety-one-day T-bill plus 3.25 percent (so does LAL), and offers no deferments.

Other competitors have entered the broader graduate and professionals market, proliferating private loans, each with unique terms, all of which change (not simply the interest rate) with some frequency so that no particular feature is likely to remain the same over a two- or three-year cycle. As of 1989–90, CONSERN offered 15-year unsecured loans up to $25,000 a year based upon the borrower's and/or cosigner's creditworthiness, with the variable interest rate based on three-month commercial paper, an origination fee of 3.5 percent, and a processing fee of $45. Repayment was to begin 30 days after disbursement, although payment of principal (but not interest) could be deferred for up to four years while enrolled in law school. CONSERN loans cover the cost of all levels of education (lifetime maximum of $100,000 per borrower) and may be used by a continuing student to pay outstanding costs for a prior period of enrollment. Staffords, SLSs, and LALs cannot pay off past bills.

The Student Loan Marketing Association's (also known as SALLIE MAE) Grad Ed Financing Plan covers law students residing in only a handful of states (most of those with large numbers of practitioners) who have good credit histories with a maximum loan of $7,500 a year (no more than $45,000 in overall educational debt), a 91-day T-bill plus 3.5 percent interest rate (but no cap), a 6 percent origination fee, and a 15-year term of repayment with the greater of $50 a month or accrued interest paid off during law school. The New England Education Loan Marketing Corporation (NELLIE MAE) had, as of 1989–90, various programs with different rates but a common annual maximum of $15,000 to be paid back over 20 years beginning 45 days after disbursement, subject to deferral of principal.

Since the market is favorable (law or medical students are excellent long-term customers with whom banks are eager to develop relationships), the possibility of more products coming on stream is high. The vendor simply has to do careful comparison shopping, trading more funds in school (lower origination fees or guaranty fees) for easier repayment later (lower interest rates, more deferment, longer term) or vice versa.

The bottom line, of course, is that the more you borrow from private sources, the more you must repay, and the more unmanageable your debt burden could become. To sell your soul for the ability to make it through law school now, only to have to give the bank devil its due later may or may not be a good deal. The choice is yours, based upon your life plan and values.

Law school is not a cheap commodity. Tuition and fees must be paid, which are modest only in public law schools. You have to pay for room and board, which are substantial everywhere but are a precondition of staying alive whatever you do. You have to forgo nearly three full years of potential job income, although that may not be as much of a barrier as it might seem. You have to pay for the cost of financing your education in part, at least, through debt.

But there is a real reward—a distant pot of gold at the end of the learning rainbow. Even more important, there is the ability to develop skills that will enable you to contribute to the enhancement of society as well as to your own personal well-being. You bought this book. This is just the first of the many significant investments you will have to make if you are to become a lawyer.

NOTES

1. Table F-2, Summary, Tuition Over the Past Ten Years, in Memorandum QS8889-46 from Kathleen Grove, Assistant Consultant on Legal Education to the American Bar Association to Deans of ABA-Approved Law Schools (hereafter "Grove" or James White, Consultant, hereafter "White"), January 30, 1989.

2. Bureau of Labor Statistics, U.S. Dept. of Labor, CPI Detailed Report Data for November 1987, Table 3 at 16, January 1988.

3. Table F-2, cited in note 1.

4. Derived from Table F-2, cited in note 1.

5. Table J-6, Student Living and Book Expenses, 1988–89, in Memorandum QS8889-60 from Grove, May 23, 1989.

6. Derived from Table F-2, cited in note 1.

7. Derived from Table J-6, cited in note 5.

8. *College Placement Council Salary Survey,* July 1989.

9. Social Security taxes are calculated throughout at 7.65 percent of the first $50,000 of earnings, while income taxes are calculated for a single person assuming a personal exemption of $2,000 and a standard deduction of $3,000 and rates of 15 percent for the first $17,850, 28 percent above that up to $43,150, 33 percent above that up to $71,000, then back to 28 percent for the remainder.

10. Estimated BLS Moderate Twelve-Month Consumption Budget Standards, December 1989 in *GAPSFAS News and Notes* 4, December 1988.

11. National Association for Law Placement, *Employment Report of Recent Law School Graduates (The Class of 1988)* 31, October 1989.

12. 2 *The Washington Lawyer* 14, July–August 1988, citing survey by Altman & Weil.

13. "Wage Spiral" in *ABA Journal* 26, June 1989.

14. Law School Admission Council, 89–2 *Law Services Report* 19, May–June 1989.

15. Pub. L. No. 99-498, Sec. 480(d)(2)(c), 100 Stat. 1268 at 1474 (1986), 20 U.S.C. 1087 vv.

16. H.R. Rep. No. 861, 99th Cong., 2d Sess. 416 (1986).

17. Table J-2, Overview of Scholarship Programs at 174 ABA-approved Law Schools, 1988–89, in Memorandum QS8889-56 from Grove, February 22, 1989.

18. *Id.*

19. Compare Table J-1, Revised Figures on Federally Guaranteed Student Loans as a Percentage of Tuition and Fees, in Memorandum QS8384-6A from White, December 19, 1983, with Table J-2, cited in note 17.

20. Compare Table J-2, Overview of Scholarship Programs at 170 ABA Law Schools, 1983–84 in Memorandum QS8384-43 from White, March 19, 1984, with Table J-2 cited in note 17.

21. Table J-4, Overview of Loan Funds at 174 ABA-approved Law Schools, 1988–89, in Memorandum QS8889-58 from Grove, February 22, 1989.

22. Table J-4, Overview of Loan Funds Other Than FGSL's at 168 ABA-approved Law Schools in Memorandum QS8485-20 from White, March 15, 1985.

23. Table J-3, Overview of Work/Study Student Employment Funds at 174 ABA-approved Law Schools, 1988–89, in Memorandum QS8889-57 from Grove, February 22, 1989.

24. *Id.*

25. *Id.*

26. *Id.*

27. *Id.*

28. See Table J1-A, Revised Figures on Federally Guaranteed Student Loans as Percentage of Tuition and Fees, 1981–82, in Memorandum QS8182-6A from White, February 26, 1982.

29. Based on $490 million in law student Staffords and SLSs as compared to $10.75 billion projected for the programs' volume nationwide in fiscal year 1988, Gwendolyn Lewis, *Trends in Student Aid: 1980 to 1988* (College Board, 1989).

30. Table J-3, cited in note 23.

31. Table J-5, Grants or Scholarships from External Sources at 174 ABA-approved Law Schools, 1988–89, in Memorandum QS8889-59 from Grove, February 15, 1989.

32. *Id.* It should be noted that there are several small private sources of scholarship aid that do not derive from the law schools themselves but about which law schools will inform you. See Law School Admission Council, *Financing Your Law School Education* 37–41 and 45–48 (second edition, 1987).

33. Table C-1, Fall 1988 Law School Enrollment in ABA-approved Law Schools, Full-time & Part-time Enrollment, in Memorandum QS8889-14 from Grove, February 22, 1989.

34. The programs appear in 20 U.S.C. Secs. 1071-1087-2 (Stafford); 20 U.S.C. Sec 1078-1 (SLS); and 20 U.S.C. Secs. 1087aa-1087gg (Perkins).

35. Pub. L. No. 99–498, Sec. 473, 100 Stat. 1268 at 1455 (1986). 20 U.S.C. 1087 mm.

36. *Id.* Sec. 476(b)(1)(A), 100 Stat, and sec. 480(a), 100 Stat, at 1463 and 1472 (1986). 20 U.S.C. 1087 pp and 1087 vv.

37. *Id.* Sec. 476(b)(1)(A)(i)–(iv), (4), 100 Stat. at 1463, 1464 (1986). 20 U.S.C. 1087 pp.

38. *Id.* Sec. 428A(c)(2), 100 Stat, at 1384. 20 U.S.C. 1078-1.

39. STATISTICAL ABSTRACT OF THE UNITED STATES 1986, Table 795, at 477 and Table 264, at 155.

40. Pub. L. No. 99-498, Sec. 428C(c)(1)(C), 100 Stat. 1268, at 1391-92. 20 U.S.C. 1078-3.

41. *Id.* Sec. 428(c)(2)(A), 100 Stat. at 1392. 20 U.S.C. 1078-3.

42. See Maureen McCloskey, LOAN REPAYMENT ASSISTANCE PROGRAM REPORT (NAPIL, 2nd ed., Aug. 1988) for a comparison of the sixteen programs then in existence.

43. Letter from Michael Caudell-Feagan, Executive Director, NAPIL to author (April 29, 1989).

44. American Bar Association/Law Student Division and NAPIL, An Action Manual for Loan Repayment Assistance, 1989.

45. Stephen Yandle, Assistant Dean, Yale Law School, "Career Options Assistance Program (COAP)," January 4, 1989.

46. American Bar Association Standards for the Approval of Law Schools, Interpretation of Standard 305(a)(iii), August 1980.

47. American Bar Association Section of Legal Education and Admissions to the Bar, *A Review of Legal Education in the United States, Fall 1988, Law Schools and Bar Admissions Requirements* (1989).

PART TWO

The Law School Experience

CHAPTER 4

Psychological Problems
of Law Students

Bernard L. Diamond, M.D.
UNIVERSITY OF CALIFORNIA, BERKELEY

> I will not say with Lord Hale, that "The
> law will admit of no rival," . . . but I will
> say that it is a jealous mistress, and re-
> quires a long and constant courtship.
>
> —Joseph Story, 1829

The law student enters law school with the expectation that, in the space of three years, he* will learn the substance of the law and that he will acquire a self-image of a lawyer. Inevitably, the student is disappointed and becomes frustrated and depressed. Depending upon his predisposition and temperament, he may blame himself, he may blame his school, or he may blame both.

He is almost immediately confronted with a new and strange teaching method—the Socratic method—which is guaranteed to rob him of his self-confidence and lower his self-esteem. The student discovers that law school teaches very little about the practice of law and the skills of lawyering. There is great preoccupation with legal decisions by higher, or appellate, courts, but little attention is given to the technique of interviewing the client. He may not learn the law, but he will, at least, learn the different forms in which the law may appear and where to search for the legal answer to a question. But such knowledge will be of no help

*The author's use of the masculine pronoun should in no way be considered as discriminatory.

63

when he discovers that the professional practice of law often requires nonlegal answers to human problems whose very existence seems not to be recognized by the legal curriculum.[1]

It is surprising that with such a mad system any students survive. Yet they do, for in most good law schools three quarters, at least, of the entering students can expect to graduate three years later. Most of these graduates will pass their bar examination (although some will have to take it more than once) and become full-fledged lawyers, committed to lifetime careers as attorneys. Judging by the results, "Though this be madness, yet there is method in't."

The Identity of the Lawyer

In recent decades much attention has been given by psychologists and psychiatrists to the problem of identity. The concept of identity and the identity crisis was developed by the psychoanalyst Erik Erikson and it has proved to be one of the most fruitful instruments for the understanding of the emotional problems of youth.[2] It is essential that the youth achieve a satisfactory sense of identity— someone "who had to become the way he is, and who, being the way he is, is taken for granted."[3] It is clear the choice of occupation plays a most important role in the achievement of such a successful identity.

Failure to establish a stable sense of identity leads to serious emotional problems—identity diffusion (often termed identity crisis) —and may result in symptoms of anxiety, depression, withdrawal, or even complete psychological breakdown.

A prime function of the law school process is to give the student a firm sense of identity as a lawyer. One important way to establish a professional identity is to identify with a successful teacher who offers a role model. A young man naturally tends to imitate those whom he admires and respects and with whom he shares common interests. Interestingly enough, there is an even greater tendency to identify with those one hates and fears. Whenever a person is threatened, physically or psychologically, he is apt to imitate the characteristics and behavior of the aggressor. Such a defense mechanism performs a valuable protective function.[4]

Dr. Andrew Watson, psychiatrist on the faculty of the University of Michigan Law School, describes the difficulties of this process of becoming the lawyer:

> In short, students expect to be taught how to behave like lawyers, which includes gaining the practical tools for performing the various tasks which they think lawyers perform. They will also be interested in understanding what "ethical behavior" consists of, though they cannot yet define clearly what they mean by it.
>
> Another anticipation which students bring to law is that they will emerge from their education *feeling* like a lawyer. Once again, though they cannot define it, they expect to be assisted in developing what we have called a lawyer's identity. Their naive layman's images of lawyers need to be transmuted into highly accurate concepts of what a lawyer actually is. At the beginning, they will confuse the internal and external values and images of role and identity. This confusion will cause them much distress during the early months of their training.[5]

Certainly, one way of acquiring a professional identity is to perform the activities of the professional in the ways that professionals customarily do. Unfortunately for the law student, modern law schools provide only the most limited opportunities for such practical experience. In this respect law students are denied the kinds of opportunities that medical students take for granted. Very early in the medical student's education he begins to examine real, live patients who already look upon him as a doctor. Long before he graduates he will become familiar with the hospital world and its multifarious inhabitants. By his senior year he will be actually treating patients (under close supervision) and feeling very much like a doctor, despite the limitations of his clinical knowledge.

A further advantage for the medical student is that most of his clinical teachers will be active practitioners. In fact, the medical school itself, with its clinics and university hospitals is actively engaged in the practice of medicine. The medical student thus has the opportunity to identify with teachers who unambiguously model the role of the practicing physician, surgeon, or specialist. He need only imitate his teachers to guarantee his future professional success.

Law students, on the other hand, are confronted mostly with

teachers who perform few, if any, lawyering tasks. His teachers usually consult with no clients and try no cases, nor do they sit on the bench. From the student's vantage point, his teachers' only nonteaching occupation seems to be writing textbooks and law review articles. This encourages the best and the brightest of the law students to do likewise. But the majority of law students have no such literary ambitions (or talents), and they are well aware that lawyering consists of something quite different from the observed activities of their professors.

As a psychiatrist, I was trained in the conservative medical model: an intensive, scientifically oriented premedical program, then medical school with its laboratories, clinics and teaching hospitals, followed by three postgraduate years of psychiatric hospital residency training. Especially in the residency training, the education process consisted almost exclusively of doing—of diagnosing and treating psychiatric patients. I early felt like a doctor and I was more sure of what I was practicing then than I am now after many more years of professional development and diffusion.[6]

Despite my twenty-five years' experience on a law school faculty, I have never gotten over my amazement that law students are given so little opportunity to do what lawyers do. Granted, in recent years the development of so-called "clinical" programs makes some gestures toward this type of education. But, at best, the clinical programs and their associated legal-aid clinics, their fieldwork, and their courtroom visitations are only a minor portion of the law student's education. Further, the student is quite conscious of the fact that the most prestigious professors do not participate in the clinical programs and that no matter how successfully he functions in the legal-aid clinic it will not enhance his status in the class hierarchy. This low esteem of clinical education still exists despite the urging twenty years ago of the then dean of Harvard Law School, Erwin Griswold, that legal education must include training in the human-relations skills so necessary for the practice of law.[7]

But giving lip service to the concept of education for human-relations skills without providing experience in which such skills could be acquired does no good. Clinical legal training is still given short shift, and the more prestigious the school the more likely it is that clinical education will be disparaged. Even Griswold refuses to acknowledge that clinical education can provide the human-relations skills he earlier advocated with such vigor.[8]

Dr. Alan Stone, a psychiatrist who is a professor at Harvard Law School, states the case for clinical education very well:

> . . . it is the clinical milieu which provides the best possibility for law students to begin to learn essential human relations skills. Cases like those . . . [in a book] do have some utility, but often they neither have the psychological depth nor the complexity that allows for rigorous analysis; nor do they involve the students personally in a way which permits the psychological elements to come to life and be comprehended at the level of emotionally significant learning. At best they lend themselves to an abstract and limited conceptual analysis which must be made on the basis of insufficient data diluted by speculation.
>
> In contrast, the student's experience with human problems in the legal clinic always has the potential of being emotionally real. A student is directly involved in a case and can explore its social and psychological implications in as great a depth as his motivation allows. If those who control legal education believe that students should develop human relations skills in law school then the legal clinic is the single best vehicle for doing so.
>
> Clinical legal education, moreover, has important psychoanalytical benefits in addition to providing a setting in which human relations skills can be learned. A well-run clinical program can offer an arena for the realistic implementation of some of a student's activist values and for the exercise of altruistic and egalitarian motivations.[9]

The Socratic Method

Very soon after entry into law school the student is confronted with a method and style of teaching for which he has no preparation in his undergraduate education. Most of his previous experience has been with the lecture system, where he passively absorbed the words of wisdom of his professors, supplemented with prescribed readings. All that was required of him was to regurgitate the appropriate answers in examinations. In the better universities he was encouraged to demonstrate that he knew how to read and write by submitting a number of term papers for which he was rewarded with an A grade more for his originality than for the profundity and logical precision of his thought. Recitations were considered "high school stuff." The nearest would be the upper-division seminar where once during the term he would give an oral presentation for which he had ample time for preparation and for which nothing but the mildest criticism would be expected.

As described by Stone[10] the Socratic method is unique to American law schools and was the creation of one man, Christopher Columbus Langdell, who was Dean of Harvard Law School in the late nineteenth century.

> For Langdell, the Socratic dialogue was a necessary adjunct to the case method of studying. Believing that law was a "science" consisting of a cohesive body of clearly discernible "principles or doctrines," he felt that the dialogue was the best way to help the student elicit these principles. But Langdell refused to have these principles laid out before the student; rather, it was necessary that "the student judge all material for himself, scrutinize instances closely, accept no other man's judgment until he had judged its logic for himself."[11]

I know of no better description of the varieties of Socratic method than that of C. A. Peairs, Jr. Its subtleties require direct quotation:

> 1. Doctor [used here in its true medieval sense of teacher] may simply ask leading questions and receive the indicated answers, proceeding smoothly and orderly through the material along a predetermined set course. This differs from lecture only in that it takes longer, and offers the listener the variety of two voices for the monotony of monologue; but it must be a poor lecturer who cannot devise at least equivalent leaven, and all in all, this procedure does not have much to recommend it as a substitute for lecture.
> 2. Doctor may ask elucidative questions until student takes an erroneous or indefensible position, and then attack that position with argumentative questions, or, with the student's position as a starting point, ask questions leading from it to a point where the error becomes palpable. This *reductio ad absurdum* process is useful in inducing caution in expressing opinions; but when the elementary thought training has been accomplished, this proce-

dure may prove oppressive rather than catalytic, as students may become chary of approaching the open area of the law, or undocumented policy questions, through reluctance to advance their own ideas without authority, or even to think for themselves.

3. In variation of the second process, doctor induces student to state, or agree with different rules or judicial statements of wide acceptance, and then leads him in the same fashion from that starting point until he meets himself in the road, coming in the other direction. This process is very useful in teaching the analytical and critical process, and in demonstrating that independent thought may often be better than acceptance of prior dictum, as well as in restoring mortality to some youth's false legal hagiarchy; but is seldom adequate to cover all points which must be treated in a course, and is most effective when loose ends are tied up in a summary lecture at the end of each chapter of topic covered.

4. A fourth method—let Socrates' shade not be too distressed at its inclusion—I shall call the pure case method, in which doctor (a) calls for statement of assigned case—of course, pinning down analysis of facts, issue, reasoning, and dictum by cross-questioning as usual; (b) puts hypothetical cases; and (c) asks for opinions, criticisms, and disagreements, without leading at all as to the answers expected, but only as to the areas and aspects of the problem to be considered. Here the teacher approaches most closely the function of the medium and lecture is, so to speak, in aphelion. The difficulties in this method are: first, in resisting the temptation to lead by putting obvious cases in juncture with the tough ones, and mixing deceptive leading toward wrong positions with a sequence of cases which approach the obvious, to baffle attempts to determine doctor's own opinion by analysis of his method; and second, in resisting student attempts to break the process by direct classroom-question or by desperate corridor campaigns to obtain under-the-counter trots and hints, as the last refuge from the library itself.[12]

Certainly, if Anna Freud's principle of identification with the aggressor holds as true for the educational process as it does for the developmental process of the child, the Socratic method must provide the major source of the lawyer's notorious insensitivity to the fine points of human emotional relationships. The Socratic method is a marvelous device for the emphasis of the purely logical, abstract essence of the appellate case. The deductive precision of such Socratic dialogue can further the illusion, claimed by Langdell, that law is a true science.[13]

Dehumanizing Tendencies

Somehow, in the preoccupation with legal logic, the humanity of the participants in the legal process is lost. I was struck by this a long time ago when I first became interested in the historical development of the laws concerned with criminal responsibility of the mentally ill. As everyone acknowledges, the single most important case in the development of the concept of criminal insanity is that of Daniel M'Naughten,[14] out of which came the ubiquitous M'Naughten rules of insanity.[15]

I became intensely curious as to what eventually happened to M'Naughten after he was convicted. Was he really insane? Or was his defense of insanity a clever scheme for the concealment of his political motives, as was so vehemently believed by his intended victim, Prime Minister Robert Peel, and by Queen Victoria? M'Naughten's trial was the sensation of the Victorian era. The legal and historical references to the case number literally in the thousands. Yet a long and thorough search failed to provide the slightest clue as to what happened to the famous defendant. Obviously, no one before me thought it of any interest or importance. I finally hit upon the solution of writing Bethlem Hospital,[16] England, and I was able to obtain copies of M'Naughten's original hospital records. Yes, M'Naughten really was insane. He remained confined in institutions for the criminally insane until his death in 1865. Throughout those twenty-two years he continued to demonstrate ample clinical evidence of mental illness.[17]

Similarly, in an extraordinary, often-cited California case of 1907, a man was adjudged to be a "homicidal maniac" and committed to a state hospital for the insane. Within seconds after the judicial declaration that he was insane, he shot and killed the sheriff who had arrested him. He was tried for murder, found guilty *and sane*, and was sentenced to death. The California Supreme Court upheld his conviction and the penalty, affirming the principle that the rule of insanity for purposes of commitment is quite different from the rule for determining criminal responsibility. I found it hard to believe that a man as mentally ill as he would actually be executed, but I could find no clue as to his ultimate disposition in the law books. I finally had to check through the records of executions at San Quentin Prison to learn that he had been hanged there in 1909.[18]

Why this extraordinary lack of interest in the people who are subjects of the leading cases? It is as if a deliberate effort were being made to dehumanize the law, to transform the law into an abstraction that has no relationship to an individual. I would like to see law reports illustrated with photographs of all the participants, including the victim, the defendant, the attorneys, and the judge. Perhaps then the student might grasp the fact that the legal process is concerned with real, live human beings. To my knowledge, no modern law book is illustrated except those dismal anatomical texts used for reference by personal-injury lawyers. This has not always been so. I own a 1562 Flemish criminal-law book[19] illustrated with many beautifully detailed engravings depicting in fascinating visual form each and every crime described in the book.

I tend to agree with Dr. Alan Stone that recent criticisms of the Socratic method are vastly overdrawn.[20] For example, Duncan Kennedy claims that law professors are a group of sadists destroying the mental health of students.[21] Nevertheless, the absence of the human element in the cases which form the core of the Socratic dialogue together with the instructor's insensitivity to the personal feelings of the students can only encourage the student to do likewise with his clients when he graduates. Only too often, the young lawyer adopts the style of aggressive, sarcastic interrogation toward his own clients, creating in them the same feelings of harassment and anxiety that he himself experienced in law school.

The remedy, in my judgment, is not to abandon the Socratic method, but rather to complement it with human and humanizing experiences. A well-managed and closely supervised clinical program is ideal for that purpose.

Who Are the Law Students?

In a discussion of the educational process by which law students are transformed into lawyers, due consideration must be given to the characteristics of law students *before* they enter law school. It has always been taken for granted that some kind of important alteration must be made in the thinking and feeling of the student that will change him into a suitable image of the lawyer. Surprisingly, this may not be necessary.

An empirical study of Walter Steel, Jr., attempted to locate differences in student attitudes as they relate to the practice of criminal law.[22] Steel assumed that entering first-year students would show marked differences from students in their final year. There were no such differences detected. The entering students consistently demonstrated lawyerlike attitudes, strongly suggesting that law students start with a higher level of legal sophistication and sense of identity as a lawyer than law schools credit them.

There have been a number of generalizations about the personalities of law students—the kinds of persons who decide to become lawyers.[23] It is particularly difficult, at this time, to accept any such generalizations because of the changing character of law school students. This has come about because of two distinctly different factors: first, the greatly increased competition for entry into law school; and second, the increase in the so-called activist students.

Before World War II, entry into law school was a painless procedure. Stiff competition for admission existed only for a very few prestigious schools, such as Harvard and Yale. Satisfactory completion of a four-year college program guaranteed admission to a very good law school. Many very adequate law schools accepted all students who had completed two years of college. Then, as now, there was no requirement for any particular type of prelegal college program. The would-be lawyer could decide as late as he wished in his undergraduate program and was practically assured entry into an adequate law school. As a consequence many persons entered law school because they had failed to make some other, earlier, occupational choice. Entry into other programs which might attract the upwardly mobile, ambitious student, such as medicine, required years of specialized undergraduate preparation, and competition for admission to those graduate professional programs was intense.

To be sure, there were problems about staying in school. All are familiar with the apocryphal tale of the law professor who embellished his opening lecture to the freshman students with the command to look to their right and their left, for the students sitting next to them would not survive beyond the first year. Actually, survival in law school was not all that difficult. But many students did fail simply because they had little interest in the concentrated application which the study of law requires. They should not have been in law school in the first place.

Increasingly, in the last three decades, the competition for admission to law school has become greater. Now, in the better law schools, it may be as difficult to be admitted to law school as it is to enter medical school. Applicants to each good law school number in the thousands for the few hundred openings in the first-year class. Even the second-rate law schools may have two or three applicants for each opening. Most law students now have oustandingly high scholastic records as undergraduates and have scored high on the Law Student Admissions Test (LSAT).

Accordingly, today, law students tend to be more intelligent, more sophisticated, and more aware of what it means to be a lawyer. They are firmly driven toward a high social status, and they are well aware that a profession, rather than business, is the modern route to such status with its power and monetary rewards. They are used to competition, and the requirement of dedicated application to their studies does not frighten them. Yet, inevitably, with such increased capacities goes increased anxiety. Fear of failure and concern with after-graduation employment possibilities lead to intensely competitive attitudes. Consequently, the less secure student is still likely to respond with the expectation that he is doomed to flunk out even though the failure rate in his school may be less than 10 percent.

This is particularly true for the ethnic minority student. Many prestigious law schools encourage the admission of third-world students, and some schools have special admission programs by which minority students may enter with distinctly lower undergraduate scholarship records and lower LSAT scores than are required for white students. Despite the encouragement at the admission level, the minority student will often be required to demonstrate the same writing and speech skills more typically associated with the middle-class white student. Law school studies are still closely tuned to traditional middle-class attitudes, skills, and values. The minority student may find it hard to compete on that level. Even if able to do so, he may firmly believe that such middle-class achievements are to be disparaged rather than emulated. These minority students, with the white activist students who share their views, present a new experience for the law school faculty and the faculty response is not always temperate and productive.

Dr. Andrew Watson stated in 1968:

> In addition to the important intellectual tools, students bring a whole set of ingrained, family-fostered, psychological images which will be crucial to their healthy and successful development as lawyers-to-be. These images are the models from which the student derives much of his motivation and measures his success. Nachmann reports several family background characteristics present to a statistically significant degree, which differentiate lawyers from dentists and social workers. All have hypothetical connection to the "central characteristics of the lawyer's work":
> 1. The prominence of verbal aggression.
> 2. The concern with human justice.
> 3. The exercise of privileged curiosity into the lives of others.[24]

But the Barbara Nachmann study referred to was written in 1960, and it is questionable whether the same findings would be true today.[25] I am confident that as the conventional interests, motivations, and values of the legal profession change, so will the dominant personality patterns of the students. Obviously, for the law schools to continue to successfully train successful lawyers will require that their curriculum and teaching methods change appropriately.

Even before the third-world and white-activist students were pressuring law schools into more emphasis on "relevant" studies, there was evidence of significant shifts in the relative status of the different legal specialties. In the first half of the twentieth century, high-prestige law was closely focused upon money and property. Big business and high finance commanded the finest legal talent, and law review students confidently looked forward to a career within large law firms that catered to those interests. Law concerned with people—criminal law, family law, civil rights, and the like—was strictly low-status. Few of the top students expressed any interest in such areas of law; criminal law was reserved for the bottom of the class; family law for the women students; civil rights for the tiny group of radicals who managed to infiltrate the schools.

Although the shift in hierarchies in the practice of law is not as dramatic, it is markedly different in the better law schools of today. Now, it is not at all unusual for the business students and the best teachers to have a strong interest in "people law." Where formerly an outstanding law graduate might consider a job in the public defender's or the district attorney's office only for the purpose of obtaining valuable trial experience, or as a first step toward a career in politics, now such a student may unabashedly express his interest and concern for the people enmeshed in the criminal-justice process. Many a radical college student who has reconciled himself to the unlikelihood of a political revolution enters law school with the specific goal of becoming an agent of social change. The traditional law review now competes with the journals of ecology and of civil rights for the editorial services of the best students. Women law students, much more numerous than formerly, no longer see themselves as restricted to family law or as behind-the-scenes memorandum writers for the large firms.

Law faculties are also changing. Some of the top law schools now appoint psychiatrists and psychoanalysts to their faculties. Sociologists and anthropologists are beginning to assert their right to participate in the legal-education process. The new law school dean may well have specialized in criminal law before his rise to eminence. Demands for affirmative action favoring minorities and women now extend to the faculty as well as the student body. Such changes in the law schools must presage comparable changes in the professional practice of law, or else the educational process will be sadly out of step with the profession it educates for. I do not fear this will happen, for an accommodation is likely to be reached before a profession as influential and powerful as law loses control over its own educational institutions. Whether the law schools will retreat to more traditional and conservative positions or the character of lawyering will change remains to be seen.

The Stress of Law School

At the same time that law schools offer more challenges and opportunities for a wider variety of people with quite different motivations than they would have had forty years ago, the dilettante who chooses law because he can think of no other occupation, or the undisciplined student who seeks the status of a professional but cannot apply himself diligently, will find law school a most difficult and unpleasant place. Law school is easiest for the students who genuinely like law and what law is all about. They like to read and study, they like to analyze logically and precisely, and they are articulate, both in speech and in writing. They enjoy dispute and argument, and they can hold their own in any Socratic dialogue. Such students have only one psychological problem in law school: they are accustomed to being at the top of their class. Law schools are likely to have many such students and obviously they cannot all be at the head of the class. Some such very capable and bright students become depressed and discouraged when they find themselves in the number two or three position. This ailment is self-curing. The arrogant adolescent attitude behind such disappointment is quickly dissipated by a more realistic appraisal of one's abilities relative to those of one's classmates.

More serious are the doubts, misgivings, and self-recriminations of the student who finds law school so different than he expected that he entertains serious doubts about his ambition to become a lawyer. Sometime during the first year he may go into a real funk, finding himself unable to concentrate in class and unable to sleep at nights. His inability to keep up with his studies only accentuates his belief that he is unfit for a career in law. Again, it has been my experience that such a condition is self-healing. But it takes much longer—it may even take the full three years of school and some time in practice before one fully appreciates that the right choice was made after all. In the meantime a few hours spent with a sympathetic counselor or psychotherapist may be extremely helpful. By one means or another, such a student must acquire the basic insight that one can be eminently suitable for a particular profession without, at the same time, feeling at all comfortable or harmonious with the educational process which leads to that profession. One can always take comfort in the possibility that, in this time of rapid change, it is the law school that is out of tune, rather than the student who doubts the wisdom of his choice.

Some students may find that difficult situations arise in their personal lives. A disappointing love affair can wreck a student's motivation and capacity for study faster than a nervous break-down. Fortunately, the student who persists will survive and his capacity for hard work will return together with his self-esteem as soon as he engages in a new emotional relationship of comparable depth. But some students are confronted with economic and emotional demands by their family situation of a kind which would devastate even the strongest. As law schools seek out students who do not come from well-behaved, conventional, middle-class families, difficulties sometimes arise which are beyond the comprehension of the most sympathetic faculty advisers.

Law school faculties are beginning to recognize the affirmative-action recruitment and special admission programs which bring minority students into the school are of little value if strenuous efforts are not made to keep those students in school and make sure they eventually graduate. This often requires considerable flexibility and willingness to give attention to the individual student's particular situation. In the past, law schools, with their "make it or out" philosophy of education, could get away with such indifference to the humanity of their students. That seems much less true now, for the pressure to succeed with affirmative-action programs is very strong. One hopes that schools which develop humane, understanding policies toward their minority students will also extend it to their nonminority students. After all, psychological and situational problems are not restricted to minorities.

Pregnancy and the care of young children cause problems for women students, and few law schools are equipped to be of help. Leaves of absence, with guaranteed readmission, should be the right of the pregnant student. Child-care centers may become as important a component of the university as the student health service and must be available to the children of both the men and the women students. For now, the responsibilities of the care of young children can fall on the father as much as on the mother, and the lack of child-care facilities can make intensive study impossible.

Many large universities now provide excellent counseling and psychotherapeutic services to their students. It is my impression that law students are more reluctant than others to utilize such services. A prideful arrogance which insists that one handle one's own problems unassisted can be very destructive. Often such pseudoindependence is fostered by the faculty, who neither understand nor are sympathetic to such means of psychological help. Advice to "buck up" and "straighten up" with sarcastic remarks about the possible unsuitability of the student for a legal career are never helpful to the seriously emotionally depressed student. Neither are false words of encouragement of the "Don't worry, everything will be all right tomorrow" type. Emotional depression which persists more than a few days and is accompanied by difficulty in concentration, accentuation of self-doubts, and lowered self-esteem is a serious condition which requires professional help. There should be no hesitation in seeking such help, because depression is very much a treatable and curable condition.

Fortunately, law students seem to have relatively few problems with excessive use of alcohol and abuse of drugs. There are, of course, the weekend drunks, and a few students become trapped in the use of "speed" and other stimulants as a desperate aid to intensive study. Use of cocaine has become chic in some social circles, but it and the hard narcotic drugs have not been prevalent among law students. Use of marijuana is quite common and some students report that its relaxing effect facilitates concentrated study. This is probably more illusory than real, but in the amounts and frequency used by law students, it has not seemed to impede progress in school.

Frankly, psychotic breakdowns such as schizophrenia also tend to be uncommon among law students, as compared with other graduate students. Such a breakdown, when it does occur, is always a most serious matter that requires immediate psychiatric attention. Withdrawal from school is generally necessary, and consideration of return is contingent upon many factors. If there is evidence of particular vulnerability to the type of stress prevalent in the law school and that such stress played a significant role in the precipitation of the psychotic break, return to school may be very ill-advised.

Law students, to my observation, seem to be a well-adjusted

group who adapt remarkably well to what at times is an almost intolerable stress. The incessant demand for competitive high performance may well take its psychosomatic toll later in life. Surely, if the pace of law school is compulsively maintained throughout the lawyer's professional life, a price will have to be paid in the form of heart attacks, high blood pressure, and other stress ailments. Hence, it is not too early for the student to learn the use of recreation and social activities as a form of relaxation and diversion from the pressures of school. For many, the traditional counterbalance of intensive physical exercise will be most useful. Others may find that relaxation techniques such as transcendental meditation are useful. People differ widely as to what they find relaxing and diversionary. I think most law students have learned before they reach law school what methods work best for them. However, it is important that the student not allow the competitive atmosphere of the law school to push him into the abandonment of the recreational methods which have worked for him in the past.

NOTES

1. For a nice illustration of how "the law" may not determine the advice the lawyer provides for his client to see Probert and Brown, "Theories and Practices in the Legal Profession," 19 *University of Florida Law Review* 447, 450 (1966–7).

2. Erik Erikson, *Identity, Youth and Crisis* (New York: Norton, 1968). This book contains the fullest description of Erikson's theories of identity.

3. Erik Erikson, "The Problem of Ego Identity," 4 *Journal of the American Psychoanalytic Assn.* 56, 68 (1956).

4. Anna Freud, *The Ego and the Mechanisms of Defense* (1966).

5. Andrew Watson, "The Quest for Professional Competence: Psychological Aspects of Legal Education," 37 *University of Cincinnati Law Review* 91, 106 (1968).

6. It is interesting, however, that my mother never did think of me as a "real doctor." To her, a psychiatrist who treated only the mind could never be a "real doctor" regardless of his professional training and degrees.

7. Erwin Griswold, "Law Schools and Human Relations," 37 *Chicago Bar Record* 199 (1956).

8. Erwin Griswold, "Hopes—Past and Future," 21 *Harvard Law School Bulletin*, 36, 40 (1970).

9. Alan Stone, "Legal Education on the Couch," 85 *Harvard Law Review* 392, 429 (1971).

10. Note 9 *supra*, at 406.

11. *Ibid.;* citations omitted.

12. C. A. Peairs, Jr., "Essay on the Teaching of Law," 12 *Journal of Legal Education* 323, 337 (1960).

13. See, for a general discussion of the nonscientific foundation of law, Bernard L. Diamond, "The Scientific Method and the Law," 19 *Hastings Law Journal* 179 (1967).

14. *Daniel M'Naughten's Case,* 10 Clark & Fin. 200, 8 Engl. Rep. 718 (1943). The correct spelling of the name *M'Naughten* is much in doubt. In most modern references it is usually spelled as *McNaghten,* the least likely to be the correct way. See Bernard L. Diamond, "On the Spelling of Daniel M'Naghten's Name," 25 *Ohio State Law Journal* 84 (1964).

15. Opinion of the Judges on Crimes by Insane Persons, 26 *Legal Observer or Journal of Jurisprudence* 273 (1843).

16. From which comes the word "bedlam."

17. Bernard L. Diamond, "Isaac Ray and the Trial of Daniel M'Naghten," 112 *American Journal of Psychiatry* 651 (1956).

18. People v. Willard, 150 Cal. 2d 543 (1907).

19. Iodoco Damhouderio, *Praxis Rerum Criminalium Iconibus. . . . , Antwerp,* 1562.

20. Note 9 *supra,* at 409.

21. Duncan Kennedy, "How the Law School Fails: A Polemic," 1 *Yale Review of Law & Social Action* 71 (Spring 1970).

22. Walter Steel, Jr., "A Comparison of Attitudes of Freshman and Senior Law Students," 22 *Journal of Legal Education* 318 (1970).

23. See, for example, Watson, note 5 *supra,* at 94.

24. *Ibid.*

25. Barbara Nachmann, "Childhood Experience and Vocational Choice in Law, Dentistry, and Social Work," 7 *J. Counseling Psychology* 243 (1960).

CHAPTER 5

Advice for Minority Students

Charles R. Lawrence III
STANFORD UNIVERSITY

Strangers in a Strange Land

Because I am one of the all too few minority professors teaching law school, I am often asked to speak to groups of minority students who are thinking about applying to law school or are about to enter their first year of study. I am always struck by the fact that they are haunted by the same fears, anxieties, doubts, and questions that I was when I entered law school twenty years ago. Why am I here? Am I really smart enough to cut it in this law school? Just who are all these white folks who look so comfortable and at ease? I wonder what they're thinking about me? Will my professors be racists? Will they give me a fair chance? What the hell is a tort, anyway? Are the other minority students feeling as uncomfortable and alienated as I am? Does the fact that I have these feelings mean I'm turning into some kind of crazy paranoid?

Of course it is important to recognize that you are not going crazy, that all first-year students, including the preppy-looking white folks, are beset by fears and anxieties. But it is really important to face up to these feelings and the realities from which they stem, so that you may become their master rather than vice versa. Harriet Tubman, the great underground railroad leader and abolitionist, once referred to herself as a "stranger in a strange land." It is a fitting description for all minority students entering law school. Law schools are part of America. It would be foolish to think that one could escape the realities of American racism in law school. Our life experiences in America have made us different from our white colleagues, and we face a different reality. We must learn to use those differences positively to change that reality.

Admissions

Many minority students wonder whether they should apply to law school. They are discouraged by the fact that their Law School Admissions Test (LSAT) scores may not be as high as those of their white classmates. Someone has told them that the Supreme Court held, in the *Bakke* case, that special admissions programs for minorities were illegal, and that law schools are no longer making a special effort to recruit and admit minorities. They have heard that there are already too many lawyers and worry that they will have trouble finding a job.

If you've been told that the *Bakke* case outlawed affirmative admissions programs for minorities, you should set the source of your information straight. The Court did say that admissions programs which employed a quota violated the law, but it also said that schools may consider the race of an applicant as a means of identifying those persons who will bring a special experience, perspective, or talent to the school. Most law schools recognize that a racially diverse student body makes for a more enriching educational experience for all. And most admissions committees understand that if they mechanically utilized test scores as the only criterion for admission, they would miss some of the best and most interesting students. Many law schools are not doing as much as they should to support the vigorous recruitment and admission of minorities, but the programs still exist. If you are thinking about applying to a particular law school, you should contact the appropriate minority student organization at the school for information and help. At many schools, these organizations participate in recruitment or act in an advisory capacity to the admissions committee and can be most helpful to you both in assessing your chances and helping you with the application process.*

*For a list of publications and programs that will be helpful in the admissions process, see "Suggested Resources and Readings," p. 91.

Law schools do not require a specific undergraduate major or course of study. It is important, though, that your transcript contain some serious-sounding liberal arts courses such as history, economics, political science, or physics. Admissions committees are suspicious of basket-weaving majors. It is also a good idea to take several courses that require a heavy dose of reading and essay work. You will want to do everything possible to strengthen your ability to express yourself clearly in writing. Most law school applications require a personal statement containing autobiographical information and your reasons for wanting to attend law school. Take the time to write a thoughtful, clearly-written statement, and be sure your essay is free of grammatical or typographical errors. It is usually the admissions committee's only sample of your own work. Try to include information and background material that will make you stand out. Remember, almost all of your competition will have won awards or held student office. Personal experiences, something about your family, or an insight gained while traveling or working on a summer job, may be the things that make you sound most interesting. Try to convey the real you.

You should begin the process of applying for financial aid at the same time you begin the application process. . . . Be sure that the financial aid office has received your application. Ask for a written verification that it is complete. Most law schools seeking to attract minority law students understand that they will probably require some financial aid. But from the student's perspective, the financial aid is rarely enough, and indeed it may often be inadequate. Minority students frequently find that they are forced to operate on an especially tight budget. If you find yourself in this position, do not feel that you are alone or that it is insurmountable. Many practicing minority attorneys came from families of minimal means, but in some way managed to get through law school.

Surviving by Excelling

Each of us has had a grandmother or an aunt or an older brother who once told us that we'd have to be better than the white man and work twice as hard to get ahead. This was certainly true for our grandparents. And, despite significant advances in the fight against racial discrimination and the belief among many whites that affirmative action programs have resulted in so-called reverse discrimination, it remains true today. What we must remember is that our grandmother's words were an admonition of the need to strive for excellence and not a justification for failure.

Some minority students use the reality of racial discrimination as an excuse for their own lack of effort or fear of personal failure. They rig the game from the beginning by saying, "I don't really care. The law is the white man's game," or "Why should I really try when these racist so-and-so's aren't going to give me a chance anyway." They seek temporary comfort in the fact that if they do not measure up, they will have a ready-made excuse. Because there is some truth in these rationalizations for minimizing our endeavors, we are all tempted to assume this attitude from time to time. But we should struggle against the temptation of achieving the shallow victory of fulfilling our own prophecy. Racial discrimination in law school, like that we face in the larger society, should be fought by excelling in whatever game we have chosen to play (be it practicing law or grass roots organizing), and by using our excellence to make the game a fairer one.

Professors

Many students are somewhat intimidated by professors and reluctant to speak to them after class or visit them in their offices. Minority students often feel particularly hesitant to approach faculty members. They are concerned that their professor will have stereotyped preconceptions about their abilities or be insensitive to their problems. There are, of course, some professors who are difficult to talk to as well as those who continue to harbor racist attitudes. But the problem is to find a way to suspend your own judgments and preconceptions so that you can make the best use of the educational resource professors provide. Be an aggressive consumer. Force yourself to talk to professors after class or visit them during their office hours. Compile a list of questions about points raised in class or the casebook which you do not understand. Write an answer to an old exam question and arrange to have the professor correct it and go over it with you. It is natural for you to be fearful that you will reveal your ignorance and engender the professor's contempt. Remember, exams are usually graded anonymously, and if you learn from your mistakes before the exam, you won't be ignorant when it counts.

Furthermore, personal contact with professors can often work the other way. The professor may well be impressed with the way you present yourself and recognize attributes you possess that have not been apparent in class. Many white professors have a genuine desire to play some role in the integration of the bar and would welcome the opportunity to feel that they had identified and encouraged a promising minority student. A colleague at a prestigious East Coast law school once suggested that minority students institute an "adopt-a-professor plan," where each of them would select a professor with whom to establish a personal relationship. He reminded them that the best white students have always recognized that when it came time to apply for judicial clerkships or prestige jobs, who one knew was as important as what one knew. If you've developed a good relationship with your professors, it's also likely that you've learned a good deal more in the bargain.

Fellow Students

Other students are your most valuable and readily accessible educational source. Many students find that they learn more in study groups with other students than they do in class, and the friends they make among their peers in law school often become important professional contacts at later points in their careers.

Minority students often find it difficult to establish the appropriate balance between establishing the contacts and networks among their white peers, which will give them the fullest access to the benefits offered by the mainstream of the profession, and maintaining the solidarity with other minority students, which provides them with support in an alien environment and a political base from which to make their needs known. I am a firm believer in the importance of active participation in and support of minority student organizations and other informal mutual support networks. Without the political work of these organizations few of us would have the opportunities we have today. They also provide a place of refuge from the assaults of law school life, with classmates to whom no explanation need be given.

If you are clear about the nature of your commitment to your own ethnic group, however, you will not feel ambivalent about your associations with white classmates. Study groups and other relationships should be formed on the basis of mutual needs and benefits, not race. When selecting study partners, avoid the loud-mouth know-it-alls and look for the classmate who is secure enough in his or her intelligence to share knowledge and to respect the ideas you have to offer.

Studying and Exams

In the final analysis, doing well in law school means doing well on law school exams. Professor Derrick Bell, Dean of the Law School at the University of Oregon and the Harvard Law School's first black professor, has written an excellent article entitled "Law School Exams and Minority Group Students." This article can be found in 4 *Black Law Journal* 304–13 (Winter 1981). You should ask for it in your law library and read it at the beginning of your first year.

Among other things, Professor Bell suggests that for most minority students the technique required to write good law school exams involves skills which must be learned through consistent practice. Many students who do poorly on exams complain that they "knew the law" as well as classmates who did well. Often in undergraduate courses they succeeded by memorizing the facts or rules and regurgitating them on the exam. But this does not work with most law school exams. One must learn to answer one or more questions containing a hypothetical fact situation in essay form. This involves an analysis like the one you would be expected to do were a client with the same problem to walk into your office. In order to write a good law school essay exam, you must learn to recognize and isolate the legal issues that must be discussed and to organize a clearly written answer, one that identifies the important facts and then applies rules of law you have learned to the issues they raise.

These techniques of analysis and organization are seldom directly taught in class. That is, your professors will not tell you how to spot an issue in a fact pattern or how to organize an answer that applies the relevant facts to the applicable law. They expect you to discover how to do these things by observing the way judges do them in the cases you read, and by listening to the questions and answers in the classroom discussion. Acquiring these skills of analysis, organization, and argument will be particularly difficult for those students who have not been exposed to them at earlier stages in their education. They cannot be learned by watching others. You must engage in the process yourself. The main message here is that you are likely to need hard and continuing work on these techniques, beginning not the week before exams, but on a regular basis throughout the year.

Some law schools have organized tutorial programs that focus on exam-taking. These courses involve the administration of regular practice exam questions. The students' answers are individually critiqued by a faculty person or a teaching assistant, who discusses the answer with the student alone or in a small group setting and then returns the answer to the student to be rewritten. These programs have proved much more successful than tutorials, which have focused solely on substantive course material. You should organize to request such a program if your law school does not already have one.* If this is not possible, you should work informally with other students by writing answers to old exams and then asking your professor to go over the answers with you in a small group.

Because preparation for exams involves a continuing and consistent effort from the beginning of the school year, it is especially important to develop good study habits. Organize and schedule specific study times for each course and stick by them. Use your time efficiently. Sitting and staring at your casebook or rapping

---

*For a description of an excellent tutorial program see: Kupers, J., "A Model Supportive and Retentive Program," in Brown, S. E., *Law School Admissions Study* (San Francisco: Mexican-American Legal Defense and Educational Fund, 1980).

with friends should be minimized. Sometimes setting short-term goals for yourself can help maintain your concentration (i.e., I will allow myself a trip to the water fountain when I've read, briefed, and understood the next two cases). Be an active not a passive learner. Force yourself to articulate what you've learned. If you can't say it out loud or write it down so someone else can understand it, you haven't learned it yet. Use your study group to force each other to articulate what you have learned during the times you studied on your own.

Study principles, not rules. Rather than trying to memorize case names or rules, try to ascertain and understand the basic principles in each section of the casebook. Look at the Table of Contents and ask yourself why the editor included the case in this section. What legal principle is the section trying to teach? How is the principle applied in this case? In what ways is the case the same as or different from other cases in the same section? Try to imagine other fact situations to which the principle would or would not apply. Try to outline each chapter in four or five pages. Rely on your text, your own class notes, and personal outlines. Do not depend on commercial outlines. Some of them can be useful in giving you an overview of the subject matter, but we learn by doing, and your own efforts in condensing a difficult subject area into a short outline will do much more to improve your analytic ability than reading the result of someone else's work.

The first year of law school will be your hardest and your most important. Be prepared to give up your social life for a year. Tell your friends you're going into hiberation. It will be worth it in the long run.

The Profession

Before you decide to go to law school you should try to meet and talk with some minority lawyers. In areas where there is a significant minority population, you should be able to find a chapter of one of the minority bar associations. Members of these organizations are usually more than happy to talk to young people who are seriously interested in becoming lawyers about their own experiences in law school and in the profession. Minority lawyers continue to be greatly underrepresented in the bar. Of the nearly 550,000 lawyers in America in 1980, fewer than 23,000 were minorities. (Minorities constituted 16.8 percent of the population, but only 4.2 percent of the lawyers.) This means that despite the so-called glut of lawyers, there are still many minority communities where there is a crying need for attorneys. This problem is exacerbated by the fact that many individuals in these communities cannot afford a lawyer and by the Reagan Administration's attack on government-funded legal services.

Minority students should remain open to the possibility of pursuing any of a wide variety of kinds of practice. It is important that all of us find ways to be of service to the communities from which we came, but this can be achieved in a number of different settings. During a period where it is increasingly difficult for all law graduates to secure employment, we must find effective ways to represent our constituencies wherever we find ourselves. Many sectors of the profession, including the most prestigious law firms and law school faculties, remain lily-white, or with only token minority representation. These institutions must be encouraged to act affirmatively to recruit and hire minority graduates, and minority students must aspire to, prepare for, and apply for these jobs as well as judicial clerkships, and jobs with government agencies, legal services, public interest groups, smaller firms, and business. Don't wait until you graduate to begin job hunting. Make contacts among lawyers near your school or home. A successful experience on a summer or part-time legal job may impress your employer and be more important than any grade on your résumé.

Both law school and the practice of law require an ability to adapt to and function in a highly pressured environment. For the minority person who must also deal with the continuing stress of American racism, it is both a more difficult and a more rewarding task. If you can take the heat, join us. Lord knows we need you.

SUGGESTED RESOURCES AND READINGS

Admissions and Financial Aid

The Council on Legal Education Opportunity
1800 M Street, N.W., Suite 290, North Lobby
Washington, D.C. 20036

NAACP Legal Defense and Educational Fund, Inc.
99 Hudson Street
New York, NY 10013

Ms. Caroline Putnam
Catholic Scholarships for Negroes, Inc.
73 Chestnut Street
Springfield, MA 01103

Herbert Lehman Educational Fund
10 Columbus Circle, Suite 2030
New York, NY 10019

Earl Warren Legal Training Program
10 Columbus Circle, Suite 2030
New York, NY 10019

Mexican-American Legal Defense and Educational Fund
28 Geary Street
San Francisco, CA 94108

National Hispanic Scholarship Fund
P.O. Box 748
San Francisco, CA 94101

Puerto Rican Legal Defense Fund
95 Madison Avenue
New York, NY 10016

Mr. John C. Rainer, Director
American Indian Scholarships, Inc.
P.O. Box 1106
Taos, NM 87571

Special Scholarship Program in Law for American Indians
P.O. Box 4456—Station A
Albuquerque, NM 87196

Indian Fellowship Program
United States Department of Education
400 Maryland Ave., S.W.
Washington, D.C. 20202

JACL
Thomas T. Hayashi Law Scholarship
1730 Rhode Island Ave., N.W.
Washington, D.C. 20036

Digest of Minority Student Programs at Various ABA-Approved Law Schools.
(Single copies of this publication may be obtained without charge from Staff
Director, Section of Legal Education and Admissions to the Bar, American
Bar Association, 1155 East 60th Street, Chicago, Ill. 60637.)

N. J. Dickenson and R. N. Swanson, *Financial Aid for Minorities in the Law,*
Garrett Park Press, 1980

Annual Register of Grant Support 1982–1983. A Marquist Professional Publication

Minority Opportunities in the Law for Blacks, Puerto Ricans and Chicanos,
Christine Clark, Ed., Law Journal Press, 111 Eighth Ave., New York, N.Y., 10011

S. Brown & H. Vasquez, *Pluralism in the Legal Profession: Models for
Minority Access* (San Francisco: Mexican-American Legal Defense and Education Fund) (See esp. Chapter VIII: "Financial Assistance for Minority Students.")

Surviving and Excelling

D. A. Bell, Jr., *"Law School Exams and Minority-Group Students,"* 7 *Black
Law Journal* 304–13 (Winter 1981).

J. P. Daves, *"How to Make It Through Law School: A Guide for Minority and
Disadvantaged Students,"* Conch Magazine Ltd. Publishers (1982).

University of Toledo Law Review Symposium, 1970 *Toldeo Law Review*
Numbers 2 and 3, see especially Bell, *"Black Students in White Law Schools:
The Ordeal and the Opportunity,"* at page 539.

The Profession

La Raza National Lawyers Association

National Bar Association
(Organization of Black Lawyers)
2109 E Street, N.W.
Washington, D.C. 20037

Puerto Rican Bar Association

Roles of the Black Lawyer: A Symposium; Career Patterns of the Black
Lawyer: A Roundtable, *The Black Law Journal* Vol. VII No. 1 (1977).

Prof. Ralph Smith, "The Invisible Lawyer," 8 *Barrister* 42 (Fall 1981).

James A. Thomas, "Career Patterns of Black Yale Law School Graduates: From Young Blacks to Old Blues," 7 *Black Law Journal* 131–7 (Fall 1980).

Geraldine Segal, *Blacks in the Law* (University of Pennsylvania Press, 1982).

H. Edwards, "A New Role for the Black Law Graduate—A Reality or an Illusion," 69 *Michigan Law Review* 1407 (1971).

CHAPTER 6

Issues of Special Concern To Women and Parents

Carole E. Goldberg-Ambrose

UNIVERSITY OF CALIFORNIA, LOS ANGELES

Lawyers like to portray the law as a female. The symbol of justice is a blindfolded, goddesslike woman holding scales. Overworked lawyers refer to the law as a "jealous mistress." By contrast, until quite recently, the legal profession itself has been overwhelmingly male. Although women are no longer denied entry to law schools and legal practice, they constituted only 3 percent of all lawyers in 1970, and only 12.4 percent in 1980. By 1990, slightly more than 20 percent of all lawyers will be women.[1]

These statistics tell us that the sexual composition of the legal profession has changed dramatically since 1970. Nevertheless, in view of the history of discrimination against aspiring women lawyers, women contemplating legal careers may properly ask whether the law schools and the profession will treat them fairly and with sensitivity. Some women also may wonder whether these male-dominated institutions will accommodate their desires to learn about sexism in the law and to enlist the legal system in the struggle against gender oppression throughout society. Others may be concerned about the extent to which law school and a legal career are compatible with childbearing, child rearing, family life, and traditionally "feminine" values and characteristics. Older women returning to school after their children have grown or their marriages have ended may wonder whether they will be welcome. This chapter will attempt to address these issues by describing law school admissions practices, structural barriers to legal study for women, the law school experience, job opportunities in law, and the structure of the profession as they specially affect women.

Of course, some of these concerns are not unique to women. In particular, although women disproportionately bear primary child-care responsibility, men increasingly are assuming a greater role as parents. A survey of Stanford Law School students conducted in 1981 revealed that almost half the men expected to share child-care responsibility equally with their partners (although the numbers of hours they expected to spend on child care each week was significantly lower than the number of hours the women expected to spend).[2] Thus some of the issues in this chapter will be addressed as concerns of parents, male or female.

Admission to Law School

Until recently, exclusionary law school policies, combined with the legal profession's image as a male preserve, discouraged many women who might otherwise have chosen law as a career. As of 1963, women comprised only 3.8 percent of law school enrollment.[3] But, coinciding with the most recent resurgence of the women's movement, passage of important antidiscrimination laws, and a general increase in the size of the profession, there has been a sharp rise in the number of female law school applicants and enrollees. Between 1965 and 1975, the student population of accredited law schools nearly doubled, but the number of women in these schools increased more than ten times, from about 2,500 to 27,000. By 1985, women were 40 percent of all students at accredited schools, and today women actually outnumber men at some law schools.[4] Percentages of women seem to be somewhat higher at newer law schools less oriented to training for corporate practice.

The law schools have not resisted this wave. They have tended to treat the increasing number of applications from women in a nondiscriminatory manner. Because of the recent surge of law school applications, many law schools are relying increasingly on numerical indicators, such as LSAT scores and grade point averages, in which female applicants have done at least as well as males. Increasing the weight attached to grade point average does help younger women more than older applicants, however. The "inflation" of all grade point averages over the past fifteen to twenty years has meant that applicants who received their college degrees before that time compete at a disadvantage. Some law schools have acknowledged this phenomenon and adjusted their admissions "formulae" accordingly, despite the difficulty in measuring the inflation precisely and accounting for it accurately. Older students should inquire whether schools to which they have applied have made such necessary accommodations.

Apart from grade "inflation," "reentry women" may worry about the reluctance of law schools to admit older students. This fear may reflect misperceptions about the demography of many law school student bodies. For example, in 1979–80, more than 10 percent of the entering class at New York University Law School had been out of college five years or more.[5] Between 1983 and 1988, the number of second-career students at Marquette Law School in Milwaukee, Wisconsin, increased by 30 percent, and the median age of entering students rose from 23 to 26.[6]

Although law schools have not fought the wave of female applicants, neither have they sought to amplify it through preferential admissions policies. Law schools that have had special admissions criteria for minorities generally have not given similar special treatment to women's applications. Some schools, however, may include women with early or unusually burdensome family responsibilities, histories of abuse, or parental resistance to their education in a special admissions category for disadvantaged students of all types.

During the late 1960s and throughout the 1970s, recruitment efforts rather than preferential admissions were the standard law school approach to increasing female enrollments. These affirmative efforts included seeking out women at coed schools during recruiting, having a female accompany male recruiting officers, holding conferences and programs for female undergraduates, mentioning the school's interest in female applicants in application materials and recruiting brochures, and featuring pictures of women in school catalogs. Since 1980, however, law has become almost a "normal" postgraduate choice for young women straight out of college,[7] and these recruitment efforts have diminished. Nevertheless, women's law groups, particularly at schools where female enrollment has risen more slowly, may still seek out female applicants and contact female admittees to encourage them to attend their school. If you are considering a law school with female enrollment below 40 percent, you may want to ascertain whether the school cares enough to engage in such recruitment efforts.

Structural Barriers to Legal Study for Parents

Parents with substantial child-care responsibility have difficulty attending school full-time during the day or part-time at night. The time required to satisfy parental obligations precludes full-time study; and part-time evening education takes the parent/student away from the home when the student's spouse and children are likely to be home. Part-time day legal education and law school–connected day-care centers would alleviate hardships for such parents. Nevertheless, the law schools, particularly the selective, accredited schools, generally have not been responsive to these needs.

Many of the faculties at accredited law schools fear that part-time study is inconsistent with the necessary level of intensity of legal education or with maintaining their institution's "elite" image. Although they might concede that a limited number of places for part-time students would not endanger the seriousness of the educational endeavor, they find it difficult to allocate those places among needy students who want to work part-time, disadvantaged students, and parents with substantial child-care responsibilities.

Nevertheless, some law schools have responded to pressure from women who have been disproportionately disadvantaged by this policy. A 1976 survey of law schools accredited by the American Bar Association revealed both confusion and variation in the availability of part-time day legal education.[8] As many as thirty-five schools may have either a formal part-time day program or may allow such study in exceptional circumstances on an individual basis. For example, Temple Law School has been able to achieve higher than average percentages of women students because it has a part-time day program and a part-time extended-day program aimed primarily at returning women with child-care responsibilities.[9] Yet many of the schools that have part-time programs fail to describe these options in their catalogs. Moreover, opportunities for part-time day study are not as widely available in the top ranked law schools as in those with fewer resources and lower prestige. Student/parents should press the law school of their choice to disclose or initiate such part-time alternatives.

For the most part, law schools have also failed to demonstrate a willingness to commit limited resources to the provision of day-care facilities for their students. According to a 1972 survey conducted by the Association of American Law Schools (AALS), only one law school had a child-care center and only 30 percent were affiliated with universities that offered day care for all students.[10] This study has not been updated, but in 1983–84, Professor Richard Chused of Georgetown University surveyed 102 law schools about their provision of child care for *faculty,* and his findings were similar to the results of the 1972 study.[11] He ascertained that only three of the schools operated their own facilities, and approximately 25 percent of law schools on university campuses had some access to university child-care facilities. (This access was often quite limited because of long waiting lists for admission to university-wide child care.)

Anecdotal evidence suggests that law schools and their affiliated universities are beginning to respond to the growing national clamor for more and better child care. For the past ten years the University of California at Davis has had a student-run child care co-op for infants less than one year old, located in a part of the student lounge. Hastings College of Law in San Francisco initiated and supports a child-care center near the law school that has places for children of law students and children who live in the surrounding neighborhood.

Of course, some parents with time-consuming child-care responsibilities do complete full-time legal study at institutions that lack day care. Especially after their first year of study, which usually follows a day-long schedule set by the law school, these parents can arrange their classes to consolidate and minimize hours spent at school. However, law schools truly concerned with redressing the underrepresentation of women in the legal profession should undertake to reduce the hardships these parents undergo.

The Law School Experience

Historically, the predominantly male law school faculties and students have treated women with indifference or hostility that reflected men's stereotyped views of women's capacities and proper roles. Male faculty members sometimes have harassed women students to test the women's responses under pressure or made insensitive comments about women who appeared in the cases studied in class. Other professors, acting out of a misplaced sense of chivalry, refused to call on women students. Furthermore, to the extent professors have convinced themselves that women attend law school frivolously and occupy the places of more deserving males, they have not assisted female graduates in obtaining judicial clerkships and desirable jobs in practice. This refusal to serve as all-important "mentors" for female students has hurt women, especially in pursuing careers in legal education. Often the behavior has reflected the professors' lack of social comfort with female students and fear of sexual connotations. For similiar reasons, and also because of competitive anxiety, male students have sometimes acted resentfully toward women students, especially those women who have done well, and have excluded them from collective study and discussion.

Female students receive much better treatment these days, although the old attitudes and practices pass away slowly. Increases in both the percentage of female students and the percentage of female faculty members are partly responsible for the improvement. With the greater numbers of female students came organized protests against the sexist behavior of professors and an alteration of the social dynamics of the law school environment. As sociologist Rosabeth M. Kanter has pointed out,[12] when women are a small proportion of the law school community, their unusualness makes them more visible, which may lead to pressures to hide their achievements or to underachieve. The women are more likely to be excluded from informal peer networks, to be reminded constantly of their differences, and to be trapped in stereotyped roles. In a study of two law schools during the 1970s, one where women were 22 percent of the student population and another where they were 33 percent, researchers found that women participated more and performed more successfully where they were a higher percentage of the student population.

Nonetheless, contemporary studies continue to document women's lower rate of participation in class discussions,[13] and anecdotal accounts by women students confirm these findings.[14] One of these studies, surveying students at five different law schools, suggests that some law professors are continuing to use illustrations and humor offensive to women.[15]

In recent years feminist writers have been asking whether law study runs against the grain of traditionally female ways of knowing and moral reasoning. They emphasize that law school trains one to be combative rather than conciliatory, abstract rather than concrete or contextual, logical rather than feeling, and concerned with the application of hierarchical rules rather than the maintenance of human connectedness. Drawing on contemporary research in feminist philosophy and psychology, they speculate that women's typical responses to moral/social dilemmas tend to emphasize all the things that law training avoids or leaves out.[16] Interviews with non-random groups of female law students reveal feelings of alienation and resigned accommodation to a system of male-oriented legal study and practice, with these feelings often related to the distance between the women's individual approaches to legal problems and what they believe law school expects of them.[17]

Because the views of male law students have not been similarly recorded, we cannot be sure that expressions of alienation and frustration are unique to women law students, or that women's law school experience is any worse than men's. In fact, a recent study of male and female law students at Stanford suggests that women and men admire the same qualities in their professors, are equally satisfied (or dissatisfied) with their law school performance, and equally successful in achieving the highest grades.[18] When recent University of New Mexico Law School graduates were surveyed, it turned out that the academic performance of females was at least as good as males; females reported that they participated at least as often as males in cocurricular activities, such as law review and student government; both females and males said they had been equally supported by other students; and females said they felt at least as supported by faculty as males. Overall levels of satisfaction with law school generally, and teaching techniques in particular, were the same for men and women. Women graduates did not find law school more challenging to their values, more lonely, less receptive to their ideas, more deficient in training in negotiation and counseling, or more alienating for failing to provide adequate role models.[19] The only finding of sex difference in law school experience appears in one study of five different law schools, in which significantly more men than women reported a belief that professors respect other students' opinions and comments.[20]

What I wish to emphasize is that the feminist critique of law study often fails to recognize that many elements of good legal thinking and practice benefit from the typically female characteristics that feminists identify.[21] Lawyers don't just enter situations after an injury has occurred or a transaction has disintegrated. They are also involved in the constructive work of fashioning mutually satisfactory economic, institutional, and personal arrangements that adequately protect their clients. And even when litigation is necessary, a combative, rule-focused approach is often not the most expeditious, cost-conscious, or long-term satisfying way to solve client problems. Law faculties (especially clinical teachers) have always presented these elements of lawyering to their students to some extent; and feminists legal scholars are heightening faculty awareness of the need to foster collaborative, problem-solving approaches in the classroom.[22]

The growing number of women law faculty and deans has also been important in changing the views of male faculty, challenging the stereotypes held by male students, and re-envisioning the project of law study.[23] Although the personalities of these women vary, most have been sensitive to the problems of women students and have encouraged them to excel. The percentage of tenure-track law school faculty who are women jumped from 1.7 percent in 1967 to 15.9 percent in 1986–87. Over one third of nontenured but tenure-track faculty are now female.[24] Moreover, while women used to be hired primarily to teach courses on Women and the Law or Family Law, they are beginning to penetrate other fields. In 1986, 11 percent of the Corporations teachers, 13 percent of the Tax teachers, 16 percent of the Civil Procedure teachers, and 12 percent of the Evidence teachers at AALS law schools were women.[25] Some schools have better hiring records than others, however. About one fifth of AALS schools surveyed for 1986–87 had 12 percent or less of their faculty slots occupied by women, and these schools were disproportionately represented among schools in the South and the West, schools in metropolitan areas with populations under 250,000, and highest prestige schools.[26]

Turning to law school chief administrators, the percentage of AALS law school deans who are women climbed from 3 percent in 1974 to 6 percent in 1988.[27] Investigating the position of women in the administration and on the faculty of law schools you have applied to is another way to go about gauging whether you will feel comfortable attending that school.

Like the treatment of female students, law school curricula have historically reflected traditional assumptions about the nature of women and their proper roles. Recent years have witnessed analogous changes in these curricula, in the direction of greater attention to women's social reality and their legal concerns. Several different kinds of developments are identifiable. First, course materials in courses not expressly devoted to sex discrimination are being scrutinized by female faculty and students to see whether legal issues affecting women are slighted, and whether cases and hypothetical problems present women stereotypically, for example, as housewives, helpless widows, or crazy drivers. A thorough study of casebooks in Criminal Law has revealed that topics of particular concern to women (e.g., abortion, rape, spousal battering, the parental duty of care, and spousal conspiracy and marital duress) are largely neglected, sex discriminatory rules are rarely identified as such or discussed, apparently neutral rules that are based on male experiences, perceptions, and values (e.g., the doctrine of self-defense) are almost never explained in that way, and the realities of women's lives are rarely appreciated in the formulation of legal doctrines affecting women. Furthermore, cases involving women as defendants are hardly ever examined to see whether they embody stereotypes and depart from the usual procedural or substantive rules in ways that generally benefit men.[28]

As feminist legal scholars pursue their exciting work of uncovering the male "tilt" in all the basic law school subjects, deficiencies in traditional course materials will become more and more apparent. Some progress has already been made, as Constitutional Law books are featuring sex-discrimination cases, Family Law courses and casebooks are confronting fundamental questions about how sex roles are reinforced by the laws of marriage and divorce, and Evidence courses are raising questions about the assumptions underlying treatment of victims in rape prosecutions. But until casebooks are revised to incorporate fully these new perspectives, the burden will be on law faculty to produce supplementary course materials and to think carefully about how they present their subjects.

Second, courses, seminars, and clinical programs have been added to the standing law school curriculum at about half of all AALS schools to redress the lack of attention by lawyers to problems of sex discrimination and sexist assumptions in the law. Approximately 75 law school faculty members were listed by the AALS in 1986–87 as teaching or having taught such a course. (There are approximately 154 law schools accredited by the AALS, and some law schools had several faculty who teach such a course.)[29] Several more or less traditional law school casebooks on the subject have facilitated teaching these courses. Courses in Employment Discrimination and Poverty Law are also available at a number of schools. These additions to the curriculum not only provide training for people who want to devote their legal careers to challenging sex discrimination but also offer a new perspective on the operation of the legal system and on traditional legal analysis. Undergraduates who have pursued curricula in Women's Studies may want to investigate whether law schools in which they are interested will enable them to continue their studies with a focus on law.

The offerings that are "clinical" in nature also provide learning through work on actual or simulated cases. Typically they involve interviewing, research, or memo writing for a government agency (such as the Equal Employment Opportunity Commission), a nonprofit public-interest law firm that specializes wholly or partly in sex discrimination cases, or the clients of a clinic established by the law school. A series of local, regional, and national conferences on Women and the Law, held annually, brings together faculty, students, and practitioners concerned with issues that arise in these new legal studies.

One reason why the law school experience for women has improved in terms of faculty composition and curriculum is that female law students at most schools have organized into strong law women's unions. If you have questions about the experience you can expect at a particular school, you should find out if such an organization exists and contact its members if it does. These organizations often distribute useful (but unofficial) information about their schools, as well as information about their surrounding communities to ease your adjustment to law school. They can also provide emotional support and contacts with upper-class women or programs involving female practitioners once you are enrolled. Law school is often a trying experience, for males and females alike. But women may feel additional strain because of role conflicts and the need to excel in order to overcome lingering job discrimination. Law women's unions are places where women can share their efforts to cope with all these pressures.

Job Opportunities

At least two kinds of questions about job opportunities for lawyers especially may occur to women. One is whether a woman faces discrimination in the job market or on the job, either because she is a woman, or because of her age if she is returning to school after many years. A very different kind of question is whether jobs exist for individuals interested in devoting their careers to combating sex discrimination.

Employment Discrimination and Available Remedies

Now that women constitute almost half of all law school graduates, opportunities for employment at the entry level have increased for women in practically every area of law practice. Judicial clerkships, including those with the United States Supreme Court, are widely available to women. According to a recent survey of large law firms, women are being hired as associates in proportion to their representation in law school graduating classes.[30] Nonetheless, women lawyers continue to experience sex discrimination in entering the job market and securing advancement. A 1983 survey of 605 lawyers conducted by the American Bar Association (ABA) revealed that both males and females believe that women face a tougher job market.[31] Women interviewing for jobs as attorneys are still sometimes asked about their husbands' jobs, their methods of contraception, the seriousness of their law study, whether they think they can face tense negotiating or litigating situations without crying, and how their husbands or boyfriends feel about their having lunch or going to out-of-town meetings with male clients.[32] Women are still sometimes excluded from law firms, denied partnerships, or confined to behind-the-scenes work or to work in fields typed as "feminine," such as trusts and estates, matrimonial law, and juvenile law. They still report being denied opportunities to serve in the judiciary, to receive mentoring, or to participate in bar associations and more informal networks of the business community and the profession.

Such discriminatory treatment has stemmed from sexual stereotypes held by male attorneys—for example, that female attorneys are undependable because they will leave jobs to follow men in their lives or to raise children; that they will be unwilling to devote enough energy to law practice in view of family demands; that they are insufficiently aggressive to function successfully in certain capacities, such as labor negotiator or courtroom advocate; or that they are too emotional and not logical or business-minded enough to perform adequately as lawyers except in "women's" fields. Such stereotypes, partly the result of the small percentage of women in the profession, are clearly overgeneralizations and in some instances demonstrably false.

Comparative studies of the legal profession have found that around the world women are overrepresented in the lowest ranks of the legal profession, *whatever* kind of work that entails.[33] Thus women's unsuitability for particular legal work cannot explain their presence in all these different fields. The explanation must be found instead in discrimination or self-selection, and self-selection may itself be influenced by pervasive social stereotypes about appropriate male and female roles and behavior, as well as by the structure of the profession.[34] Studies of individual law school alumni populations do indicate that women are more likely than men to interrupt or slow their career for childbirth and child rearing, and that women lawyers work slightly fewer hours per month than men.[35] Most noteworthy, however, is the high percentage of women as well as men who are devoting long hours to their careers, despite the extra burdens women assume when they have families.

Some evidence of job market discrimination against women lawyers can be found in statistics about the representation of women in different areas and at different levels of the profession. According to the 1988 report of the American Bar Association's Commission on Women in the Profession, "The 'higher' echelon positions—in terms of remuneration, power and prestige—are still disproportionately held by men."[36] Although women have constituted at least one third of all law school graduates for the past eight years, women are only 25 percent of all associates in private practice and only 6 percent of all partners (and increasing their representation among partnerships at a rate of only 1 percent a year). Some, but not all, of this gender-based disparity can be explained by the fact that women have only recently entered the profession in large numbers. The ABA Commission found: "Of all lawyers admitted to the bar between 1971 and 1979, 71 percent of the women and only 48 percent of the men were associates as of 1980."[37]

Women constitute a little over 7 percent of all state and federal judges; and at the federal level the percentage of judges who are women actually has declined in recent years. In government practice women are overrepresented. Thirteen percent of all women lawyers but only 7.2 percent of all male lawyers work for federal, state, or local governments.[38] However, those in the management of government practice (one of the few possibilities for career advancement) are disproportionately male.[39] Finally, studies of lawyers' income show that women in comparable categories of practice earn less than men who graduated approximately the same time they did.[40]

Some recent studies of younger alumni of particular law schools suggest that stratification in the types of practice male and female lawyers engage in may be diminishing. A survey of University of Michigan alumni from the late 1970s found that 70 percent of the men, compared with 44 percent of the women, were in private practice five years after graduation, and 21 percent of the men, compared with 37 percent of the women, were in government service, legal aid, or offices of corporate counsel. The gap between the proportion of women and the proportion of men working in private practice was closing rapidly, however.[41] Younger male and female graduates of Stanford and the University of New Mexico tend to find themselves in the same types of practice and in law firms of similar size when they engage in private practice. The only significant sex-based differences between male and female graduates of these schools tend to be in the subject area of practice. Male Stanford graduates were much more likely than females to practice corporate law. Greater proportions of University of New Mexico males practice substantially in corporate law, criminal law, personal injury, and real-estate work, whereas greater proportions of women practice in the areas of domestic relations and natural resources.[42]

Once on the job, women lawyers may have to contend with other forms of discrimination—sexual harassment and denigrating treatment from coworkers, opposing counsel, and the judiciary. Task forces established by the ABA and the supreme courts of states such as California, New Jersey, New York, and Rhode Island have been holding hearings to determine whether women attorneys are subjected to disrespectful treatment that differs from the treatment accorded men. The most common types of biased conduct are addressing women in familiar terms, commenting on their personal appearance, making sexual or offensive remarks, failing to treat women seriously, and lesser tolerance for women's behavior than for comparable behavior by men.[43] These patterns of discrimination create what is usually described as a "double bind" for women—if they are assertive and driven, they risk being labeled arrogant and abrasive; if they are softer and more compassionate, they risk being judged incompetent and uncommitted.

There is some reason to believe that biased conduct and these consequent dilemmas will diminish as the number of women participating as litigants and judges increases. In the meantime states are beginning to develop judicial education programs to sensitize judges to sex bias, and a few are beginning to enforce norms of professional conduct that require judges both to refrain from expressions of gender bias and to prohibit others in their courtroom from exhibiting such bias.[44]

Modern concern about sex discrimination in the profession focuses on the upper levels of practice precisely because discrimination at the entry level has diminished; and while the profession remains stratified on the basis of gender, women are increasingly found at all levels and in the entire range of legal specialties. It would be a mistake for any woman to curtail her ambitions because of the fear that opportunities will be denied her based on her sex. First, while studies comparing male and female lawyers' satisfaction with their work sometimes report that women are less satisfied, the fact remains that a large majority of *both* male and female lawyers are quite satisfied with their professional lives.[45]

Second, remedies for sex discrimination are increasingly available in administrative fora and in the courts, and organizations of women lawyers are available to provide general pressure against biased behavior. The legal remedies have included those directed at law school placement offices and those directed at legal employers themselves. Under federal legislation, as well as under the policies of the ABA and AALS, law schools (where much interviewing for entry-level legal employment occurs) may not provide facilities for employers that discriminate on the basis of sex. Law school sanctions against nonconforming employers have varied from sending a letter to the interviewing employer, barring the employer from use of the facilities, and contacting other schools to urge them to bar their facilities to that employer as well. Federal and state laws also directly prohibit employers from discriminating, including decisions to admit associates to partnership.

Women have used these laws successfully to combat sex discrimination in law firms, and the very existence of these laws exercises a restraining influence. Settlements with some of the largest Wall Street firms have included provisions mandating that a certain percentage of all associate openings be offered to women and that firm events not be held in clubs that bar women. Bar associations, such as the one in Los Angeles County, have also resolved not to hold their meetings in clubs that exclude women.

Blatant discrimination has all but vanished, leaving camouflaged bias in its place. Given the subtle and subjective judgments that prospective employers must make about the qualifications of lawyers seeking jobs and promotions, it is often simply too difficult and costly to prove in court that discrimination in hiring or promotion has occurred. Furthermore, women lawyers are often fearful that complaints of discrimination will brand them as "troublemakers" and hinder their careers.[46] Thus the pressure exacted by law schools and organizations of women lawyers may ultimately be more important in restraining discrimination than actual litigation.

Finally, while the informal exclusion of women from mentoring, traditional bar organizations, and private clubs still exists, it is a little early to assess how significant such disadvantages will be in determining women's ultimate progress in the profession. Knowledgeable observers of the legal profession report that it is moving in the direction of greater emphasis on acquiring business and large client bases, at least in the big law firms that increasingly dominate law practice.[47] Informal networks may be particularly important for success in this environment. At the same time, local, state, and national groups of women lawyers are creating their own networks and even linking their organizations with the growing numbers of women in business, other professions, and the offices of corporate counsel. Furthermore, more and more senior women lawyers are available to perform invaluable mentoring functions. By both helping one another and by forcefully challenging bias in the broader legal community, the swelling number of women lawyers can hasten an end to gender bias in their profession.

Age discrimination may well be a more serious problem than sex discrimination for the older woman returning to school. Law firms in particular seem to be worried about the age of their associates. They profess to fear that older associates will become impatient with the pace of promotions, that their personalities and life-styles will not be as malleable, and that they will not take orders well from partners younger than themselves. The older student is thus denied individual consideration on her or his own merits.

Unfortunately the legal remedies available against age discrimination are not as comprehensive as those against sex discrimination. Federal and state laws prohibit discrimination against individuals between the ages of forty and sixty-four, but there are no laws concerning age below forty. Some, but not all, law schools have fuller policies against age discrimination by employers using their placement facilities. Older women therefore should prepare well for interviews and anticipate the prospective employer's objections.

Opportunities to Practice Feminist Law

Legal positions for people who want to challenge sex bias are not legion. The problem is not a shortage of legal grounds for bringing sex discrimination lawsuits or a general dearth of feminist legal causes. Federal and state laws offering women the opportunity to sue over discrimination in employment, housing, credit, insurance, and education are plentiful. The problem is rather that the potential female clients tend not to be wealthy. Therefore legal fees for such suits must generally come from the money recovered, *if* there is a victory. This source of income is uncertain and delayed, making it imperative that feminist attorneys find alternative sources of income.

A few groups of feminist attorneys have attempted to solve this problem in the context of private practice. They supplement their income from sex-discrimination cases with the income from more lucrative matters, such as domestic relations cases, which they try to handle from a feminist perspective. The lawyers in some of these firms also attempt to alter traditionally sexist attorney-secretary relationships by sharing more of the unpleasant responsibilities; they also try to eliminate traditional barriers between lawyer and client by being more open and less controlling.

Several other groups of active feminist attorneys have obtained foundation funding or private contributions to support their women's rights work in the setting of a nonprofit organization. Examples include the Women's Legal Defense Fund in Washington, D.C., and the Women's Law Fund in Cleveland, Ohio. In addition, some general public-interest law firms, such as the Center for Law and Social Policy in Washington, D.C., as well as longtime organizations such as the ACLU, devote a significant portion of their time to sex-discrimination cases and related legislative work. UCLA School of Law's placement office maintains a computer printout of all nonprofit organizations that devote a significant amount of their resources to women's rights, and the list comes to over forty such organizations. These institutions rarely have comfortable sources of funding, however, and hence few positions exist. If a permanent position with such an organization is not feasible for you, you may be able to obtain a student externship that allows you to work there for a semester; and some law schools have student-funded scholarships that can be used for work with such groups during the summer.

Finally, some feminists choose to work for a government agency that has responsibility for enforcing sex-discrimination legislation or promoting the concerns of female victims in battering and sexual-abuse cases. Such agencies exist at federal, state, and local levels. For example, many prosecutors' offices in large cities have specialized units that devote themselves to sexual-assault cases. Jobs with these agencies offer less freedom to the feminist attorney, however, because the ultimate government authorities are predominantly male and not always feminist. Many female attorneys who cannot avail themselves of any of these alternatives cope with the difficulties of establishing a feminist practice by choosing a more traditional job and volunteering their time and skills to cases, bar-association committees, and other organizations concerned with women's issues.

The Structure of the Profession

Sex discrimination is not the only obstacle facing women in law. The very way the profession is practiced conflicts to some extent with traditional notions of women's proper family roles and personal characteristics. As men and women have challenged the correctness of assigning these roles and characteristics exclusively to women, it has become appropriate to identify these "structural" obstacles to success as impediments to parents with substantial child-care duties and to people embracing traditionally feminine values.

The idea of a professional "career" assumes that the professional can single-mindedly devote the first ten to fifteen working years to the career. Its model is the husband who can relegate the time-consuming functions of raising children and providing familial warmth to a wife who does not work outside the home. It follows that without some change in the concept of a successful career or in the "proper" family roles for parents, lawyers with significant child-care responsibilities cannot achieve success professionally, or can do so only by assuming the burden of two exhausting roles.

Historically, many women responded to this dilemma by forgoing family life altogether. A 1983 ABA study of male and female lawyers found that 32 percent of the women, compared with 8 percent of the men, were never married; and 69 percent of the women, compared with 24 percent of the men, had no children. (The sample of female lawyers was considerably younger than the male sample, however, with three fifths of the women under 35 and one third of the men over 45.)[48] Studies of more comparable samples of male and female law school alumni, focusing on younger graduates, reveal much smaller disparities between the percentages of males and females married and having children, with one survey of graduates of five different law schools finding that a higher proportion of women than men had children.[49]

Ironically, this increase in the number of women attorneys with children has occurred at a time when the demands of private practice have become even more consuming.[50] A 1988 survey of one hundred New York City law firms showed that billable hours of associates had risen by an average of nearly one third since 1983.[51] At the same time there has been no apparent reduction in the allocation of child-rearing burdens between men and women.[52] Women still have the bulk of responsibility, although men's reported attitudes, if not their current practice, suggests that they would like to take more time off after the birth of each child.[53]

As more women enter the profession, pressure to restructure the practice of law to accommodate parenting is becoming acute. The option of being "superwoman"—drafting documents in the labor room and returning to work the next day—is seen as fundamentally unfair to women. Women law school graduates are beginning to grill job interviewers about their childbearing and child-rearing leave policies, as well as about their policies concerning flexible hours and part-time work. Government agencies, such as one U.S. Attorney's office that allowed two lawyers each to work three-fifths time,[54] have been among the first employers to offer the options of part-time careers and job sharing. Law firms are also increasingly receptive to "part-time" arrangements for parents (which often means a forty-hour rather than a sixty-five-hour work week!), and even "per-deal" arrangements with compensatory time off.[55] A 1982 survey of law firms that interviewed at Stanford Law School revealed that 66 percent of firms with maternity policies or experience allowed, or would be likely to allow, part-time work.[56] However, these options are probably more readily available for lawyers who have established themselves in their jobs on a full-time basis; and we do not yet have enough experience to know how unconventional work arrangements will affect the timing or likelihood of attaining partnership status.

Some law firms that are unwilling to reexamine the demands of law practice are at least willing to provide practical responses to the needs of parents. They have provided benefit plans to assist in payment for child care, home computer terminals, and dictation facilities, and, in a few highly publicized instances, firm-sponsored day care (especially on an emergency basis).[57]

It is important to note that even where part-time work has not been possible, many lawyers with primary responsibility for children have been able to progress rapidly in their careers.[58] One surprising result of a study of University of Michigan graduates was that the women with children seemed to be more satisfied with the combination of their family and work life than any other group of women or men.[59] There are many possible explanations for this phenomenon, ranging from the possibility that women expect less to the possibility that a combination of responsibilities puts less pressure on any one aspect of life and provides valuable perspective. Sociologist Cynthia Fuchs Epstein attributes some of women lawyers' success with the difficult task of managing work and family life to the fact that lawyers are professional problem solvers. Whatever the explanation, women lawyers will continue to press for changes in the legal profession to make the roles of active parent and committed lawyer more compatible. They are likely to find support in this endeavor, as men and women alike begin to decry the modern evolution of the legal profession into a more grinding and bureaucratized form of work.

Associated with the conflicts between professional careers and family life has been the contrast between the cultural ideal of femininity and the core of attributes thought to be necessary for most professional roles. As sociologist Epstein has pointed out, preferred female attributes in America include, among others, "personal warmth and empathy, sensitivity and emotionalism, grace, charm, compliance, dependence, and deference." Yet the characteristics typically associated with fulfillment of a lawyer's role are deemed masculine: "persistence and drive, personal dedication, aggressiveness, emotional detachment, and a kind of sexless matter-of-factness equated with intellectual performance."[60] Must a woman, then, discard all traditionally feminine characteristics and values if she is to function successfully as a professional in the legal world?

Historically, women reconciled these conflicts through their choice of a "female" specialty in the law or by taking a secondary role in a husband-wife law partnership. Today's women are strongly resisting such limitations. Some have assimilated the preexisting values of the profession, joining men in the push for high prestige and high monetary rewards. These women are aided by the fact that the women's movement and the increasing number of female lawyers have challenged the notion that male and female characteristics come in mutually exclusive bundles. Other women, however, have joined with some men in questioning whether the practice of law is necessarily incompatible with all the "feminine" characteristics. Legal scholars, judges, and practitioners are increasingly interested in negotiation, mediation, and conciliation as alternatives to the adversarial method of resolving disputes. Public-interest law and government practice are alternatives to private practice that caring men, as well as women, seek out. And appropriate sensitivity to one's client is a lesson of good lawyering taught in clinical programs in the law schools. Thus both women and the profession are feeling the effects of women's recent influx into the law.[61]

I personally encourage women to enter the legal profession. A legal career offers women financial independence and practical competence. Beyond that, the legal profession as a whole can benefit from greater receptivity to traditionally feminine values, as well as from the consciousness of oppression derived from the women's movement. Because lawyers step so easily into politics, the legal profession is also a road to political power for women. Although hostility, discrimination, and role conflicts may confront the woman who pursues a legal career, the growing influence of women within the profession promises to reduce these problems.

NOTES

1. "ABA Report: Women in Law Face Overt, Subtle Barriers," *N.Y.L.J.*, August 19, 1988, at 2, col. 3.; C. Epstein, *Women in Law* 4–5 (1983).
2. "Law Firms and Lawyers with Children: An Empirical Analysis of Family/Work Conflict," 34 *Stanford Law Review* 1263, 1280 (1982).
3. C. Epstein, *supra* note 1, at 53.
4. *Id.*, at 54–55; B. Curran, K. Rowich, C. Carson & M. Puccetti, *Supplement to the Lawyer Statistical Report: The U.S. Legal Profession in 1985* at 66 (1986).
5. C. Epstein, *supra* note 1, at 45.
6. C. Mentkowski, "Students Are More Mature," 61 *Wisconsin Bar Bulletin*, Number 11, at 58 (1988).
7. C. Epstein, *supra* note 1, at 44.
8. The results of this survey are reported in S. Gottlieb, "The Feasibility of Part Time Day Legal Education," 30 *Journal of Legal Education* 291 (1979).
9. M. Angel, "Women in Legal Education: What It's Like to Be Part of a Perpetual First Wave, or the Case of the Disappearing Women," 61 *Temple Law Review* 799, 826 (1988).
10. The results of this survey can be found in S. Bysiewicz, "Women in Legal Education," 25 *Journal of Legal Education* 503 (1973). Eighty-one of 124 AALS-accredited law schools responded to the questionnaire survey.
11. R. Chused, "Faculty Parenthood: Law School Treatment of Pregnancy and Child Care, 35 *Journal of Legal Education* 568, 571 (1985).
12. R. Kanter, "Reflections on Women and the Legal Profession: A Sociological Perspective," 1 *Harvard Women's Law Journal* 1, 10–11 (1978).
13. T. Banks, "Gender Bias in the Classroom," 38 *Journal of Legal Education* 137 (1988); Project, "Gender, Legal Education, and the Legal Profession: An Empirical Study of Stanford Law Students and Graduates," 40 *Stanford Law Review* 1209, 1242 (1988). Whether these results signify women students' alienation or simply their disinterest in dominating classroom discussion is uncertain.
14. C. Weiss & L. Melling, "The Legal Education of Twenty Women," 40 *Stanford Law Review* 1299 (1988).
15. T. Banks, *supra* note 13, at 144–45.
16. C. Menkel-Meadow, "Portia in a Different Voice: Speculations on a Women's Lawyering Process," 1 *Berkeley Women's Law Journal* 39 (1985).

17. J. Foster, "Antigones in the Bar: Women Lawyers as Reluctant Adversaries," 10 *American Legal Studies Association Journal* 287 (1986); J. Elkins, "On the Significance of Women in Legal Education," 7 *American Legal Studies Association Journal* 290 (1983); C. Weiss & L. Melling, *supra* note 14.

18. Project, *supra* note 13, at 1241–42. There were greater differences among male and female graduates, suggesting that women's and men's reactions to law school have become more similar over time, or that memories may distort earlier experiences.

19. L. Teitelbaum, A. Sedillo Lopez, J. Jenkins, "Law School, Law Practice & Gender: Some Questions, Some Data, and More Questions," unpublished manuscript at 47–55 (1989). This particular law school has a higher than average percentage of female and minority faculty.

20. T. Banks, *supra* note 13, at 143.

21. C. Menkel-Meadow, *supra* note 16, at 50–55.

22. S. Wildman, "The Question of Silence: Techniques to Ensure Full Class Participation," 38 *Journal of Legal Education* 147 (1988).

23. C. Menkel-Meadow, "Feminist Legal Theory, Critical Legal Studies, and Legal Education or 'The Fem-Crits Go to Law School,' " 38 *Journal of Legal Education* 61 (1988).

24. R. Chused, "The Hiring and Retention of Minorities and Women on American Law School Faculties," 137 *University of Pennsylvania Law Review* 537, 548 (1988).

25. B. Levin, "Testimony before American Bar Association Commission on Women in the Profession," 89–2 *Association of American Law Schools Newsletter* 11 (April 1989).

26. R. Chused, *supra* note 24, at 548–50.

27. B. Levin, *supra* note 25, at 11–12.

28. N. Erickson, "Sex Bias in Law School Courses: Some Common Issues," 38 *Journal of Legal Education* 101, 104–113 (1988).

29. *Id.* at 103, note 11.

30. Project, *supra* note 13, at 12–24.

31. B. Winter, "Survey: Women Lawyers Work Harder, Are Paid Less, but They're Happy," 69 *American Bar Association Journal* 1384, 1385 (1983).

32. R. Siegel, "Presumed Equal," 17, No. 4 *Student Lawyer* 22, 26–31 (1988); "ABA Report," *supra* note 1, at 2, col. 5.

33. C. Menkel-Meadow, "Feminization of the Legal Profession: The Comparative Sociology of Women Lawyers," in R. Abel & P. Lewis, *Lawyers in Society: Comparative Theories* 196 (1989).

34. D. Rhode, "Perspectives on Professional Women," 40 *Stanford Law Review* 1163, 1181–92 (1988).

35. D. Chambers, "Accommodation and Satisfaction: Women and Men Lawyers and the Balance of Work and Family," 14 *Law and Social Inquiry* 251, 268–69 (1989) (surveying graduating classes of the University of Michigan from the late 1970s); Project, *supra* note 13, at 1243–46; L. Teitelbaum et al., *supra* note 19, at 68–70.

36. "ABA Report," *supra* note 1, at 2, cols. 3–4.

37. *Id.*; S. Goldberg, "Is This All There Is?—Women and Job Satisfaction," 74 *American Bar Association Journal* 72 (June 1988) (reporting a 1984 survey of 3,000 lawyers of all ages).

38. "ABA Report," *supra* note 1, at 2, col. 4. The proportion of black women practicing for the government or in public-interest law is 48%. N. Burleigh, "Black Women Lawyers: Coping with Dual Discrimination," 74 *American Bar Association Journal* 64, 67 (June 1988).

39. "ABA Report," *supra* note 1, at 2, col. 4.

40. D. Chambers, *supra* note 35, at 284, note 111; L. Teitelbaum et al., *supra* note 19, at 57–59; S. Goldberg, *supra* note 37.

41. D. Chambers, *supra* note 35, at 285.

42. Project, *supra* note 13, at 1243–45; L. Teitelbaum et al., *supra* note 19, at 55–57.

43. Note, D. Round, "Gender Bias in the Judicial System," 61 *Southern California Law Review* 2193, 2203–04 (1988).

44. *Id.* at 2219–20.

45. Project, *supra* note 13, at 1222, 1245–46; D. Chambers, *supra* note 35, at 274; S. Goldberg, *supra* note 37.

46. D. Rhode, *supra* note 34, at 1192–96.

47. J. Kaye, "Women Lawyers in Big Firms: A Study in Progress Toward Gender Equality," 57 *Fordham Law Review* 111, 113–16 (1988).

48. B. Winter, *supra* note 31, at 1385.

49. D. Chambers, *supra* note 35, at 262–64; L. Liefland, "Career Patterns of Male and Female Lawyers," 35 *Buffalo Law Review* 601, 607 (1986).

50. Kaye, *supra* note 47, at 1141.

51. Zeldis, "Survey Shows Associates Work 29% More Hours Over 5 Years," *New York Law Journal*, October 11, 1988, at 1, col. 3.

52. D. Chambers, *supra* note 35, at 265–68; L. Liefland, *supra* note 49, at 614.

53. "Law Firms and Lawyers with Children" *supra* note 2, at 1285–89 (one-fifth of Standford male students responding to survey reported that they would like to take a combination of part-time work and leave for at least one year after the birth of each child); D. Chambers, *supra* note 35, at 279.

54. *See* C. Epstein, *supra* note 1, at 366.

55. J. Kaye, *supra* note 47, at 123–24.

56. "Law Firms and Lawyers with Children," *supra* note 53, at 1275.

57. J. Kaye, *supra* note 47, at 124.

58. For stories profiling successful women lawyers, see V. Quade, "Twelve Success Stories," 69 *American Bar Association Journal* 1400 (1983); B. Repa, "Is There Life After Partnership," 72 *American Bar Association Journal* 70 (June 1988).

59. D. Chambers, *supra* note 35, at 272–74.

60. C. Epstein, *Woman's Place: Options and Limits in Professional Careers* 20 (1972).

61. C. Menkel-Meadow, *supra* note 16.

CHAPTER 7

Advice for Lesbians and Gay Men

Rhonda R. Rivera and
Robert L. Eblin
OHIO STATE UNIVERSITY

No sane person should plan to attend law school without serious forethought. Law school and the practice of law are absorbing, sometimes overwhelming experiences for nearly everyone who attempts them. Gay men and lesbians, however, must weigh some special matters when considering a legal education and career. From choosing a school to landing a job, a gay person's sexual orientation does make a difference. While gay persons should not avoid the legal profession out of fear of discrimination, evaluating some of the challenges they will face may make their law school experience more rewarding and ease their entry into the legal profession.

A caveat: The authors of this chapter are both "out," politically active gays who personally believe that being "in the closet" is psychologically destructive, no fun, and quite a waste of energy. We do recognize that some people feel very secure, if somewhat cramped, living in a closet. We have tried to include advice for those people as well as more liberated gay persons.

Gays and Lesbians Should Go to Law School

Despite what you may have learned in your high-school civics class, the American legal system is not a bastion of equality and fairness populated solely by kind and just officers of the law. Like the rest of American society, the legal profession is influenced by racism, sexism, elitism, and homophobia. The law generally discriminates against gay people; moreover, the legal profession frequently discriminates against gay attorneys. Combating this discrimination, we believe, is the reason why gay people *should* go to law school.

The Juris Doctor is a versatile, empowering degree. Aside from rioting in the streets (exciting, but dangerous and illegal), the most effective way to change the system is from within. The more lesbian and gay attorneys there are, the more impact we can have on the legal system. The more gay folk who "make partner," the easier it will be for the next generation to get jobs. The more gay people who are elected or appointed judges, less often will laws be interpreted to discriminate against gay people.

Opportunities abound for gay and lesbian attorneys to serve the gay community and the public interest. Because gay relationships are almost universally unsanctioned by the law, gay persons have special needs concerning tax and estate planning and child custody; persons with AIDS (gay and non-gay) are faced with numerous legal problems in the course of their illness; many lesbians and gay men are faced with employment and housing discrimination on a daily basis.

Gay and lesbian attorneys can also get high-paying jobs in large firms and lead a comfortable existence solving the legal dilemmas of corporations. We suggest those who choose this latter career remember three things: First, pro bono (free) work is good for the soul and the community. Second, gay and lesbian law students make fine summer associates and should be hired in great number. Third, the organizations and attorneys who are in the trenches working to advance your rights as a gay person need and deserve your financial support.

So whether your interest is in toiling to advance the civil rights of gay persons or in becoming a slick corporate attorney, you can do it as a gay person, and if you decide you want to, you should go to law school.

How to Choose a Law School

This country has more than 170 law schools, varying in academic reputation but very much alike in how and what they teach. For most prospective law students who are gay, the sensible approach is first to identify those schools you would like to attend. Consider factors such as location, cost (public versus private), size, educational focus and reputation, and the makeup of the student body. Once you have drawn up a list of fifteen to thirty schools, go back and evaluate the schools from the perspective of a gay person.

You can begin with the school's nondiscrimination policy. The policy is almost always printed in a school's catalog or application. If it is not, call and ask for a copy. Does the policy include sexual orientation? At this writing, more than one third of American law schools have nondiscrimination policies that do include sexual orientation. If a school does not have such an official nondiscrimination policy, you may not care to attend the school. (And you should write a letter to let them know *why* you will not attend!)

If the school does have a nondiscrimination policy, look for signs that it is taken seriously. At some schools, firms and government agencies (e.g., the military and the FBI) that discriminate against gays are banned from on-campus recruiting of law students.

Many law schools also have a gay and lesbian student group. If none is listed in the school's catalog, call and ask whether one exists in either the law school or the university at large. Ask for contact names and follow up to find out how gay students are treated at the school. Give them a call or visit and introduce yourself. Realize that even if no such student group exists and the college office cannot give you the names of any gay students, gay and lesbian students *are* there. Gay and lesbian students are in *every* law school; they just may not be out to the administration. Another suggestion for finding gay people at a law school: Contact the National Lesbian and Gay Law Students Association (see address on p. 129) to see if any members attend the school you are considering.

Also investigate the student chapters of the National Lawyers Guild and the ACLU in law schools. These organizations and their members are often gay-supportive.

Gay faculty also populate every law school, although openly gay faculty are not yet a universal phenomenon. Check the biographies of professors usually found in school catalogs. Clues to look for are courses or writings on sexual orientation law, sexual privacy issues, or AIDS law. If all else fails, call the school and ask. If you make a contact, follow up. If convenient, visit the school and the professor. (A friend on the faculty is always a good thing to have!) Gay persons interested in a career in gay rights activism may find it especially helpful to attend a school with active, openly gay professors.

The inability to locate gay students or faculty does not mean that you should avoid a particular school, but it does mean you should have some other strong reason for attending. Law school is challenging. Being gay in law school is more challenging, and it makes good sense to choose a school where you are not going to be the lone gay figure.

Admissions: Gay Can be Good

Admission to law school is not much of an issue for gay men or lesbians for both practical and policy reasons. First of all, the majority of laws students are admitted on the numbers (quantifiable academic indicators). Secondly, unlike blacks or women, gay folk are not recognizable by their photos or, in most cases, by their résumés. If a gay person announced their sexual orientation in their admissions materials, the announcement would be irrelevant in almost all law schools today.

If your application falls in the middle, being neither automatically accepted nor denied, what you put on your résumé and essay will likely be reviewed by members of the admissions committee.

Feedback from gay law students and admissions committee members at law schools around the country indicates that applicants who are out are more likely to be viewed favorably than to be discriminated against. Obviously this situation is not true at all law schools. The Law School Admissions Council has no official policy on this issue.

Moreover, whether you are accepted or denied admission by a school, your sexual orientation per se is likely to be a minor factor. Merely stating that you are gay or lesbian on your application, while a brave political statement, is not as significant as listing accomplishments or leadership in gay politics or gay organizations.

In any case, mentioning gay activities will set you apart from the thousands of other applicants being reviewed, and that difference is usually a good thing in the giant shuffle of paper that makes up law school admissions.

Being "Out" in Your Law School

Whether one should be "out" anywhere is a highly personal choice. "Being out" also means different things to different people. Leading the gay student organization is very different from letting a few close classmates know of your sexual orientation. Bringing a same-sex date to law school functions is more "out" than socializing in gay bars.

If a gay student organization exists at your law school, by all means join. The vigor of any student organization varies from year to year. Your organization may consist of only a few loosely knit members socializing together or it may be actively involved in advocating change in the law school and the world at large. If you are not happy with the group, work from *within* to change it. Your participation is important. Besides, safety lies in numbers.

If gay students are not organized at your school, form a group. Usually all it takes is a note to the Dean or the Student Bar Association and someone willing to be your faculty adviser. Forming a gay student organization will give you an "official" platform from which to address issues in your school. The organization will also be listed with other student groups in school catalogs and orientation materials, drawing in more gay and lesbian students in subsequent years. Use your organization to educate the larger student body about the concerns of gay and lesbian law students, to advocate for equal treatment of gay persons under the law, and as a base for socializing.

If you are not prepared to join or form a gay student group, at least do not retreat into the closet when you begin law school. Ideally, all lesbians and gays would be completely out in law school: willing to discuss gay issues in class, willing to bring lovers and partners to law school functions, willing to be active in combating discrimination in law school and the larger world. Unfortunately we do not live in an ideal world, and coming out can be a scary process. It will take time to develop a support network—and to pinpoint those who will not be supportive—but you will feel better about yourself if you are not spending energy trying to hide a key component of your personality. Do not be silent when peers make jokes at the expense of "fags" and "dykes." Ask how the law applies to gay couples when both the casebook and the professor blithely presume universal heterosexuality. Many of your classmates will respect you for not hiding your sexual orientation. You will undoubtedly find that some of your best friends are not gay, but are supportive and gay-affirming.

Of course, some of your classmates will *not* be supportive. A few will be incontrovertibly homophobic: Never turn your back to them. However, many are simply ignorant. They have never known, up close and personally, an out gay person. These classmates may have an image of gay people that consists largely of negative stereotypes. With patience and persistence, sometimes those views can be changed. The result: a more supportive environment for gays (and for you) at your law school.

Make Law School Bearable:
Maintain an Outside Life

If you let it, law school will consume your every waking minute, as well as your dreams while you sleep. You should take law school seriously, but you should not forsake all contact with the outside world. Guard your mental health.

First, watch out for your relationship. Law school has an unhealthy effect on marriages and other intimate relationships. If you have a life partner when you go to law school and plan to keep him or her, you must find a way to nourish and protect that relationship. Being gay will make this job more difficult because your relationship often will be unrecognized and not supported. Find other gay couples in the area with equivalent situations, i.e., one person in an all-consuming program. Check out the gay medical-student organization and similar graduate organizations. Develop a life outside the law school for you as a couple.

Even if you are single, creating a life outside law school is necessary. The constant heterosexual presumption is grinding; stereotypes and myths abound even from supposedly liberal students and professors (i.e., "Some of my best friends are . . ."). Find lesbian and gay lawyers who lived through the experience; cultivate their friendship (they will also be helpful for job hunting). Today many cities and states have gay and lesbian bar associations to help you (see partial list on p. 129). Also make a conscious effort to stay in touch with family and non–law school friends. They will keep you grounded in reality.

Finding a Job

Job hunting is rarely described as a pleasant experience. A large amount of time, money, and energy is spent by employers and applicants. Because appearances often seem to be all-important, both sides try to put on a happy face while sweating in expensive suits and tight shoes. (It's sort of like entering the Miss America pageant: No matter how well developed your plans for achieving world peace, you'd better have great legs.) Universally disliked or not, job searching is a fact of life and should be approached carefully.

The closeted gay person has little to worry about when looking for a job—if you plan to stay that way for the rest of your life. If working in a firm where you can keep a picture of your lover on your desk is not important to you, you can stride through the interview process as though you were not gay. But even closeted gays have some issues to consider: How does the firm treat men and women who remain (apparently, at least) unmarried after age thirty? What is the firm's policy on employees with AIDS? If you later decide to come out (or are found out), will you be asked to leave?

The truth is, many firms and other employers remain prejudiced against openly gay employees, or at least in *hiring* openly gay employees. Once hired and productive, gay people somehow seem less threatening, less "stereotypical." So how should gay law students who are out approach the job search?

First decide what type of legal work you would like to do. Do you want a job with a large firm? A government agency? A gay-rights firm? Use the resources available in your placement office to investigate specific employers. Consider factors such as pay scale, the amount of time demanded of employees, client base, areas of law practiced, and opportunities for promotion.

Drafting your résumé is the next step. We suggest writing two: one listing all of your relevant activities as a gay person, one not. In some cases, listing gay activities will be to your advantage. Gay-rights firms, obviously, will be delighted to know that you chaired the Gay and Lesbian Law Caucus at your school. A growing number (but still a minority) of mainstream law firms will also consider gay activities a plus, just as they would consider leadership in the Student Bar Association.

Identifying employers that will not react negatively to an "out" résumé is not always simple. Some employers are clearly hostile to gay and lesbian employees, e.g., the military, the FBI, and the CIA (no matter what they say). You can get hired, no doubt, if you are closeted, but these organizations spend hours and dollars trying to ferret out gay persons. We suggest you avoid them unless you are masochistic.

A few firms have sexual orientation included in their nondiscrimination policies, but they are rare. You can do some investigating by asking around, but information you get may be unreliable. Your placement office is also unlikely to be of much help in this area.

The second résumé comes in handy in situations where you want to control disclosure of your sexual orientation. If you are not identified as a gay person on your résumé, you cannot be prescreened on that basis. Coming out in an interview allows you to gage the reaction of the interviewer, immediately answer any questions, and otherwise present a positive image. You may even wish to wait until you are called in for a second round of interviews before coming out. By then the firm has a greater investment in you. During a day of six or seven interviews you may get a better sense of the firm's likely reaction to your coming out and who may be a good person to tell. If anyone asks why you neglected to mention your term as treasurer of the National Lesbian and Gay Law Students Association on your résumé, tell them the truth: Gay persons are frequently discriminated against in employment, and you felt better about disclosing that information when you could discuss it face-to-face.

While you probably do not want to work in a firm that discriminates against gay persons, you should take action if you believe that an employer discriminated against you during the recruiting process. Lodge a complaint with the employer itself and your school's placement office. Find out if other students (including other minorities and non-gay women) experienced discriminatory treatment by the employer or its representatives. If your school takes its nondiscrimination policy seriously, the employer may be barred from recruiting on campus. Such a bar usually gets publicity (especially with calls to the local press) and is always embarrassing to employers (just ask the military, the FBI, and the CIA).

Admission to the Bar

One's morality is a criteria of admission to the bar in all states. No bar rule in any state speaks of morality specifically in terms of homosexuality. However, since some persons, if not a majority or Americans, regard homosexuality as immoral per se, law students seeking admissions to the bar are often worried. In fact, your sexual orientation will probably not in any way affect your admission to the bar. The most recent case addressing the issue read, "private non-commercial sex acts between consenting adults are not relevant to prove fitness to practice law." Moreover, the American Bar Association recently endorsed gay-rights laws, which protect lesbians and gay men in employment, housing, and public accommodations.

Caveat: A different result might be obtained if one is convicted of a sexual offense and hence has a criminal record. Bar admission forms require the truthful reporting of criminal records. If you have a criminal record, regardless of the crime, we suggest consulting the bar admissions committee before entering law school.

Get Involved in Gay Rights Legal Work

Gay people are and should be active in all areas of the legal profession. Gay people are judges, tax specialists, litigators, divorce lawyers, and, of course, law professors. Some gay attorneys devote their entire practice to securing the rights of gay people. *All* gay attorneys should give some of their time to the gay community. Almost any gay organization can use legal assistance, as can many gay individuals. Persons with AIDS, who face myriad legal challenges over the course of their illness, are frequently in need of pro bono representation.

You can begin helping while in law school. For example, summer clerkships now exist with Lambda Legal Defense and Education Fund in New York and Gay and Lesbian Advocates and Defenders (GLAD) in Boston. These kinds of opportunities will increase. Many AIDS organizations furnish legal services, and these organizations now hire (or need volunteer) law clerks.

So do some good for your community and for your soul: No matter where you work or study from nine to five, make some time for volunteer AIDS and gay-rights work. Gay people have made significant progress in gaining acceptance and civil rights in the twenty years since the Stonewall riots in New York, but the struggle continues. Make sure you play a part in the next twenty years.

RESOURCE LIST

Lesbian and Gay Bar Associations

National
National Lesbian and Gay Law Association
14 Beacon Street, Suite 720
Boston, Massachusetts 02108

California
Bay Area Lawyers for Individual Freedom
P.O. Box 1983
San Francisco, California 94101

Lawyers for Human Rights
P.O. Box 480318
Los Angeles, California 90048

Illinois
Lesbian and Gay Bar Association of Chicago
3225 North Sheffield Avenue
Chicago, Illinois 60657

Massachusetts
Massachusetts Lesbian and Gay Bar Association
P.O. Box 2901
Boston, Massachusetts 02101

New York
Bar Association for Human Rights of Greater New York
P.O. Box 1899
Grand Central Station
New York, New York 10163

Ohio
Ohio Human Rights Bar Association
P.O. Box 10655
Columbus, Ohio 43201

Pennsylvania
Philadelphia Legal Professionals for Human Rights
P.O. Box 58279
Philadelphia, Pennsylvania 19102

Washington, D.C.
Gay and Lesbian Rights Committee
District of Columbia Bar
1707 L Street N.W.
Washington, D.C. 20036

129

Gay and Lesbian Rights Law Firms

Gay and Lesbian Advocates and Defenders (GLAD)
P.O. Box 218
Boston, Massachusetts 02112

Lambda Legal Defense and Education Fund
666 Broadway
New York, New York 10012

National Center for Lesbian Rights
1370 Mission Street
San Francisco, California 94103

National Gay Rights Advocates
540 Castro Street
San Francisco, California 94114

CHAPTER 8

The Messages
of Legal Education

Sylvia A. Law
NEW YORK UNIVERSITY

I am always pleased when people I like and respect decide to go to law school. The study and practice of law can powerfully illuminate our understanding of the collective arrangements that define our individual and social life. Legal training enables people to support themselves through work involving enriching human relationships and intellectual challenge. Legal skills can be used to help realize our visions of a just society. Although these possibilities make the study and practice of law attractive, the reality of practice can be much different. Many young lawyers, particularly associates in corporate firms, work for the relatively privileged to preserve a status quo in which material wealth and political power are distributed unfairly and *everyone* is oppressed by hierarchical and alienated relationships.

One fact, more than any other, influences the personal and professional choices facing lawyers and law students today, and the collective choices that we face as a society. It is that we live in a world in which there are gross disparities in the distribution of money, political power, and the personal opportunity for significant life choices. In the United States, the richest fifth of the population receives 40 percent of the personal income, whereas the poorest fifth receives 5 percent of the personal income. Disparities in the distribution of unearned wealth, political power, and personal power over important life choices are probably even greater that the disparities in the distribution of income.[1] On a

131

world scale the disparities are greater still. The United States has 6 percent of the world's population and consumes 40 percent of the world's resources.

Despite the gross disparities in the distribution of resources and opportunities, Americans share a common culture. We all see the same ads urging us to buy. We all have similar desires to have those things that we believe will make life more beautiful and comfortable. We share common desires for interesting, creative, and useful work for ourselves and our children. Because we share a common culture, we feel the disparities in wealth, power, and opportunity more acutely.

Gross inequality in the distribution of material resources produces a situation of insecurity for everyone. People at the bottom are most obviously insecure; they face the daily uncertainty of not knowing where the next meal will come from or whether they will be able to buy their children shoes. Any unexpected expense is a disaster. Most "middle-income" Americans also face economic uncertainty. Jobs that were once secure and well-paying are now disappearing as multinational corporations seek the highest profits, without regard to the consequences for jobs or communities. In 1981, 34 million Americans had no financial protection against the risk of hospitalization.[2] These are not the poorest people, for they are protected by public health insurance. These are low- and middle-income workers and ex-workers. Even the rich are insecure. God forbid that you should not make it to the top. Or that, having made it to the top, you should somehow make a misstep that will cause you to slip from a position of privilege.

The disparity in the distribution of wealth and power, particularly in a time of deep economic insecurity, is a major factor motivating people to go to law school. These disparities also pose a central challenge to our social and legal arrangements. Are democracy, equality, personal security, self-actualization, or solidarity possible in a world in which material goods and political power are distributed in such a wildly uneven way? Are these disparities the inevitable cost of material growth, progress, and innovation?

Unfortunately, thought about the legal profession and legal education often mystifies rather than illuminates our understanding of these social relations, and increases, rather than decreases, perceptions of personal insecurity. This can be illustrated by examining first, the way in which legal education is organized, particularly in the first year of law school; second, the intellectual content of the law itself; and third, the lessons of legal ethics for a lawyer's choice of life work and for the attorney-client relationship.

Legal Education: The First Year

Five characteristics of the first year of law school engender a sense of personal insecurity in students and hinder them from using the study of law as a means of understanding and affecting the world in which we live.[3]

First, the required curriculum of the first year is virtually identical in every law school and has been for most of this century. In contracts, torts, property, and procedure we study disputes between private individuals; criminal and constitutional law focus on issues of public power. Although some teachers attempt to place the cases in a larger social context, the selection of subjects emphasizes the private and the individualistic. All of these courses have a strong common law orientation. All deal, almost exclusively, with the opinions of appellate court judges. The proscribed first-year curriculum plainly does not exhaust that which is interesting in the law. There is no course dealing with the law governing any form of organization—corporations, families, or labor unions. There is no course dealing with the way the legislative and executive branches function; nothing on state and local government; nothing on public taxation or expenditures. We study abstract principles as presented in appellate cases, with little effort to place these abstractions in an empirical and historic context or to connect the principles with the concrete skills and work of lawyers.

The benign explanation for this phenomenal uniformity is simply the weight of history. Many in American legal education today recognize that the content of the first year reflects no eternal verity. But it is much easier to reach a negative consensus than it is to make specific affirmative change. But, whatever the justification, the effect of the present arrangement is to give first-year students a distorted view of what the law is and little training in the skills that lawyers use.

Second, almost all first-year study takes place in very large classes. I find that it is simply not possible to have the sort of exchange I associate with learning in a group of 120 people. The numbers prevent students from knowing each other or developing a sense of community. One justification for the large class is that it is valuable for students to learn to articulate and defend assertions —at the edge of their comprehension—in front of a large group of people. This may be a useful skill, but exclusive reliance on large classes is impossible to justify in educational terms. Duncan Kennedy says of the law school classroom:

> The sense of autonomy one has in a lecture, with the rule that you must let teacher drone on without interruption balanced by the rule that teacher can't do anything to you, is gone. In its place is a demand for a pseudo-participation in which one struggles desperately, in front of a large audience, to read a mind determined to elude you . . . (The) classroom arrangement suggests at once the patriarchal family and a Kafka-like riddle state.[4]

The classroom experience generates insecurity and passivity.

A third feature of law school life is that, apart from legal writing, students are evaluated exclusively on the basis of written examinations, graded anonymously. Written exams, however well-designed, test a narrow range of skills, knowledge, and characteristics relevant to the practice of law. More important, the grading process defines a power relationship between grader and graded that is fundamentally inconsistent with true education.[5] Law school purports to encourage students to disagree with cases, with professors, and with each other. But our practice says that there is a right answer and that what matters are not the skills of legal practice or an understanding of the way that law shapes social relationships, but rather spotting issues and writing a coherent first draft under pressure. The effect of exams and grading is to take a group of people all of whom were smart and competent when they arrived at law school and to sort them into a pecking order in which almost everyone "fails." The process reinforces the student's sense that it is both inevitable and just that someone else will define your worth, and will find you wanting.

You will quickly learn that the reason exams and grades matter so much is that they are important to the firms. The firms want students sorted into a hierarchy. And legal education is relentless in defining hierarchical relations and persuading people to accept that as just. People in the legal profession believe in the hierarchy of law schools, and believing makes it true. Within each school, grades define the pecking order. Grading is defended as a meritocratic alternative to allocating opportunities through ranking based more directly on race, sex, religion, and family connection. But there are less painful, more effective ways to measure competence in particular subject matter. More important, we should evaluate a much wider range of skills and characteristics—hard work, responsibility, the ability to listen, research and writing skills, persistence— through more cooperative forms of education such as the work that now takes place in clinics and first-year writing programs, and in much legal practice. Law schools should not simply teach technical skills. A complex and troubled society needs people to think deeply about the relations between law and our social arrangements. Even the most practically oriented lawyer will benefit from this kind of thinking. But grading as it is practiced in law schools today does not contribute to either technical competence or reflective thought.

A fourth important feature of life in the first year of law school is that within the first few weeks, before students have a chance to probe the mystery of the law on the most rudimentary level, the placement process begins. The very term *placement* conjures up a static and ordained world in which, if you are good and lucky, you will be "placed," rather than a world that we are creating together. The reality is that it is much more difficult to find a job doing work that is socially useful, or even socially neutral, than it is to find a place in the service of concentrated corporate power. Firms hire months in advance. Public interest organizations and small firms do not have the financial stability that permits such advanced planning, and public interest jobs are more difficult to find. Students interested in pursuing public interest work are often confronted with a choice between a secure, well-paying job offered months in advance, or waiting in the hopes that if they hustle and are lucky they will be able to find a minimally paid position doing socially interesting work. The placement process exacerbates the anxiety of first-year students.

Placement and the anxiety it generates are not necessary. I believe that law schools could and should take collective action to keep the firms and the placement process at bay at least until the second semester of the first year, though many students and teachers would disagree. We could and should take action within law schools to provide financial support and loan forgiveness to students who have incurred debts to finance their legal education and who seek to do socially useful work at submarket rates. Congress could and should provide increased funds for socially useful legal services and subsidize loan forgiveness for lawyers who have incurred debt and choose low-paying public service work.[6]

A fifth and final universal characteristic of the first year of law school is that students are expected to work very hard. At NYU we require first-year students to take more credits that we will allow them to take in subsequent years. The benign explanation for this is that the first year defines the ideology of legal education. It is much easier for a faculty to agree to add something than it is to agree to delete. But the excessive work pressure has the function of making students feel out of control. Law students often feel they must make a choice between school and their friends, the movies, music, and novels. Obsessive work habits and the sense that you lack control over your own life are extremely conducive to encouraging students to pursue particular types of work.

In short, what we do in the first year of law school purports to be a value neutral meritocracy, but it has the effect of generating insecurity and hierarchy, and of pushing students in particular directions. We not only fail to help students to function independently or to work cooperatively, we affirmatively promote the belief that individual worth is defined by individualistic competitive evaluation. We not only fail to help students acquire the concrete skills of legal practice or knowledge of the role of the law in defining concrete institutional arrangements, but we engender a sense of incompetence that encourages the belief that people need an organization of superiors to tell them what to do. Doing well in the insecurity and hierarchy of law school prepares people to accept a place in a firm. The fact that there are commonsense justifications for these arrangements simply makes it more difficult to challenge them.

Concepts of Law

The intellectual content of the concepts of the law and of the substance of legal education reinforce some of the same messages that are implicitly reflected in the way life is organized in the law school. Historically there are three major lines of theoretical thought about the function of the law, each with a corresponding methodology for legal education. These are: legal formalism, legal realism, and critical legal thought.[7]

The formalist theory, which largely informs the study of the first year, conceives the common law as a coherent, principled whole that allows the just settlement of particular disputes to be predicted or derived by a process of logical deduction from a few general principles reflected in the cases that went before.[8] The theory is that once you understand the basic principles of negligence or offer and acceptance, you can then deduce the just result in a particular dispute, or the right answer on a law school exam.

The formalist view of the law embodies commonsense notions of evenhanded justice—like cases should be treated alike. It reflects, to a large degree, the way many judges think about their work, though good practitioners are more likely to believe that cases are won or lost on the facts and the lawyer's ability to present a claim as factually and emotionally sympathetic. Its methodology for legal education is convenient because core principles can be understood simply by reading cases; anonymous exams are an appropriate method for determining whether students have grasped the core principles and the process of deduction from those principles.

There are many problems with the formalist approach to the law, which have been explored in depth by the legal realists and pragmatists of the early twentieth century and the contemporary work of the critical scholars. First, the formalist principles incorporate highly controversial value assumptions, often without explicit discussion or acknowledgment. For example, the formalism of the late nineteenth century assumed that the core value of the law is free, individual self-assertion within the context of the free-enterprise system. Torts cases of this period often invoked notions of "progress" or "development" in holding that entrepreneurs could only be held financially responsible for injuries resulting from their activities if the injured person could prove fault.[9] Holmes thought it *self-evident* that "the public generally profits by individual activity. As action cannot be avoided, and tends to the public good, there is obviously no policy in throwing the hazard of what is at once desirable and inevitable upon the actor."[10] It is possible to make radically different assumptions, for example that people should generally be held responsible when their actions cause injury to others.[11] Although few people still blindly accept as universal truth that what's good for General Motors is good for America, the common law that we study in the first year today developed, in a complex way, out of cases accepting this very equation. The formalist approach requires that we accept controversial assumptions as givens from which the fair and consistent result in a particular case can be derived. It discourages probing of these core assumptions.

A second problem with formalism is its failure to recognize that the legal system of a complex society incorporates a large number of core principles, which are often in conflict. For nearly every principle there is an equally well-established counterprinciple.

Finally, the syllogistic process of deducing concrete results from core principles, or from congeries of conflicting core principles, is so imperfect that the outcome of most particular cases is uncertain. It is not possible to make accurate predictions of outcome, much less meaningful assessments of justice, within the confines of deductions from prior cases. Nevertheless formalistic theory and practice encourage the belief that the status quo is just because it is required by established principles.

In recent years a new version of formalism has appeared in works exploring the connections between law and economics. Such works, which are undeniably fascinating, always begin with certain assumptions.

(N)o one knows what is best for individuals better than they themselves do . . . (T)he function of the prices of various goods must be to reflect costs to society of producing them, and if prices perform this function properly, the buyer will cast an informed vote in making his purchases; thus the best combination of choices available will be achieved."[12]

Beginning with assumptions such as these, the analytic tool is then applied to problems in contract, torts, property, and even family or criminal law.

Of course the "model" of the informed consumer casting his vote in the free market election often bears little relationship to reality. It assumes competitive sellers when in fact there are many barriers to free competition, from government regulation to monopoly control. It assumes that the things we want can be purchased individually, when in fact many valuable things such as clean air and safe streets can only be purchased collectively. It assumes that consumers can make informed choices when we all know that is often not possible. It sidesteps all questions about existing and persisting inequalities in the distribution of wealth.

And finally, it encourages the belief that life can be reduced to a series of commodity exchanges. Health care involves not a healing relationship between two people but a transaction in which a medical provider sells a service to an insured.[13] Our visions compete in a "market-place of ideas." Lawyers do not work with others to create a more just society but rather sell their labor for a price.

This new formalism is subtly seductive. With a few unquestionable premises leading to ineluctable conclusions, it offers the potential for an analysis that is consistent and pervasive. But it is also inadequate and misdirected. We cannot analyze complex social problems in terms of a few assumptions about the function and operation of the free market. We cannot come to grips with our common problems, or understand the operation of the law, by simply substituting definitions and deductions for values and facts.[14]

The second major approach to the law and to legal education is legal realism or pragmatism. The development of legal realism was a direct response to the inadequacies of the formalist approach. Realist theories reflect a basic mistrust of rules, abstract concepts, deductive logic, and mechanical application of doctrine.

Legal realism is, according to its proponents, not so much a philosophy or theory, but rather a "method" which Jerome Frank called "experimental" and which Karl Llewelyn calls the "descriptive or the technological branch of the discipline."[15] Realists were influenced by two metaphors: scientific method and skilled craftmanship. Frank urged that legal education focus on the reality of the lower courts where most cases begin and end. Karl Llewelyn sought to achieve both increased technical competence and greater professional commitment to the public good by immersing students in the concrete details of legal work. He urged that teachers reject the abstract analysis of the rationalizations presented in appellate decisions and rather attempt to understand cases as the facts presented themselves to an attorney. Realists sought to enable students to understand the process by which judges reach decisions and recognized that the process was closely linked to personal bias and intuition, as well as the formal application of principles.

This tradition is also still alive and well in American education. We see it, for example, in clinical programs and in upper-level seminars in which students are immersed in the facts as well as the law of a particular area of human activity.

The realists challenge the traditional formalist assumption that individual self-assertion is the core value of a just legal system. They believe that value choices cannot be made on the basis of a priori assumptions, and that other value choices are possible. The pragmatists/realists rather advocate more apparently neutral values of "workability," "efficiency," and "least waste."[16] Perhaps the best symbol of this attempt is the metaphor of the social engineer—a craftsperson who embodies both scientific rationality and the skills of practical implementation.[17]

The problem with the realist approach to the law is that value choices are still unacknowledged. "The metaphor of social engineering substitutes a technocratic slogan for what ought to be a reasoned moral choice. It assumes a bureaucratic perspective within which—once it is fully adopted—there is much less moral choice available."[18]

Both formalist and pragmatic/realist approaches to the law assume a broad-based commitment to shared social values. The formalists make this assumption explicit, whereas the realists make the assumption in more subtle form. This criticism of the pragmatic/realistic tradition is as old as the tradition itself. Randolphe Bourne, in a debate with John Dewey in 1919, argued that pragmatism can only work in "a society at peace, prosperous, and with a fund of good will."[19] In any serious crisis, the philosophy of intelligent and efficient control does not meet social needs. Pragmatic education does not give people "a coherent system of large ideas, or a feeling for democratic goals. They have, in short, no clear philosophy of life except that of intelligent service, and the admirable adaption of means to ends."[20] Pragmatism assumes a social consensus—shared value commitments—at least among those who are able to express their opinion. It is increasingly difficult to accept the pragmatic idea that there are widely shared values, within which questions of public policy can be settled by rational technique. The social consensus, if ever there was one, has broken down. There are sharp divisions with respect to basic values, and even sharper conflicts of interest between various groups within the society.

The third and most recent school of thought about the law and legal education is critical legal scholarship. The critical scholars, building upon the work of the realists, demonstrate both the incoherence of particular legal doctrines and that "there is no such thing as the skill of legal analysis in the way most . . . faculty think there is."[21] Roberto Unger, a leading critical scholar, explains that to date the principle agenda of the critical legal scholars has been to "critique the attempt to impute current social arrangements to the requirements of industrial society, human nature, or moral order."[22] By demonstrating that present social and legal arrangements are in no way preordained, the critical scholars make it possible for us, individually and collectively, to begin to assess what constitutes substantive justice. Critical scholars have shown many of the ways in which the law, and particularly traditional legal distinctions between government and market and market and home, perpetuates oppressive relations of illegitimate hierarchy and alienation.[23] Abstact and empty legal "rights" have been used to placate the just anger of working people and black people demanding change.[24]

But, Unger continues, critical scholars "have yet to take a clear position on the method, the content, and even the possibility of prescriptive and programmatic thought . . ."[25] There are today sharp divisions among critical scholars on this issue. Some in the critical movement focus exclusively on the "irrationalist enterprise" of criticism, urging that alternative visions and social forms are possible only when prevailing concepts are exposed as incoherent.[26] Others believe, like Camus' Sisyphus, that "people break out of their accustomed ways of responding to domination by acting as if they could change things," despite powerful theoretical arguments that they cannot.[27] Unger urges that, "We would fall into an error that we criticize in our adversaries if we imagined our conceptual activities as a substitute, even a substitute source of insights, for practical conflict and intervention."[28]

The difficulty is that a law student or lawyer who engages in "practical conflict and intervention," particularly in alliance with the most oppressed, must inevitably invoke arguments, skills, and rights that are inconsistent with a purely critical enterprise. Our legal heritage—including the noble ideals of equality, freedom of dissent and conscience, and democracy—*has* been used to oppress people. But it may also contain the seeds of our liberation, and people who engage in practical conflict must often act as though they believe that these grand ideals are possible to achieve.

There is a second division among critical legal scholars. Some believe it is important to recognize that our legal and cultural arrangements oppress some people—the poor, women, blacks, working people, the handicapped—in ways that are particularly vicious. Other critical scholars believe, as one dedicated welfare rights lawyer put it, that "the oppression of the Harvard Law School is *identical* to the oppression of the Roxbury welfare center."[29] Our culture does oppress everyone. Law professors, as well as students, are constrained by the hierarchy of the classroom. Wall Street partners, as well as domestic servants, often do not find rich human community in their work and are unable to work for goals they believe important. Significant social transformation can only be accomplished by majoritarian constituencies. It is therefore vital to understand social problems in terms of commonality rather than division. Further, it is important to struggle against injustice wherever we are, including within the corporate law firm or the elite law school.

But the view that Harvard Law professors are oppressed in exactly the same way as the homeless and the hungry is only a half-truth. It denies the fact that sharp disparities in the distribution of wealth preclude community, and political and economic democracy. People with a larger degree of political and economic power have greater capacity to exercise autonomy in their daily lives. As Tallulah Bankhead once observed, "Honey, I been rich and I been poor, and rich is better." I believe that it demeans the pain of poverty to assert that it is exactly the same as the oppression of the executive suite.

The point to notice in entering law school is that legal education has not resolved conflicts in social values. Legal education often denies that value conflicts exist. Law school is not going to provide a "coherent system of large ideas" to assist you in resolving the dilemmas that confront a thinking person in dealing with sharp disparities in the distribution of wealth, political and social power, and resulting insecurity. We all need to develop some sort of philosophy of our lives together with others whose lives and ideas we respect. Law school is not designed to help. It is vital for law students to engage in work on the issues that inspired them to go to law school. Press your school to provide opportunities to expand your knowledge of the areas of human life that you find exciting and important. Do not let the individualist, competitive ideology of the first year discourage you from pursuing more cooperative forms of work that are available through clinics. Work with others.

Legal Ethics

The messages implicit in the way that law school is organized and in theoretical thought about the nature of the law are also reflected in principles of legal ethics. The prevalent view of legal ethics is that an individual attorney is entirely free to represent anyone he or she chooses, without fear of criticism from within the profession. Abe Fortas, former Supreme Court Justice, put it like this:

> Lawyers are agents not principals; and they should neither criticize nor tolerate criticism based upon the character of the client whom they represent or the cause that they prosecute or defend. They cannot and should not accept responsibility for the client's prac-

tices. Rapists, murderers, child-abusers, General Motors, Dow Chemical—and even cigarette manufacturers and stream polluters— are entitled to a lawyer; and any lawyer who undertakes their representation must be immune from criticism for so doing.[30]

Furthermore, the conventional view is that a lawyer is also largely free to determine, in the exercise of professional expertise, the way in which the client's interests are to be represented. Fortas argues that the client should not be "permitted to dictate or determine the strategy or substance of the representation, even if the client insisted that his prescription for the litigation was necessary to serve the larger cause to which he was committed."[31]

I could not disagree more strongly with what I perceive to be the prevailing view of legal ethics. I disagree with the notion that a lawyer is not responsible in choosing the clients for whom he or she will work. I also disagree with the notion that a lawyer, once having entered into an attorney-client relationship, is free to decide what is in the client's best interest.

In deciding whom you are going to work for, particularly in a period of history in which there are real and sharp divisions of values in a society, you must make a personal moral choice. Lawyers and nonlawyers alike should have some sort of philosophy of life and should work to make their life have meaning within that philosophy. Commentators on legal ethics point out that the adversary system can function properly and fairly only if everyone in our society who needs legal representation actually receives it, and the Code of Professional Responsibility recognizes as "axiomatic" that lawyers have an obligation to assist the profession in fulfilling its duty to make legal counsel available. But this general responsibility of the profession does not seem to impose any obligation on any particular individual within the profession. In short, neither professional education nor professional ethics provides any answer to the question "To what ends should I use my legal skills?" Indeed, the prevalent view of legal ethics would seem to say, because everyone is entitled to as much legal talent as they can buy, you can work for anyone you choose and meet your obligations as a professional. Even if this is all that is required of you as a professional, I would submit that we all have an obligation to ourselves and to each other to try to make sense of our lives in deciding to what ends we will use our legal skills. In becoming a professional, we do not stop being human. As humans we have some responsibility to work toward objectives that seem to us useful.

Even though the generally accepted view is that a lawyer is an agent in relationship to his or her client, the prevalent ethic, as expressed by Mr. Fortas, is that the lawyer is a special sort of agent who has the power to decide what is best for the client. I also disagree with this. A lawyer has a special skill and power to enable individuals to know the options available to them in dealing with a particular problem, and to assist individuals in wending their way through bureaucratic, legislative, or judicial channels to seek vindication for individual claims and interest. Hence, lawyers have a special ability to enhance human autonomy and self-control.[32] Far too often, however, professional attitude, rather than serving to enhance individual autonomy and self-control, strips people of autonomy and power. Rather than encouraging clients and citizens to know and control their own options and lives, the legal profession discourages client participation and control of their own legal claims. Rather than exposing the social and personal value judgments inherent in legal decisions, professionals tend to mask decisions as technical and to make decisions for the client. Lawyers have no particular expertise in making social or value judgments for their clients. In general, the bar has about as much or as little in the way of coherent social philosophy, and personal self-interest, as anyone else.

The lawyer does, however, have a special skill and ability in dealing in the legal system. Perhaps the most important job of a lawyer at this point in history is to build, or to rebuild, democratic processes—to enable individuals to exercise more power and control over their own lives. However, if lawyers are to serve this function, they must recognize that selecting a client or a job is a personal moral choice, and once having agreed to represent a person or organization the lawyer should work to enable to do what the client sees as important rather than simply imposing the lawyer's decisions on the client.

Is it unrealistic, or at least unsympathetic, to recognize, on the one hand, that law students today are subject to enormous pressures growing out of the insecurity and injustice generated by gross disparities in the distribution of wealth and power, and to suggest, on the other hand, that law students have a high degree of responsibility in addressing these issues and making decisions about their own careers? Maybe. However, I am as certain as I am of anything in this world that there will be more joy in your life and a greater day-to-day sense of personal and professional satisfaction if you develop a personal and political philosophy and try to work in accordance with it.

Ralph Nader suggests that while in law school you should simply ignore the question of how you are going to make a living, and rather try to figure out how, assuming that you had a source of support, you could use your legal talents and skills in the most effective way to do work which seems to you important. I think this is good advice. Nicholas Johnson, former Commissioner of the FCC, suggests that the question of how to hustle money to support yourself is essentially a legal question. If you have developed your legal skills with the enthusiasm and passion that can only come if you are working in a context that makes sense to you, when the times comes to support yourself, you will be able to figure out how to do it. I think that this is also good advice. Most important, nurture a group of friends who share your values. Friendship requires time and effort; lawyers and law students are crippled when the organization of their lives leads them to believe that they do not have time for friendship. We need our friends to help us figure out what we think. None of us can do it alone.

NOTES

1. I am indebted to the late Edward V. Sparer for this and many of the other ideas in this essay. See, for example, Sparer, "Potential Disaster in National Health Plans," 2 *Just Economics* 3 (1974); Sparer, "Gordian Knots: The Situation of Health Care Advocacy for the Poor Today," 15 *Clearinghouse Rev.* 1 (1981).

2. National Health Law Program, *Hard Facts: The Administration's 1984 Health Budget*, p. 15 (1983).

3. This discussion of law school life is illuminated by Duncan Kennedy's writing and work. See, for example, "Legal Education as Training for Hierarchy," in D. Kairys, ed., *The Politics of Law* (1982). (Hereinafter *Training for Hierarchy*.) Professor Kennedy is one of the leading theorists of critical legal studies, and has made enormous contributions in applying critical insights to legal education. See nn. 22 *et. seg. infra*.

4. *Training for Hierarchy, Id.* at p. 42.

5. R. Meisler, *Trying Freedom* (New York: Harcourt Brace Jovanovich, 1984).

6. See, for example, R. Pollack, "Lawyers for the Poor." *The New York Times*, June 17, 1983, p. 34.

7. I am indebted to Professor Rand Rosenblatt, Rutgers University Law School —Camden, for the discussion of the formalist and realist traditions. For an excellent treatment of the points summarized here see Note, "Legal Theory and Legal Education," 79 *Yale Law Journal* 1153 (1970).

8. See, for example, E. Root, "Some Duties of American Lawyers to American Law," 14 *Yale Law Journal* 63 (1904).

9. For discussion see D. Kennedy, "Form and Substance in Private Law Adjudication," 89 *Harvard Law Review* 1685 (1976).

10. O. Holmes, *The Common Law*, M. Howe, ed., (Cambridge: Belknap Press, 1963) p. 77.

11. James and Gray Shulman, *Cases and Materials in Torts* (1976) demonstrate not only that other assumptions are possible, but also that they are embedded in our common law tradition.

12. G. Calabresi, *The Costs of Accidents* (New Haven: Yale University Press, 1970), pp. 69–70. R. Posner, *Economic Analysis of Law* (Boston: Little, Brown, 1972).

13. R. Rosenblatt, "Health Care, Markets, and Democratic Values," 34 *Vanderbilt Law Review* 1067 (1981).

14. A. A. Leff, "Economic Analysis of the Law: Some Realism about Nominalism." 60 *Virginia Law Review* 451 (1964).

15. K. Lelewelyn, "On What is Wrong with So-Called Legal Education," 35 *Columbia Law Review* 651 (1935), J. Frank, "Why Not a Clinical Lawyers School?" 81 *University of Pennsylvania Review* 907 (1933).

16. R. Pound, *Social Control Through Law* (New Haven: Yale University Press 1942), pp. 64–65.

17. See the discussion of John Dewey's concept of "political technology" in M. White, *Social Thought in America: The Revolt Against Formalism* (Boston: Beacon, 1957), pp. 128–46 and 243–46.

18. C. W. Mills, *The Sociological Imagination* 131 (New York: Oxford University Press, 1959, Penguin ed. 1970). See also Marcuse, "Remarks on a Redefinition of Culture," *Daedalus*, Winter 1965, pp. 190, 193–97.

19. R. Bourne, "Twilight of Idols," in *Untimely Papers* 114, 119 (New York: B. W. Huebsch, 1919).

20. *Idem* at 130.

21. Kennedy, *Utopian Proposal: Dissent from the Report of the (Harvard) Committee on Educational Planning and Development* at 34 (April 1980).

22. R. Unger, "The Critical Legal Studies Movement," 96 *Harvard Law Review* 563, n.1 (1983).

23. See, for example, F. Olsen, "The Family and the Market: A Study of Ideology and Legal Reform," 96 *Harvard Law Review* 1497 (1983).

24. K. Klare, "Deradicalization of the Wagner Act and the Origins of Modern Legal Consciousness, 1937–1941," 62 *Minnesota Law Review* 265 (1978); A. Freeman, "Legitimizing Racial Discrimination Through Anti-Discrimination Law," 62 *Minnesota Law Review* 1049 (1978).

25. N. 23 *supra.*

26. C. Dalton, "Review of *The Politics of Law*," 6 *Harvard Women's Law Journal* 229 (1983).

27. A. Camus, *The Myth of Sisyphus* (New York: Knopf, 1967); Sparer, "Fundamental Human Rights, Legal Entitlements and the Social Struggle: A Friendly Critique of the Critical Legal Studies Movement," unpublished draft, p. 64, forthcoming *Stanford Law Review* 1983.

28. Unger, *supra* n. 22 at 667.

29. Statement, Jeanne Charn, Conference on Critical Legal Studies, Camden, New Jersey, April 17, 1983.

30. A. Fortas, "Thurman Arnold and the Theater of the Law," 79 *Yale Law Journal* 988, 1002 (1970).

31. *Id.* at 996.

32. For an excellent description and analysis see P. Gabel and P. Harris, "Building Power and Breaking Images: Critical Legal Theory and the Practice of Law," 11 *New York University Review of Law and Social Change* 369 (1983).

PART THREE

First-year and Required Courses

CHAPTER 9

The First-year Courses: What's There and What's Not

David L. Chambers

UNIVERSITY OF MICHIGAN

At the great majority of American law schools, students begin with a set of required courses that bear the titles of the next six chapters: Procedure, Contracts, Criminal Law, Property, Torts, and Constitutional Law. The six are likely to be taught in ways that resemble each other on the surface. Each will have a "casebook" slightly heavier than a Chicago phone book. Each casebook will devote more pages to the decisions of courts of appeals than any other form of material, and assignments will come almost entirely from the casebook. In class, the professors will have an arched eyebrow for every confident assertion a student makes. They will lecture in varying degrees, but nearly all will call on students who have not volunteered, asking questions about the assigned cases and the issues they raise.

In a year, if you choose to go to law school, you may conceivably look back and find the following chapters like the ads for Happy Valley Estates in sunny Arizona: Lured by the promise of bracing experiences in the land of Property and Torts, you will have arrived on the site and found nothing but sand, mesquite, and a drainage ditch. I hope not. When, as he does, one of our authors exults about his subject, "At times, highly technical! At times, even arcane! But mostly, enormously stimulating!" I hope you can forgive his enthusiasm or, better yet, come to share it. For many people, the first year of law school is an intellectual sunrise, the most exciting year of their life as a thinking individual. Unlike the huckster from Happy Valley, most of us in teaching believe in what we have to sell.

Variety and Similarity
Among the First-year Courses

I can be somewhat more specific about the varieties and similarities of courses and what your teachers are likely to be trying to achieve by discussing the varieties of approaching one course, Criminal Law, as an example. In a later chapter, Lloyd Weinreb describes some of the issues that lie in wait for you in criminal law. Here I wish merely to skip across the surface, comparing approaches of teachers. I have chosen Criminal Law in part because it involves many matters you've probably thought about before law school. You've probably even committed a crime or two—stolen an apple from a farmer's orchard, drank beer before you turned twenty-one, or littered.

To provide you with some rough sense of the similarities and differences among courses, I sent a questionnaire to forty teachers of Criminal Law randomly selected from the principal available list of law teachers.[1] Twenty-five were returned completed. The sample, though random, is not large enough to permit me to speak with confidence about the exact portion of teachers that teach one way or another at schools across the nation, but such precise information would not be particularly useful to you anyway. Moreover, even though the survey was conducted at the time of an earlier edition of this book, I believe, on the basis of a more recent study of criminal law courses,[2] that essentially the same similarities and differences continue among criminal law courses today.

At all but two of the respondents' schools, Criminal Law was a required course, typically taught for three credit hours in either the first or second semester of the first year. In a few schools, but only a few, the course was given as a four-, five-, or six-hour course. (Several of the other first-year courses, particularly Contracts,

Civil Procedure, and Property, are alloted four, five, or six hours' credit at most schools.) Two-thirds of the courses were taught in classes of sixty to ninety students. Only one responder typically taught a class with fewer than fifty students; three typically taught a class of more than one hundred and ten.

For all responding teachers, the grade in the course was based primarily on a single examination given at the end of the course. A few teachers assigned a paper in addition to the final exam, a few others gave one or more quizzes or a midterm, and a few more took into account class participation, but most relied on the exam alone. (The reliance on a single exam by most law teachers is, in itself, a source of anxiety for many students because they have few clear signals about how they are doing week by week during the term.)

At my request, many of the teachers sent me copies of a recent final examination. By far the most common sort of question on these examinations was a request to discuss a hypothetical and slightly unreal situation that was both somewhat like and different from the situations in cases discussed in class. ("During a heated verbal argument between D and X, D pushed X and a fist-fight ensued. Knowing himself to be a hemophiliac, D told X . . ." or "Abercrombie coveted Basil's Terraplane Roadster . . . (H)e persuaded Basil to lend the car to him . . ." Dire events follow. But were they crimes?) You can anticipate much the same sort of questions on the examinations in most of your other first-year courses.

So much for the package. What's inside? For example, what sorts of crimes or other issues are discussed in the basic Criminal Law Course?

All who answered the questionnaire indicated that they spent time on the law of homicide, that is, the law of murder and manslaughter, most spending more than four class sessions. This intense attention to homicide is reflected in most criminal-law casebooks. No other crime received such universal approbation. On sex offenses, by contrast, most spent far less time. Similarly, although you might suspect or hope that sentencing matters—the use of the death penalty or fixed terms of imprisonment, for example—would be given substantial attention, only one teacher devoted more than four classes, and well more than half spent none whatever or only one class on all sentencing issues.

About most other subjects there was more diversity in the extent of coverage. For example, about half the respondents indicated that they spent a few class sessions on the insanity defense and half spent a few classes on the law of conspiracy, but the remaining half (not necessarily the same persons as to each subject) were about evenly split between spending no time at all and spending more than four sessions. Similarly, although about half the teachers spent a few class sessions on property offenses, such as larceny and obtaining false pretenses, which were developed in the common-law courts, six teachers spent no time on them, whereas eight spent more than four classes.[3]

Comparable variations can be expected in other first-year courses. Beyond a few matters, there is no common agreement among law teachers about the specific subject matters that must be covered in any of the courses. As a student, I had a course in Torts that never covered the law of libel and slander, and I still can't remember the difference between them or whether the difference makes any difference. Most Torts professors across the nation probably spend a fair amount of time on libel and slander under the heading of defamation. Civil Procedure courses are similarly likely to differ widely in the extent of their coverage of the problem of whether the judge in a federal court should apply federal or state law in certain suits, Property courses in their degree of emphasis on the law relating to gifts. And so on.

The variations in coverage derive in substantial part from the fact that most instructors will be using discussions of particular crimes or torts or issues in the law of contracts only in part as ends in themselves, and to an equal or larger extent as a vehicle for serving other functions. In this regard, my list of crimes discussed in first-year courses is misleading. Two professors at the same school can each discuss "homicide" for weeks but approach it in such different ways that students with the different teachers who talk to each other will hardly believe they are taking courses with the same title, let alone discussing the same sort of human misbehavior. Conversely, two courses that never deal with the same particular crime may seem quite alike to students who talk to each other because of the identical themes the teacher will have stressed.

In the questionnaire, I tried to learn about the different approaches of courses in a couple of ways. First, there was a checklist of possible areas of emphasis. Second, there was a more open-ended question, "If you had to reduce to one or two the most important functions you intend your course to serve, what would you mention?"

Most teachers, in responding to the checklist, said they placed a "great deal of emphasis" on "the general state of the law in the United States today." In the sample examinations, this emphasis was evident in the frequency of questions that called for a recollection and application of specific doctrines. On the other hand, in answering the question about the "one or two . . . most important functions" teachers hoped their courses to serve, far fewer than half stated that their central purpose was to convey an "understanding of substantive criminal law" or "the elements of common law crimes." One, but only one, saw his purpose quite bluntly as the "coverage of substantive criminal law needed for the bar exam" and only three placed substantial emphasis on the state of the law in the state in which their school was located. Doctrine it would thus appear has a secure but limited place in most teachers' views of their course. More than half the professors gave as their two most central themes concerns broader than the teaching of specific doctrines. It is these broader themes that explain the haphazard coverage of specific crimes among courses.

The first broader theme encompassed issues distinctively raised by the criminal law but larger than the concerns raised by any single offense. Professors used the course to explore "concepts of blameworthiness" or "the moral, social and ethical implications of the criminal law." For such an approach, materials about almost any criminal offense can suffice. If a teacher is interested, for example, in inducing students to think carefully about the proper role of retribution in framing rules defining criminal offenses, it may make little difference whether she chooses as her example for discussion the different degrees of homicide or the different forms of sexual assault. (On the other hand, those who are greatly concerned about sexually assaultive behavior as a critical social problem in itself may find unacceptable a course that omits materials on rape.)

Second, several respondents said they stressed issues that underlie almost all government regulation of human activity, not simply activities regulated as criminal. One stated that his central goal was "to establish the limits and limitations of law as a mode of social control" and two others used almost identical language. Another named only a slightly different emphasis, "the inherent limitations on court-made rules as problem-resolving mechanisms." A third stressed the theme of "approaching the study of law from the legislative point of view" and another "the role of statutory law in a legal system." The criminal law is, to be sure, a particularly apt subject for examining the appropriate limits of the law and the roles of courts and legislatures, but it is simply one of many subjects that could serve. For example, the same themes will probably be raised in your course in Torts in considering whether the wisest way to meet the needs of persons injured in automobile accidents is to depend on lawsuits in court in which the injured person proves the other driver at fault, or instead on a scheme of insurance that provides compensation without requiring proof of fault.

A third more general function professed by the responding teachers was the training of students in the analytic skills lawyers need. In responding to a long list of possible themes, two were checked more frequently than any others as receiving "a great deal" of emphasis and a third was not far behind: training in perceiving the functions lying behind various doctrines, training in the careful reading of appellate decisions, and training in the reading of statutes. In the boot camp of the first year, most of your five or six teachers will probably spend large blocks of time simply working on developing your capacity to read and analyze legal materials carefully, much more difficult skills to master than might be guessed in advance. Training students to try to perceive the functions lying behind rules may be regarded as similarly indispensable. Without attention to the functions rules are to serve, it is often impossible to determine how a statute should be construed in a novel situation. It is even less possible to decide wisely how common-law rules, those developed through the courts alone, should be applied in novel situations.

We have thus seen that the first-year instructors will be emphasizing concerns other than the mastery of specific doctrines or rules. It is equally important to understand that these other concerns will vary among your teachers. Although several respondents, as I've indicated, placed great emphasis on training in statutory interpretation, several others said they gave it little or no emphasis at all. Similarly, although a majority of instructors said they gave a "moderate amount" of emphasis to "the historical development of doctrine," or to "the tactical problems of attorneys," or to the "ethical problems of attorneys," several said they gave one or more of these a great deal of attention, and as many or more said that they accorded these concerns no attention whatever. All your other first-year courses are susceptible as well to such widely varying approaches.

I believe many first-year students are confused or irritated by the fact that their teachers and the writers of casebooks are only partly concerned about conveying the "law" of crimes or contracts. Some of the irritation is just. Often the teacher will fail to make clear what his or her purposes are. Criminal Law seems simply a "bait-and-switch" gimmick to snare you into learning about the close reading of cases or statutes.

Indeed, despite their titles, nearly all the first-year courses may turn out to be the same course—how to think about legal problems as American lawyers tend to think about them. Although you may come to regard this subject as the most important of all, the courses may be frustrating not so much because they are redundant but rather because you will find it more difficult to know when you have grasped a process or a way of looking at the world than when you have correctly memorized a rule. You may also feel cheated if your teacher in the service of these other goals fails to reach large areas of a subject clearly within the scope of the course's title. In fact, she may never reach the last fifteen dollars of your forty-dollar casebook.

The heavy reliance on appellate-court decisions in all your courses many also prove a slight disservice to you. Most teachers of first-year courses would probably say, if asked, that they use the opinions of appellate courts not because the holdings of the courts are so important in themselves, but rather because they are vehicles for learning to read closely, they are repositories of interesting fact situations that generate discussion, and they include one person's (the judge's) reasoning for reaching a given result, thus providing a foil for debate about the issues. Although it is probable that after the first year you will have developed a just skepticism of the wisdom of appellate judges in general, it is also probable that at some level you will have absorbed a sense that law nonetheless emanates primarily from appellate judges or, put another way, that matters with which appellate judges do not become concerned are really not law.

What You Will Have Derived from the First Year and What You Won't

If you arrive at law school overweight and unable to play the cello, you are likely to finish law school overweight and unable to play the cello. There's only so much we can do.

On the other hand, you will be different and your friends who are not law students may now find you slightly offensive.

You will know a lot you didn't know before. You will have learned the concepts of "offer" and "acceptance" in contracts and "negligence" and "contributory negligence" in torts. You will be familiar with some of the current content of the Uniform Commercial Code and your own state's or the federal court's rules of judicial procedure. You are likely to have acquired valuable ways of approaching legal issues beyond the few approaches you may have previously considered. Among your acquisitions will likely be a knowledge of some of the common sources of the law; an alertness to the need to understand the arguments on both sides of an issue; a budding capacity to frame arguments to the maximum advantage of one side of a dispute; some special language to wrap around some commonplace notions; and a developing sense of the procedures through which problems can be addressed and resolved.

These are valuable skills. Your head will never be quite the same again. As one cynical critic of law schools has commented, "Each year 100,000 students are taught to think like lawyers. Teaching someone who for twenty-one years has thought like a person to think like a lawyer is no mean achievement."[4]

For whatever you have learned, however, there is a great deal you will not have learned. There are both forms of law and skills of practitioners you are likely to have heard little about during the first year. For example, in your first-year courses, most of the appellate cases you read will have begun in a trial court as a suit between private individuals or entities or, in the case of criminal law, a suit by the state against an individual. In the United States today, however, lawyers appear daily in forums other than courts and have to impress officials other than judges. Decisions as small as whether Jones's Shoe Store should be permitted to expand its parking lot or as large as whether a public utility should be permitted to operate a new nuclear power plant are made by administrative officials or agencies, not by judges. So are decisions about electrical and natural-gas utility rates, the granting of TV and radio broadcasting licenses, the permission to mine on public lands, and decisions about an individual's eligibility for Medicaid or Social Security disability benefits. The officials and agencies charged with making these decisions use procedures for developing general rules and rendering individual decisions that are in many ways different from the approach of courts. By the same token, appellate courts reviewing the decisions of officials and agencies typically approach the process of review quite differently than they approach review of a trial judge's decision in a contract dispute between two private citizens.

Despite this, despite the enormous growth of governmental agencies within the last half century and their impact on the lives of all citizens, and despite the fact that many lawyers today devote almost their entire practice to working with such agencies and officials, few law schools introduce law students to this kind of "public law" during the first year. In nearly all law schools, this gap is addressed in the second and third years by a course in administrative law and, in most schools, by specialized courses in such matters as environmental law, energy law, or public-utility law. In most schools, however, these courses are optional. More important, the "private law" cast of the courses in the first year— Mrs. Smith sues Pop's grocery—helps imprint on students that "real law" is the sort of law they learned in those first required courses, and that the administrative law of agencies and executive officials is somehow secondary in godliness and effete in character. During your first year, you should struggle to retain perspective about the narrow vision of the sources of law to which you are being exposed. During your second and third year, you should be certain to take some courses that provide the wider focus.

An even more fundamental gap exists in most first-year curricula. The capacity to analyze legal issues, the major focus of the first year, is only one of the many skills a fine lawyer needs. Let us consider a few of the many other skills lawyers need about which you may hear rather little during your first year.

Lawyers are fact-assemblers. When they receive a new matter, they must often pull together a complex story from jumbled bits of information scattered out to the horizons of their client's vision. The facts do not come dehydrated and prepackaged as they do in the opening paragraphs of the opinion of a court of appeals. Lawyers will typically need to consider ways of looking at a situation that are very different from the way it is initially described by a client. Not many schools give students early exposure to the art of investigating and organizing factual material.

Lawyers are interviewers. They interview people who, embarrassed, devious, or blinded, reveal only part of a story. Corporate clients are often said by their attorneys to be no more likely to tell their attorneys the whole truth about a disputed financial deal than the defendant in a murder case about his whereabouts on the night the victim was shot. Lawyers need to develop a second sense, a skill at learning how to ask or ferret out what they want to know. They need to learn how to develop relationships with varied clients. They need to learn to keep alert to detecting a client's legal problems that are very different from the ones about which the client initially thought she needed advice. Few schools give early training in interviewing.

Lawyers counsel people about much more than the law. The practitioner retained by a corporation finds her advice sought on purely business matters almost unrelated to issues of law and may find it increasingly difficult to separate her role as attorney from a developing role as entrepreneur. In family matters, it is often a matter of chance whether a client has been directed initially to a lawyer, minister, or family doctor. A parent considering divorce may simply want wise counsel—not about whether he and his spouse can legally agree to joint custody, but about whether joint custody is sensible in their circumstances. To help a client reach an answer, a lawyer may well need to draw upon information from disciplines other than law. Lawyers must also learn to define their roles as counselors—when do they refer clients to others with special skills, how ardently do they try to "persuade" a client to do what the lawyer thinks best? Few law schools give early training in counseling.

Lawyers are negotiators. Most real-estate lawyers and securities lawyers rarely appear in court. Many spend the bulk of their time fashioning deals for the development of shopping centers or the merger of companies. Even lawyers who file lawsuits spend much of their time negotiating. A dispute between two large corporations or two next-door neighbors that has led to a lawsuit is far more likely to be resolved by a settlement than by a judicial ruling or a jury's award. Criminal charges are far more likely to be resolved by a plea of guilty than they are to be resolved at trial. Few schools give early training in the art of negotiation.

All this and much more are likely to be missing from your first year. But there are, after all, three years of law school. Will the gaps in the first year be addressed in the next two? Maybe yes. Maybe no. At many schools it's up to you. The vast bulk of courses offered in your remaining years of law school will provide training in substantive or procedural doctrine and the analysis of problems not covered in the first year. You will find courses in the law of corporations, taxation, conflicts of law, trust and estates, criminal procedure, and so forth. In some schools, particularly ones with small faculties, many of these courses will be required. At the same time, in most schools, it is possible to slide through three years without ever taking courses that provide useful training in many of the other lawyer skills. There is a grave danger that you will graduate from law school believing that, apart from a few mechanical matters such as how to get to the courthouse, all you need to know to be a good lawyer is doctrine and how to think about doctrine.

Many students and law teachers share an unjustified expectation that students will develop such skills in interviewing, counseling, and negotiating adequately in the first years of practice. Faculty members at many schools envision a model career pattern in which the student steps from law school into a large or middle-sized law firm, where the older lawyers nurture him or her in the practical skills of practice. The fact is, however, that large numbers of young lawyers start out immediately on their own or in Legal Aid offices or in prosecutors' offices with no elbow to work at the side of. They are immediately given substantial responsibility for matters that affect the lives of large numbers of people. Even the young practitioners who do start in a well-supervised law office are likely to serve as apprentices to lawyers who developed their own skills in an unreflective, haphazard way. It is not simply a recent development that law schools offer little such training. The senior partners didn't get any either.

What should you do about these possible gaps in your education? Here are a couple of pieces of advice.

First, don't let the prospect of incomplete training stand in the way of your absorbing as much as possible from the courses of your first year. Although it is true that many things will probably be missing, much of what is there—for example, training in careful reasoning and training in the close reading of legal materials—will be of great value to you in practice and probably cannot be mastered later if you do not master it in law school. Throw yourself into it. Get up your courage and participate in class discussions. Form a study group with others who are not quite like you and haggle over the issues raised in your course materials.

Second, give serious consideration to taking whatever courses you can after the first year that provide training in skills or exposure to the nature and structure of the legal profession. One particular sort of offering deserves mention: courses in what is commonly referred to as "clinical law." These are courses in which law students handle cases for actual clients under the supervision of instructors or private practitioners. In Chapter 19, Gary Bellow describes the sorts of clinics commonly found at law schools. Apart from recommending clinical offerings, I'd also urge you to involve yourself in extracurricular activities that permit you to work with people on their legal problems under the tutelage of those with experience.

One danger of taking only courses that operate in the realm of ideas or doctrine and shield you from real people with problems is that you are likely, while a student, to fail to see yourself as a lawyer. Throughout law school, students can refer cynically to lawyers as "they." Such detachment permits the student confidently to deny to himself that he would engage in shady practices that an extremely high portion of lawyers engage in; then later, in practice, when the opportunity for misbehavior occurs, the student will have no reservoir of pain about the issue to guide him.

I believe the law student's lack of a sense of identity as a lawyer—a sense that apparently develops much earlier for medical students who, in about their second year, start having patients who look up to them—partly accounts for the nearly universally reported restlessness of third-year law students. Especially itchy are law students who come directly to law school after college. By the last term of law school they are typically in their nineteenth consecutive year of sitting in classrooms. Students not only become bored; they become anxious as they head untested into practice. I once spoke to a young law school graduate, highly regarded by her teachers, who described her reaction to the graduation gift of a briefcase. "I felt," she said, "that I was still a child about to play dress-up."

Of course, I do not contend that you will get little from law school, even if yours is the most traditional of educations. The chapters that follow amply demonstrate the excitement which awaits you. These years may well be the most exciting time in your life as an intellectual, a Fourth of July picnic of ideas. They were just that for me. Maybe I should be a little more tempered. Actress Elizabeth Ashley, asked by a reporter how she enjoyed her return to New York City after a time away, replied, "Well, it's not as good as homemade chocolate mousse, but it's a whole lot better than grape juice." May you have more mousse than juice.

NOTES

1. A list of the teachers at the more than one hundred and fifty law schools that are approved by the American Bar Association. I conducted the survey before the publication of the first edition of this book. My belief is that the survey, if conducted today, would produce much the same results. For a sample, I picked every fourteenth teacher from a list of teachers of Criminal Law at these schools published in the American Association of Law Schools, Directory of Law Teachers 242–47 (Supplement 1975). The law teachers who responded came from schools in seventeen states. They are schools of widely varying size and widely varying standards for admission.

2. See Nancy Erickson, *Final Report: Sex Bias in the Teaching of Criminal Law* (1989) (unpublished paper).

3. In nearly all the schools, procedural aspects of the criminal law—for example, the use at trial of confessions or rights to counsel or trial by jury—are covered in advanced courses, and fewer than a third of respondents indicated that they covered such subjects at all as part of the first-year introductory course.

4. J. Auerbach, *"A Plague of Lawyers,"* Atlantic, October 1976.

CHAPTER 10

Civil Procedure

Judith Resnik
UNIVERSITY OF SOUTHERN CALIFORNIA

What the Course Is About

Traditionally the world of procedure has been divided into three categories—civil, criminal, and administrative. Those terms have been used to delineate various kinds of proceedings, and the definitions of each rely upon the existence of the others. For example, civil cases are those in which no criminal penalties (often but not exclusively incarceration) are sought. Administrative proceedings are those in which (typically) the government is a party and the case is processed in administrative agencies rather than courts. Courts, in turn, are defined as institutions that handle civil and criminal cases. However, these lines are not sharp; for example, while civil disputes often involve private citizens, in a substantial proportion of civil cases the government is a party, as either plaintiff or defendant. In all of these proceedings, be the case called civil, criminal, or administrative, someone (an individual, a group, a representative of the government) starts a proceeding against someone else (an individual, a group, a representative of the government), claiming that the other has violated some legal norm. In all three categories a third party, empowered by the state, is called upon to determine the validity of the claim. In all three categories the parties have some degree of autonomy to fashion the contours of the dispute and yet are also limited by conventions and rules. In all three categories, questions exist about

165

the power of decision makers, the constraints imposed upon them, the kinds of sanctions or remedies that might be imposed, and the ability to seek reconsideration of the decisions rendered. In all three categories the decision makers may not be required to render decisions—by virtue of settlement, negotiation, withdrawal of claim, or the pursuit of other kinds of process. And in all three categories the procedures are assessed as to whether they are fair and efficient.

Procedure is thus the study of the processes of litigation and dispute resolution in the United States. The topics covered include how lawsuits are started and stopped, what powers the decision makers have, and what the structure of courts is and has been. The issues central to procedure are value-laden. The questions to be addressed include: Why have process at all? Why care about *how* a decision is made? If process is required, how much should be provided? How formal should it be? How expensive should it be? How free should the parties be to initiate lawsuits? Who gets to litigate and who is foreclosed? And what about the decision makers— what kinds of information should be required prior to decision? What remedies should courts be able to order? How much power should judges have, and when should that power be constrained? When may decisions be reconsidered, and when should they be considered "final"?

Obviously these questions do not admit to easy, unvarying answers; ideas about procedure are deeply rooted in the social-political fabric. Court systems embody, express, and create the values held about what constitutes fair process. Procedure courses are thus laced with questions about legal policy, about constitutional theory (of what *due process* means, of when attorneys are required, of the power of courts to compel individuals to appear), and about the role of courts in this political system.

Procedure is also a course in which the question of lawyering is central, for procedural systems in the United States are very lawyer-dependent. Thus, perhaps more than other first-year courses, the emphasis in procedure is on how lawyers take a problem from the world at large and transform it into something called a "lawsuit." Because that question spans all the kinds of cases that one can imagine, students in procedure consider the procedural aspects of a wide variety of cases—from those involving a car accident to those involving a school-desegregation case, from those involving child custody to those involving antitrust litigation. The focus is on the creation of lawsuits and the role of lawyers—in relation to their clients, the courts, and the political structure. Because providing process costs money, time, and energy, the role of resources is critical to the study of procedure. Thus rules that treat all individuals as similarly situated belie the reality that some of us are richer than others, that some of us have more access to help than do others, and that some of us are more likely to be harmed than are others. Procedure courses therefore examine the costs of lawyering and the impact of rules that shift costs from one side to the other or that provide for government subsidies for litigation.

When studying litigation, it is important to remember that not all moments of discord result in the filing of lawsuits. Individuals and groups often disagree. Moveover, even when someone characterizes the discord as a "dispute," only a small percentage of such disputes result in the filing of civil, criminal, or administrative proceedings. For example, one study estimated that in disputes involving more than one thousand dollars, disputants filed lawsuits (in either state or federal court) in 11.2 percent of the cases. Of the cases filed, less than 8 percent were tried; more than 50 percent were terminated by voluntary agreement of the parties. Thus proceduralists have to bear in mind that litigation is only one of many possible responses to problems presented by clients, and the study of litigation must be linked to the study of the other options that can be pursued consecutively or sequentially.

Once a decision *is* made to file a lawsuit, a choice often exists about where to file a lawsuit. State courts are courts of "general jurisdiction," which means that they can handle all kinds of cases; while federal courts are courts of "limited jurisdiction," that is, Article III of the United States Constitution gives the federal judiciary power only over cases that fall within certain categories. In some instances the jurisdictional grants of the state and federal court systems overlap, and the two have "concurrent jurisdiction"; that is, both systems have the power to hear a case, and the parties (and most often the plaintiff, and, in reality, the plaintiff's lawyer) can pick which of the two court systems in which to file. For example, in a contract dispute in which more than $50,000 is at stake and the plaintiff is from California and the defendant from New Jersey, the plaintiff can decide whether to file in state or federal court. Similarly, in many cases seeking vindication of civil rights, the plaintiff can choose to file in either state or federal court. Students in procedure courses learn about federal statutes, rules, and aspects of practice (such as current legal doctrine, the relative time it takes to process cases, the ways in which cases are assigned to judges, and the like) that affect such choices.

Students of procedure also learn how to start lawsuits—by the filing of a document, called a *complaint* in civil litigation, an *indictment* or *information* in a criminal case, and a variety of names in administrative proceedings. After that initial document is served on the opponent, that opponent has an opportunity to respond—with an answer, a plea, or with a motion to the court to stop the case. Thereafter, most litigation systems have some rules of information exchange by which the parties give each other (and the court) information about the case. Increasingly, judges or court personnel are taking an active role in scheduling and monitoring the pretrial phases of cases—to move cases along, to urge settlement, to attempt to supervise attorney behavior. Most cases end without trial; for example, fewer than 5 percent of the civil, and 13 percent of the criminal cases filed in the federal system in 1986 ended by trial.

If cases are decided either by judges or juries, then in most instances the aggrieved party can appeal to a higher court, which has (often limited) authority to review the decisions made below. In the federal system, and in many of the state systems, there are three tiers of decision makers: a trial court; an appellate system with an obligation to review if either side appeals; and the highest court, which picks the cases that it wants to hear. At each stage the parties often have the option to withdraw. Increasingly, parties are encouraged (sometimes by the imposition of sanctions) to seek alternatives to litigation, called, these days, "alternative dispute resolution," or ADR.

What Law Teachers Teach in Procedure

There is no one way that law schools teach about the many issues described above. Almost all law schools require a first-year course that lasts either a semester or the full year and is called either Civil Procedure or Procedure. While the course explores the themes sketched above, the content and emphases of the courses vary a good deal. Some teachers use the Federal Rules of Civil Procedure as the framework for a course, while others focus upon Supreme Court case law, interpreting doctrines such as who has legal injury (plaintiffs, causes of action, standing), who can participate (party structure), what is the reach of the authority of the court (jurisdiction), what remedies can be afforded (equitable or legal relief), and when further decision making is precluded (res judicata and collateral estoppel). Other courses spend less time on doctrinal development and more on how lawyers develop a case from filing to disposition, while yet other courses have litigation materials interspersed with discussions of procedural theory. In some schools jurisdiction over individuals (personal jurisdiction) is taught in the introductory course, while in other law schools that issue is explored in upper-division courses. Some law schools have courses that focus on trial procedures, while others emphasize pretrial phases of litigation and settlement.

In short, in this area, as in many others, teachers have to make choices about what issues are central, and there is a lively ongoing debate among teachers of procedure about what stays in and what comes out. Further, as the demographics of law teaching change a bit and more women and minorities enter the teaching profession, questions about some aspects of procedure courses are raised. Many state courts have convened special task forces on gender and racial bias in the courts and in the legal profession. Topics once considered gender-neutral—such as the role of the judge, the nature of lawyering, and the allocation of work among the courts—are questioned as we debate the values implicit in the subject matter.

How Students Respond to Procedure

In some sense the subject matter of the procedure course is a bit less accessible than the other first-year courses. Much of the rest of early law school consists of reading cases to extract principles from them—all to build up a set of doctrines and rules in a particular area. In those courses the fact that a lawsuit was the basis for the opinion written by a judge is simply not the focus; the case is assumed to be there, and the issue is what one learns from the application of legal doctrines to a particular set of facts.

In contrast, courses in procedure do not assume the existence of a case. A central question for the course is: What is a case? How does one make something "out there" into something called a lawsuit? For some students the range of materials can be a bit daunting or disorienting. I have taught at several law schools and at all have heard the same question: What exactly are we supposed to be learning? The answer is to try to keep one's focus on a few questions. Take, for example, the case of Abby Gail Lassiter, who was in prison and faced with the effort by the North Carolina Department of Social Services to terminate her right to be a parent. The case, later in the United States Supreme Court, is about whether she, as an indigent, has a constitutional right to a lawyer to assist her in defending against the action.

When reading a case, students should always remember to ask:

- What happened "out there" in the world? (In the *Lassiter* case, the state was seeking to end her relationship with her child.)
- Who wants what? (The mother wanted to remain the legal parent of her child and the state wanted to free the child for adoption.)
- Who thought that getting courts into the picture would help? (The state went to court to make the factual separation of the parent and child legally permanent.)
- What court was chosen, and what response did the court make? (The state filed the proceeding in state court, and the defendant raised the claim of her Fourteenth Amendment right to counsel.)

- What role did the lawyers play, and how did they use procedure to advance their clients' interests? (The defendant initially lacked a lawyer; only on appeal did a lawyer enter the case on her behalf, and the record developed at the trial level suffered from the absence of anyone assisting her to answer the neglect and disinterest charges against her.)
- Did the procedure constrain or enable decision making that you respect? (When reading the *Lassiter* case, you will debate how much the current adjudicatory system is lawyer-dependent and whether such dependency is to be praised or decried.)

In other words, a procedure course has several agendas: to teach a law student how lawsuits can be constructed; to think about the role of lawyers in the construction and destruction of lawsuits; to consider the institution of adjudication, the role of courts in the political structure, and to explore what values are embodied in the procedural choices made. Over time the kind of questions implicit in a procedure course become easier for students to ask and to answer, and comfort with the subject matter increases.

One final point to underscore is how procedure courses and law school can distort one's focus. Learn, early on, that by and large, no one wants a lawsuit. Plaintiffs don't want lawsuits, they want what lawsuits can get them—money, land, freedom. Defendants don't want lawsuits, they want lawsuits to end as quickly as possible. Courts don't want lawsuits, either; they describe themselves as overworked (a question, by the way, for procedure courses to examine), and courts have a variety of methods to discourage either the filing or the pursuit of lawsuits. While lawyers sometimes want lawsuits as a way to make money, in theory, at least, lawyers want to help their clients, which means using lawsuits instrumentally. Thus, as you learn how to construct lawsuits, you should also remember why those lawsuits were wanted in the first place, and you should constantly be asking: Why are these "the rules"? How have they changed over time? What values are imbedded in them, and how might you want to contribute to restructuring those rules so as to enable a better process and a better outcome?

Suggested Readings

A first suggestion is that you need not feel obliged to read any of the materials listed below prior to coming to law school; once you arrive, you will have more than enough occasions to become acquainted with this literature. A second suggestion is that if you want to get a preview of procedure courses, go sit in on first-year classes at a law school. However, should you feel the need, I have provided a few of the books and articles that preview some of the issues raised in procedure courses.

Books (General)

Cover, Robert M. *Justice Accused.* (Yale University Press, 1975.)

Herrnstein Smith, Barbara. *Contingencies of Value.* (Harvard University Press, 1989.)

Kluger, Richard. *Simple Justice.* (Vintage Books, 1975.)

Books (Procedure)

Summaries/Legal Treatises

Administrative Office of the United States Courts, Annual Report of the Director (Washington, D.C.). Yearly reports providing data on litigation in the federal courts.

Fleming, James Jr., and Geoffrey C. Hazard, Jr. *Civil Procedure*, 3rd ed. (Little Brown, 1985).

Lind, E. Allan, and Tom R. Tyler. *The Social Psychology of Procedural Justice.* (Plenum Press, 1988).

Wright, Charles Alan. *Law of Federal Courts.* (West's Publishing Co., 3rd ed. 1976).

Casebooks

Cover, Robert M., Owen M. Fiss, and Judith Resnik. *Procedure* (Foundation Press, 1988).

Field, Richard H., Benjamin Kaplan, and Kevin M. Clermont. *Materials on Civil Procedure.* (Foundation Press, 1984.)

Fink, Howard P., and Mark V. Tushnet. *Federal Jurisdiction: Policy and Practice*, 2nd ed. (Michie Books, 1987.)

Landers, Jonathan M., James A. Martin, and Stephen C. Yeazell. *Civil Procedure*, 2nd ed. (Little Brown, 1988.)

Louisell, David W., Geoffrey C. Hazard, Jr., and Colin C. Tait. *Cases on Pleading and Procedure*, 6th ed. (Foundation Press, 1989.)

Articles

Cover, Robert M. "Violence and the Word." 95 *Yale Law Journal* 1601, 1986.

Eisenberg, Theodore, and Stephen C. Yeazell. "The Ordinary and the Extraordinary in Institutional Litigation." 93 *Harvard Law Review* 463, 1980.

Fiss, Owen M. "The Forms of Justice." 93 *Harvard Law Review* 393, 1978.

Galanter, Marc. "Why the 'Haves' Come out Ahead: Speculations on the Limits of Legal Change." 9 *Law & Society Review* 95, 1972.

Menkel-Meadow, Carrie. "Portia in a Different Voice: Speculations on a Women's Lawyering Process." 1 *Berkeley Women's Law Journal* 39, 1985.

Resnik, Judith. "On the Bias: Feminist Reconsideration of the Aspirations of Our Judges." 61 *Southern California Law Review* 1877, 1989.

Trubek, David M., Austin Sarat, William F. Felstiner, Herbert M. Kritzer, and Joel B. Grossman. "The Costs of Ordinary Litigation." 31 *UCLA Law Review* 72, 1983.

CHAPTER 11

Contracts

Robert L. Bard

UNIVERSITY OF CONNECTICUT

I see three prime reasons for establishing Contracts as a required first-year course: contract law remains the paradigm of a doctrinally based law system; contracts is the prime example of facilitative law—legal arrangements whereby public power is made available to individuals to facilitate their economic activities; and study of contract law provides one of the best vehicles for teaching a wide range of essential legal skills and concepts. I will be satisfied if this chapter clarifies the nature of contract law as a highly doctrinal legal structure designed for use by private citizens in consensual transactions, sensitizes students to the range of objectives being pursued in their particular contracts course, and provides some insight into the pedagogic methods being used by the professor.

Love It or Leave It

I predict that of all your first-year courses, you will react most strongly to Contracts. In fact, your experience in Contracts may well color your view of the nature of law and your capacity or desire to cope with it. To make this point, early on in the semester I ask my students if Contracts is the epitome or the antithesis of law; and then proceed to make a case for both propositions. Since contracts embodies all that is unique, fascinating, mind-blowing, and ridiculous about law and law school, you will love it or hate it. To make matters more confusing for a first-year law student, Contracts is well suited to explore many aspects of law and lawyering essentially unrelated to its subject matter. These include training students to think like a lawyer, the dynamics of judge-made law, plus a variety of important ideas that don't really belong to any particular subject matter area.

The mode of your instruction may be called a Socratic dialogue, but it will be neither Socratic nor a dialogue. It will consist of intensive grilling of students who will be held to standards of precision of thought and expression far beyond the capacity of any first-year law student. Thus, nothing you say is likely to be right. You may find that no fact or argument which you found persuasive will be deemed relevant, or, if relevant, will have the meaning you ascribed to it while briefing the case. Worst of all, any considerations that would seem to you essential for reaching rational and just outcomes in the cases under discussion may well be "demonstrated" to be irrelevant and somehow softheaded.

Of all the learning you will derive from a first-year Contracts course the rules of contract law are the least important. Some of you may be lucky enough to get a professor who has thought deeply about contract law and is determined to share some of her insights into the nature of law. With such a professor you will still learn many rules, but you will learn them not for their intrinsic importance, but to amass a sufficient basis of material to permit thought and discussion about the nature of contract law—indeed all branches of law—as a tool of social ordering. Such an approach to a first-year Contracts course seems to be very hard on students, but is extremely rewarding over a lifetime of legal practice.

Is Contract Law Necessary?

The continued need for a year-long first-year course in Contracts has become controversial. For nearly a century, Contracts was deemed the nonpareil of legal education, if not law itself. The founder of modern American legal education, Christopher Columbus Langdell, Dean of Harvard Law School, greatly aided by the theorizing of Justice Holmes, embodied his radical revision of legal education and his vision of law in a Contracts casebook. And over the intervening years there has been a concentration of the greatest legal minds on this subject. The names of Holmes, Ames, Corbin, Williston, Llewelyn, Fuller, and Gilmore come quickly to mind. Often, these same men were major contributors to jurisprudence. But in recent years the value of Contracts as a separate first-year required course has been increasingly challenged. And there now are only two major English-speaking legal thinkers—Ian MacNeil (American) and Patrick Atiyah (English)—who call contract law their intellectual home.

There are two kinds of criticisms of Contracts as a significant component of a law school's core curriculum. One is that all the major doctrinal problems of contract law have been solved to an extent that we need no longer waste five to seven credit hours in the freshman year on a subject matter whose important features may be grasped in far less time. The second is that the kind of agreements contract law is designed to support no longer play a major role in our society and, where such agreements retain some significance, the relevant contract law is better treated in the context of the specialized legal fields that still make use of them. That is, to the extent contract concepts play a major role in insurance, labor relations, international law, or secured transactions (mortgages), it is better to consider the relevant contract-law problems in courses focused on these particular subject matters rather than to waste precious first-year curriculum time on the study of general contract principles.

In large measure, the very success of contract law is partly responsible for its diminishing estate with many thinkers about legal education. That is, the law pertaining to the transactional arena whose needs brought contract law into being—commercial dealings between professional business people—has been developed to a point where there is relatively little need for further refinements in contract law to warrant concern by students or their professors. The law of Contracts, particularly as clarified and rationalized through the American Law Institute's Restatements of Contracts, and, of course, the Uniform Commercial Code, has resolved most of the difficult, important, and interesting questions that have long concerned scholars, students, and law reformers. These solutions have been bequeathed to courts, the bar, and the commercial world in such form to greatly reduce the necessity of further intensive criticism and reformation. Those problems that do remain are concentrated on the fringes rather than the center of the set of problems with which contract law has been most concerned. Consumer transactions, particularly transactions involving poor consumers, including housing rentals, now has become the prime center of attention of legal scholars seeking to restructure contract law for the benefit of the poor. But such efforts seem rather futile. Although there is some room in contract law for legislation and judicial action for the benefit of the economically and politically weak, contract law is not an effective instrument for redistributing wealth and power. This can only be achieved by direct political action—the poor need more money and power, not better laws or more lawyers. Some have argued that the very existence of contract law actually accentuates existing socioeconomic disparities. But, economic analysis demonstrates the falsity of this position. Within any given distribution of wealth, everyone is better off with contract law than without it.

Nevertheless, a strong case can be made for the continuance of Contracts's current position in the first-year curriculum. In fact, these are the same reasons why Contracts has assumed such great importance in legal education for so long. First, the law of contracts has been closely associated with the transition from a status society to a laissez-faire, capitalistic, agreement-based society. Second, of all branches of the law, contract law best fits the model of law envisioned by post-Civil War legal theorists, led by Langdell and Holmes. Its salient feature is a highly formalized, rigorous, deductive analytical system roughly analogous to those developed by the hard and pure sciences in the nineteenth century. Indeed, Langdell explicitly characterized his approach to law study as paralleling that of the sciences, with the law library substituting for the laboratory.

Actually, the association of contract law with the transition of western societies from a status to a "contract" based socio-political-economic system confuses fundamental political structure with a useful but limited technical device. The "status to contract" shift refers to the ability of individuals to choose their modes of social and economic life with a minimum of government interference. The law of contract establishes a system of government-managed rules primarily designed to facilitate economic transactions between strangers through use of a highly formalized set of legal rules. These rules are entirely unrelated to agreement-based justifications of liberal democracy, à la John Locke and John Rawls.

There is a weak relationship between modern contract law and the fundamental socio-economic structure of a given society. If a society prohibits the rearrangement of productive resources or assigns all such resources to the state which centrally dictates the use of such resources, there would be little use for contract law. This is the case because contract law is a legal tool that facilitates the reordering of the factors of production by increasing the security of private agreements designed for this purpose. Once a society transforms itself into one that permits a wide range of individual economic decision-making, it becomes quite useful to create social tools which increase the security of certain kinds of agreements. Though contract law is such a tool, its overall role is peripheral rather than central.

But even in an open society the integration of economic, social, and political activities through the use of contract law is, and always has been, a second-best solution, to be used only where more secure forms of association are unavailable. The family and nonprofit institutions such as universities, charitable foundations, and large corporations, are examples of social institutions that seek coordination without use of contractual arrangements. And, as critics of current methods of teaching Contracts point out, the trend is toward greater use of noncontractual forms of integration.

Contracts and Law as Authoritative Rules

Authoritative rules are essential components of any legal system. Rules are conduct-directing norms, telling those subject to these rules how they are to behave under particular circumstances. Authoritative rules are those conduct-directing norms which are expected to be obeyed by all citizens of a political society. Thus, law usually is conceived as a set of rules imposed by a government authority designed to direct the conduct of both private parties and various public officials when certain matters are brought to their attention.

For most people criminal law is the paradigm of a legal system. Criminal law and procedure directs the conduct of police, prosecutors, and courts. It, like all law, represents a priori decisions by a political society that certain kinds of conduct will be punished. But contract law hardly fits this model. Contract law is authoritative only to the extent that private parties have chosen to make it so. And contract law prescribes outcomes under particular circumstances only where the parties haven't chosen to direct different outcomes. The essence of contract law is that it is consensual; people choose to govern some aspect of their relationships via contract law, and only those who so choose are bound by it. But those who choose to be so bound are given the power to use the force of the state to help enforce their private promissory arrangements.

This represents a highly sophisticated relationship between private citizens and governments, thereby greatly enriching the concept of law. I often start my Contracts course by asking whether contract law or criminal law could be most easily dispensed with by any large political society. The subsequent discussion is designed to demonstrate the enormous difference between contract and criminal law. No organized society could do without criminal law, and indeed every society, no matter how primitive, has some sort of criminal law system. But so long as criminal law and property law were operational any society could dispense with contract law.

The concept of voluntary law is somewhat difficult to reconcile with the notion of law as an authoritative, conduct-directing norm. The problem is further complicated by the fact that the goal of Contracts, unlike criminal law, is not total compliance. Instead, the penalties for breach of contracts are designed to compensate victims—not to deter breaches. Thus damages often are low enough so that it frequently pays for parties to breach their contracts.

These are fundamental and sophisticated concepts, and as is so often the case with legal education, their fundamentality makes them appropriate for first-year study. However, their sophistication might call for postponement until students are more familiar with basic concepts. But postponement usually means avoidance, since few upperclass electives in Contracts are offered and even fewer students elect to take them.

Contracts as Quintessential Legal Doctrine

Although all law operates through rules, bodies of law differ in the degree that their rules fit tightly with each other and produce a conceptual system. Such systems, like contracts, are built upon a limited number of concepts, which are manipulated to create a highly dense intellectual structure, similar to mathematics or theology. This kind of system is sometimes called doctrinal law. Other bodies of legal rules, like torts and property, are not doctrinal. Rather they constitute a collection of self-sufficient, mutually independent prescriptions.

Despite the success of the legal realist school of jurisprudence, which dismantled much of the gleaming theoretical purity that Contracts enjoyed in the period between the Civil War and World War I, contract law remains the most fully developed doctrinal law system. But it is neither the only model for law, nor necessarily the most important model. Stimulating inquiry about why it is useful to use a doctrinal system for Contracts, but dangerous to do the same in developing criminal and constitutional law, is another good reason for including Contracts in the first-year curriculum.

The essence of a doctrinal system, indeed of all legal arrangements, is that it deliberately narrows the factors that may be considered by the judge in applying legal rules to particular cases. It is this feature of contract law that most frustrates first-year students. According to one scholar, law is "blind to details of subject matter and person. It does not ask who buys and sells and what is bought and sold . . . contract law is abstraction—what is left in the law relating to agreements when all particularities of person and subject matter are removed." It precludes consideration of the relative wealth and legal sophistication of the parties, the moral culpability of the breaching party, and the extent to which a failure to perform was deliberate or largely unavoidable.

In fact, law eliminates many of those factors that matter in an unlimited search for justice or truth. But this is the point. Legal rules represent a specialized way to apply agreed-upon social policies to particular cases, and such an enterprise requires a conscious narrowing of the factors relevant to each judicial decision. Karl Llewelyn's famous little legal primer, *The Bramble Bush*, expands on the very special nature of legal thinking. And, if the phrase has any meaning at all, "thinking like a lawyer" must refer to this peculiar capacity to solve problems through application of a narrow but intensive perspective.

A basic tenet of a democracy is that legislatures, not judges or legal theorists, must make the law. Thus, when judges are forced to apply old law in new situations, the rigidity of a doctrinal system protects judges against accusations of usurpation of decision-making powers allegedly belonging to the executive and legislative branches of government.

Of course, no legal systems can be administered without some judge-made law, because no set of principles, whether judge-made or legislature-made, can cover all situations. This forces judges to make law where precedents don't apply and legislative intent is undecipherable. Even in these cases, judges can obtain guidance from the manifest objectives of contract law in general, and the particular area of contract law involved in the problem at hand. Under these circumstances, the narrower the range of possible choices and the more limited the methods of adapting existing law to new situations, the less anyone need fear usurpation of legislative powers and prerogatives.

Immunization Against Contracts

Students seem to have one of three reactions to this situation. Some never seem to understand the nature of a doctrinal argument. They persist in trying to take account of every factor that seems to them to matter, and it is extremely difficult to get them to achieve the necessary narrowness of focus. For these people, Contracts is an excruciating experience. Every time they are asked to recite they find themselves (sometimes rather brutally) chopped down, and they never really know why. Or students grasp what is expected of them but totally reject the doctrinal approach as unworthy of serious consideration by intelligent and serious people. Often they extend this rejection to all of law. If this is what law is about, they argue, it is insanity.

At the other extreme, many students think they have found in Contracts the ultimate in intellectual satisfaction. Here, at last, is a set of problems for which there are *answers*. No more of this frustrating ambiguity in which no question seems to have an unequivocal answer, where there are always more factors to consider and certainty forever eludes them. Contract law, once the basic nature of the game is understood, permits application of intelligence to reach a degree of certainty that eludes them in most of their other studies.

All of these attitudes are right and wrong to some degree. Despair of ever understanding law, and therefore of ever being a good lawyer, is usually inappropriate. Most students admitted to decent law schools have the necessary intellectual capacity to cope minimally with a law school curriculum and the bar exam. The only difficult aspect of law is the fact that those who work in it—judges and lawyers—will recognize only certain kinds of arguments. Once this is grasped law loses all its terrors. Indeed, because legal systems are designed to be operated by people of average intelligence, they must be relatively simple. Neither lawyers nor judges are wholly drawn from the genius class, and it is people of average intelligence who write and apply the law. Law is a mass-marketed item, and to perform its function it must be comprehensible by a very large number of ordinary citizens.

This definitely does *not* mean that good lawyering is easy. But lawyering has surprisingly little to do with great facility in manipulating legal doctrine. In fact, very little of lawyering involves subtle pondering of difficult legal propositions. Judgment, persistence, reliability, and the ability to relate with people count the most. Intelligence is vital, but not necessarily the particular kind of intelligence that leads to A's in Contract or magna cum laude degrees. In other words, do not judge your potential as an effective lawyer by your performance in law school, particularly your performance in highly abstract subjects such as Contracts.

The reaction I most fear typically happens to better students. This is the uncritical extrapolation of values and modes of analyses well suited to Contracts problems to other arenas of social interaction. That is, the principle of excluding all but a few factors in considering the appropriateness of legal arrangements may be learned too well. Legal and judicial attitudes appropriate for commercial transactions usually are highly unfortunate for criminal and constitutional law. And area of law, like international and administrative law, which are highly undoctrinal, may be rejected out of hand. Severe criticism of the Supreme Court for failing to follow precedent is, in my view, the outgrowth of application of critiques appropriate for bodies of law, such as contract and property law, designed to produce a high degree of predictability, to legal areas such as constitutional law, which deals with questions relating to the basic ground rules of a complex society.

The message here is to take Contracts seriously, but not too seriously. That is, the utility of a highly structured rule system for many commercial transactions must be recognized. But the danger of insisting that all areas of law conform to the contract model must be avoided. Each "subject area" of law must be viewed as a special purpose tool invented by humanity to better order certain aspects of social and political life in a large society. In certain circumstances (and Contracts may be one of them) to achieve the maximum predictability the rules must be narrowly construed. In other areas, far greater flexibility is essential.

Contracts as a Trojan Horse

No matter who your Contracts teacher is, and no matter what casebook he or she uses, of one thing you can be sure—the teaching of contract law, per se, will be but a minor element of the professor's goal for the course. Worse yet, different professors have radically different notions of what the noncontract-law component of the course should include. Certainly the professor wants you to learn the basic rules and concepts of contract law, but knows, even if you don't, that you don't need six credit hours to do it. Your professor even may know that most contract rules can be learned outside of class once students have grasped the basic outline and vocabulary of contract law. But because you don't know all this, and rightfully believe that the purpose of a required first-year Contracts course is to learn contract law, you are likely to become extremely frustrated when the professor seems to dawdle on a single case or explores alternative legal formulations and never gets around to revealing which one is "right," or even worse, asks irrelevant questions such as "Why do we need contract law and what would happen if it were eliminated?" Things will further deteriorate when you compare your class with other sections and learn that their professor has already covered seventy pages while you are still immersed in the first or second case.

It is quite likely that your professor will use his or her Contracts course to teach all the essential legal skills necessary for effective case reading. Case reading certainly is best taught in the context of a doctrinal system, and contract law boasts the best-developed doctrinal system. Doctrinal systems also are extremely forward-looking—that is, each new decision must take into account its impact upon the future development of the law. This forces the decision maker in each case to weigh the long-term consequences of choosing one legal solution over another. Also, contract law is an attractive area for teaching legal skills because its objectives are rather simple: to facilitate the use of agreements as a tool of economic organization.

Contracts and Economic Analysis

Perhaps the most interesting thing that has happened to the study of contract law in the past fifteen years is the increased application of microeconomic theory to contract doctrine. Together with all areas of law closely related to economic activity, Contracts lends itself to economic analysis. Like many of the major contributions of economics to legal analysis, economics' contributions to contract law are of two types: some stem from application of relatively sophisticated microeconomic theory and others involve use of an economic perspective without reliance on the standard analytic apparatus. A good example of the former is the use of indifference curves to demonstrate the potential gains from making gift promises enforceable.[1] Similar techniques were used by the same authors to demonstrate the costs of traditional attitudes toward liquidated damages.[2]

An excellent example of the second type of economics' use is the rigorous exploration of the concept of unequal bargaining power. Unequal bargaining power is key to the analysis of the nature and consequences of contracts of adhesion—transactions in which one of the parties insists upon a standard set of terms that are offered on a take-it-or-leave-it basis. It has long been an article of faith that contracts of adhesion are effective means for translating economic power into advantageous terms of trade. In fact, by intensive probing of the concept of unequal bargaining power, without use of marginal analysis, it can be demonstrated that contracts of adhesion benefit both parties, and are not instruments of oppression by the economically powerful against the economically weak.

Learning the Basics

You will be anxious to learn everything you need to know to get a high grade in Contracts, to pass the bar, and to practice effectively. You are likely to assume that these three objectives are synonymous with learning contract *doctrine*. You will be wrong, but no one will be able to convince you of that until you become a senior.

Though students grossly overrate the importance and difficulty of learning doctrine, a minimum amount must be learned to be able to cope with more relevant aspects of Contracts. In going about learning contract doctrine you should understand that many law professors believe that students are capable of discovering the rules for themselves. Unfortunately, professors often fail to provide students with enough guidance on how to go about learning the rules. In some cases this stems from the pedagogic theory that knowledge gained with difficulty is better learned. I will accept the sincerity of those holding this view, although one always remains a bit suspicious of any expert who deliberately makes comprehension of his or her specialty more difficult than it need be. But law, like life, contains sufficient difficulties without deliberately creating more. Fortunately, the antidote to obscurantist teaching methods is readily available in the many outlines and short treatises currently in print. These will be briefly described hereafter.

Casebooks

Undoubtedly, the required learning materials for your Contracts course will be a combination of case reports, text, notes, excerpts, and questions called a "casebook." Conceivably students could rely solely on their casebooks to learn basic contract doctrine. This is particularly true of more recent books which are organized on the principle that the course's basic teaching materials should present all the principal components of contract law in the clearest possible way. But such books seem difficult to produce. Probably, the prime impediment to the production of self-sufficient teaching materials is the susceptibility of contract law to the introduction of a wide range of important and interesting legal subjects, as well as contract doctrine. Since multi-purpose books are less than ideal for any particular purpose, including the teaching of basic doctrine, students understandably become anxious and wisely, I think, supplement the casebooks with study aids.

The Uniform Commercial Code and the Restatement of Contracts

Your casebook will contain many references to the Restatement of Contracts and the Uniform Commerical Code. But it may or may not tell you where these fascinating intellectual artifacts fit in the law's seamless web. The Uniform Commercial Code is positive law. That is, it has been passed by state legislatives. In fact it has been adopted in some form by every state except Louisiana and therefore is the authoritative law for transactions covered by it. In the contracts field this means the sale of goods. I rather suspect that the density of the Code will make your initial contacts quite painful.

The Code was developed into a highly terse form over a rather long period by highly sophisticated law professors and legal practitioners. A great many of the sections interrelate, and the Code is chock full of cross-references. Occam's razor has been brutally applied to eliminate any redundancies, including redundancies that might be helpful to the uninitiated. More confusion is caused by the decision to leave many crucial doctrinal areas of Contracts to the common law, and until one is quite familiar with the Code it is often difficult to know whether or not the Code covers a particular aspect of contract doctrine. Again, the cure is patience and perhaps the purchase of a fully annotated edition of the Code. Every casebook now includes a considerable amount of material dealing with the Code, and almost invariably includes a large number of exercises and questions about it. Whether your professor assigns them or not, do not fail to do these exercises and to check them with your study group. After a bit, the basic structure of the Code will clarify itself. I recommend purchase of the annotated edition even if your casebook contains Article 2 of the Code (Sales). The illustrations and background given in the annotated edition are invaluable both for your Contracts course and subsequent practice.

The Restatement of Contracts is quite another matter. First, it does purport to be a comprehensive treatment of all of contract law. But unlike the U.C.C., it has no prescriptive authority. It is not law, but is rather a curious combination of what the law is and what the draftsmen think it ought to be, often without clear distinction between the two.[3] In many cases, judges dealing with a novel problem may be influenced by the Restatement and often cite it in support of their decision. But you must not confuse the status of the Restatement and the Uniform Commercial Code. The latter is legally binding, whereas the former is no more than suggestive. The Restatement though is full of wonderful short hypotheticals that beautifully illustrate the borderlines of each doctrine.

Outlines, Bar Review Materials, Hornbooks, Treatises

Now for the difficult business of choosing the best study supplement. There are all sorts of supplements. The most rudimentary is Emanuel's. This may be a useful outline for review, but is inadequate for in-depth study of the more intricate components of contract doctrine. By far, the best study aid is *Gilbert's Outline*. This book, written by a distinguished Contracts professor, is the best existing statement of basic contract doctrine, complete and well-organized. It is so good that I routinely assign it as the basic text for my course.

In addition there are the short treatises (often called Hornbooks). Of these, Murray is the best and Corbin the worst. And, topping the pyramid, are the two great multivolume treatises by Williston and Corbin. I would skip the short treatises, because Gilbert's provides all the complexity you can handle. And, except for those with a particular interest in the fullest treatment of a particular point of law, rarely is it necessary to consult the multivolume treatises for the purpose of coping with your Contracts course. For questions relating to the Uniform Commercial Code, the latest annotated edition of the Code itself is far and away the best source of enlightenment.

Law Reviews and Scholarly Books

Law-review articles and scholarly books constitute another source of enlightenment about contract law in general and particular aspects thereof. However, most law-review articles focus on very narrow issues and are directed toward other scholars rather than beginning law students. There are exceptions though. One of these is the late Grant Gilmore's *The Death of Contracts*, which is the printed version of lectures delivered by Gilmore at the Ohio State University Law School in April 1970. Grant Gilmore had long been the doyen of contract scholars; he combined vast learning, analytical accuity, and literary grace of an order rarely found in an intellectual discipline not known for its grace of expression. *The Death of Contracts* is unique in combining a magisterial overview of the rise and dissolution of pure contract theory with extremely useful explications of some of the most difficult doctrinal components of contract law.

A few law-review articles also can be helpful in understanding certain knotty doctrinal areas. The two articles by Fuller and Perdue, "The Reliance Interest in Contract Damages,"[4] are a must. Kessler's article on contracts of adhesion[5] is another invaluable piece.

For me, a severe limitation of Gilmore's work is that he is concerned with the development of contract doctrine largely in isolation from the social uses to which the agreements that might be supported by contract law would be put. Perspective will be restored through some contact with the writings of Ian MacNeil. MacNeil's signal contribution is his emphasis on contracts as a means to support long-term relationships rather than the one-shot ventures represented by sales. Not surprisingly, focusing upon the role of law in supporting long-term relationships inevitably will raise sharply different issues from those generated by approaches centered around sales, which has typified contract law in the past. MacNeil's thinking about modern contract law is beautifully and concisely presented in his book, *The New Social Contract.*[6]

Gilmore and MacNeil operate at a very high level of abstraction. To add body to understanding of the nature and function of contract and contract law on our peculiar variety of free enterprise capitalism, I offer the list of readings in the Appendix at the end of the chapter. I hope the headings and subheadings sufficiently indicate the nature of each of the recommended readings.

Conclusion

Contracts is powerful medicine. Although contract law is the epitome of an important variety of legal ordering, it must not be made the measure of all law. Moreover, closely articulated doctrinal systems, like contract law, are difficult to grasp, but once the peculiar nature of a doctrinal argument is learned, law school should hold no further terrors for you. And remember, many successful lawyers barely squeaked through their Contracts course.

APPENDIX

1. Contracts, Freedom and Legal Underpinnings of Society

Milton Friedman, *Capitalism and Freedom*, 1–36 (1962).

H. L. A. Hart, *The Concept of Law*, 189–95 (1961).

Lon Fuller, *The Problems of Jurisprudence*, Ch. VI (Temp. ed. 1949).

Lon Fuller, *The Morality of Law*, Ch. I, particularly pp. 19–30 (1964). Includes Marxist position on commodity exchange.

Friedrick Kessler and Grant Gilmore, "Introduction: Contract as a Principle of Order," pp. 1–15, *Contracts: Cases and Materials* (2nd ed. 1970).

Morris R. Cohen, "The Basis of Contract," 46 *Harvard Law Review* 533 (1933).

Harold C. Havighurst, *The Nature of Private Contract* (1961).

Stewart Macaulay, "Justice Traynor and the Law of Contracts," 13 *Stanford Law Review* 812, 813–17 (1961).

David Slawson, "Standard Form Contracts and Democratic Control of Law Making Power," 84 *Harvard Law Review* 529 (1971).

2. History of Contract Law and Theory

E. Allan Farnsworth, "The Past of Promise: A Historical Introduction to Contract," 69 *Columbia Law Review* 576 (1969).

Morton Horwitz, "The Historical Foundations of Modern Contract Law," 87 *Harvard Law Review* 917 (1974).

James Willard Hurst, *Law and the Conditions of Freedom in the Nineteenth-Century United States*, Ch. I, "The Release of Energy" (1956).

Grant Gilmore, *The Death of Contracts* (1974).

3. Some Insights from Other Disciplines

Economics and Contract

Richard Posner, *Economic Analysis of Law*, Ch. 1, 3, 28 (1972).

Arthur Leff, "Economics Analysis of Law: Some Realism About Nominalism," 60 *Virginia Law Review* 451 (1974).

Gordon Tullock, *The Logic of the Law*, Ch. 3–5 (1971).

Lon Fuller and William Perdue, "The Reliance Interest in Contract Damages: 1 & 2," 46 *Yale Law Journal* 52, 373 (1936), particularly pp. 52–80.

Friedrick Kessler and Richard Stern, "Competition, Contract, and Vertical Integration," 69 *Yale Law Journal* 1–21 (1959).

Stewart Macaulay, *Law and the Balance of Power: The Automobile Manufacturers and Their Dealers* (1966).

Empirical Research: The Use of Contract in Fact
Stewart Macaulay, "Non-Contractual Relations in Business: A Preliminary Study," 28 *American Sociological Review* 55 (1963).
E. Allan Farnsworth, "Meaning in the Law of Contracts," 76 *Yale Law Journal* 939 (1965).

4. The Functions Served by Legal Formalities

Lon Fuller, "Consideration and Form," 41 *Columbia Law Review* 799–814 (1941).
Arthur Von Mehren, "Civil Law Analogues to Consideration: An Exercise in Comparative Analysis," 72 *Harvard Law Review* 1009, 1015–18 (1959).

5. The Lawyer's Function in a Contract Regime

Henry Hart, Jr. and Albert Sacks, "A Notation on the Problems of Law Making Generally," in *The Legal Process. Basic Problems in the Making and Application of Law* 232 (Tentative Edition 1958).
Hart & Sacks, *Id.* "Note on the Lawyer's Function, and the Relation of Law to Other Social Sciences," at 198–206.

6. Teaching Contracts and Its Place in the Law School Curriculum

Lawrence Friedman and Stewart Macaulay, "Contract Law and Contract Teaching: Past, Present, and Future," 1967 *Wisconsin Law Review* 805.
Charles Black, Jr., "Some Notes on Law Schools in the Present Day," 79 *Yale Law Journal* 505 (1970).

NOTES

1. Goetz & Scott, *Enforcing Promises*, 89 *Yale Law Journal* 1261 (1980).
2. Goetz & Scott, *Liquidated Damages, Penalties and the Just Compensation Principle*, 77 *Columbia Law Review* 554 (1977).
3. For one explanation of the origins, purpose and effect of the Restatements, *see* Gilmore, *The Death of Contracts* (1974).
4. 46 *Yale Law Journal* 52, 373 (1936).
5. *Contracts of Adhesion—Some Thoughts About Freedom of Contract*, 43 *Columbia Law Journal* 629 (1943).
6. Yale University Press, 1980.

CHAPTER 12

Criminal Law

Lloyd L. Weinreb
HARVARD UNIVERSITY

If they were asked to give an example of law, most people would probably mention some conduct that is against the law, a crime. From one point of view, the example would be badly chosen. As law students quickly learn in their first year, if criminal law and "civil" law are two halves of the whole, the halves are decidedly unequal. Criminal law occupies a small part of a law school's curriculum and a small part of legal practice. From another point of view, criminal law is the best example, the very paradigm of law. It is not necessarily law at its most effective or, in any particulars, most enduring. But it shows the law more clearly than any of its other branches as an exercise of the authority of the state. That is what makes it, despite all the variations of content from one course in criminal law to another, an indispensable part of a legal education.

Near the heart of the major issues in criminal law is the problem of retributive justice, the deliberate infliction of harm as a response to past conduct. Some conduct may seem so obviously wrong that the appropriateness of punishment can ordinarily be assumed. Other crimes may seem to be only a matter of social engineering, so that the appropriateness of punishment depends entirely on the legislative objective. The general theories of punishment differ greatly. So-called theories of "strict justice" emphasize the past, what a person has done; utilitarian theories emphasize the hoped-for future, how punishment may improve him or his behavior afterward. In all cases, whatever the theory, the method of the criminal law raises directly a question about justice that cannot be answered without reference to the particular conduct of the person to be punished.

For that reason, individual responsibility is an overarching theme. Most of the substantive criminal law is built on two concepts: intention and act. Generally, crimes require intentional wrongdoing. Although the number of crimes, mostly minor crimes, of carelessness or inadvertence is increasing, by and large the criminal law is concerned with knaves, not fools. Some of the most difficult muddles, which may confound us even after the fullest statement of the facts of a case, arise because of the importance we attach to a person's state of mind. Does a person who burns down a building to collect insurance *intend* to kill persons who he knows are inside even though he hopes against the odds that they may get out in time? Is his state of mind relevantly distinct from that of someone who deliberately waits to burn down a building until people are inside, in order that they will be killed? To what extent, if at all, should we deal differently with a person who kills in the grip of an irrationally exaggerated rage and one who kills coldly and deliberately, albeit perhaps in response to a real wrong done to him by his victim? Should the criminal law consider only whether or not there was an intention to kill, or should it examine the intention more closely and distinguish, say, between euthanasia out of compassion for the victim and killing a bank guard in the course of a robbery?

Similar difficulties surround the concept of an act. A shopowner sells cans of commercial heating fluid containing deadly alcohol to derelicts on skid row; if he knew (or should have known) that they would drink it in disregard of the plain warning on the label, is he liable for their deaths?[1] Should criminal liability depend at all on the consequences of acts or only on the acts themselves? If two persons drive equally recklessly, should they be guilty of different crimes if one of them runs over and kills a pedestrian? When should a person be liable *vicariously* for the act of another because of the relationship between them? If a bankrobber shoots someone inside the bank, is his confederate waiting outside in the getaway car also liable for the shooting? In what circumstances is a person criminally responsible if he *fails* to take some action that would have saved another person's life?

The problems that such cases present may arise from the ambiguity of concepts like "act" and "intention" (and "causation"). Often a disagreement can be cleared up by attending closely to the way in which words are being used. It might be enough, for example, to reply to a question about the intention of the arsonist who vainly hopes that no one will be killed: "It all depends on what you mean by intention." That response is not adequate, however, if the question is how the law should dispose of his case. The conceptual ambiguities are not just a matter of the open texture of words; they cover a difference of substance that we believe is important to our purpose. In most of our affairs, we can be aware of the issue without having to resolve it definitively. The criminal law requires an answer: the defendant *is* or *is not* guilty of murder, or manslaughter, or some other crime. In actual cases, doubts are hidden within a verdict. In a class in criminal law, after the facts have been thoroughly explored, our doubts are likely to be all too evident.

The standards by which responsibility is measured in the criminal law reflect a more fundamental understanding of the meaning of individual responsibility. That is clearest in cases in which a person is not held liable for his own conduct because we do not regard it as meaningfully within his control. A young child may be said to act intentionally, but because we do not regard him as fully responsible for his behavior, his act that would be a serious crime if it were committed by an adult is noncriminal, whatever we may do to prevent him from behaving that way again. In 1954, the decision of the United States Court of Appeals for the District of Columbia in *Durham* v. *United States*[2] prompted a thorough reconsideration of individual responsibility in the criminal law and renewed awareness of its significance.

In a famous opinion by Judge Bazelon, the court abandoned the traditional test of legal insanity, which held that a person was insane when he committed an act, and therefore not criminally responsible, if, because of a "defect of reason, from disease of the mind," he did not know what he was doing or that it was wrong.[3] The court substituted a test that declared simply that a person was insane if his act was the product of mental disease or defect. Partly because the existing test of insanity had been criticized without being substantially changed for more than a hundred years, the

Durham decision touched off a prolonged and exciting debate. It quickly became apparent that the new test could be variously interpreted; at one extreme it departed little from what it had replaced, and at the other it might exculpate as insane anyone whose act could be traced to an identifiable mental "condition" even though he retained a substantial capacity to control his behavior.[4] As the debate developed, it expressed the tension between liberty and social order in an unusually explicit form. For the conclusion that a man is not responsible for his behavior not only exculpates him from criminality; it also affords a basis for subjecting him to "treatment" designed to change his behavior involuntarily. Those who advocated the Durham test on humane grounds of social conscience and social responsibility were opposed by others who resisted its implications. If by the old test society sometimes dealt harshly with persons who, without fault, were unable to control their behavior, the new test seemed to leave too much room for the society to displace individual responsibility and control behavior itself. Usually, the positions in the debate stayed well within the extremes; the controversy about the insanity defense did not force us to choose between Darwinism and totalitarianism. It would be just as misleading, however, to see in it only a technical discussion about a doctrine of criminal law. The debate reveals that not only the particular policies of the law but criminal justice itself is defined within a social context.

The issue of the insanity defense has been settled for the present by widespread adoption of a third test, recommended by the American Law Institute in its Model Penal Code. That test, which refers to a person's "substantial capacity" to control his behavior, borrows something from both of the others.[5] Not any distinguishing mental disability but only one that significantly incapacitates a person (without necessarily *wholly* incapacitating him) will exculpate him. That intermediate position, which some have described as only a cosmetic improvement on the old test, suggests another feature of the criminal law. Except in extreme circumstances when for other reasons the society has embarked on a radical course, the criminal law is likely to avoid a sharp choice between opposing tendencies in the community. It is, as James Fitzjames Stephen observed, too rough an engine to be used that way.[6]

Within a narrower compass, the study of particular crimes affords the same kind of insight into the values and conflicts of our society. During the past few years, the authority of the state to enforce standards of private morality has been tested concretely by efforts to repeal laws prohibiting certain kinds of private sexual behavior; or the use of some drugs, especially marijuana; and other activities that call immediately to mind John Stuart Mill's distinction between "self-regarding" and "other-regarding" acts, on which his defense of individual liberty depends. One cannot reflect for long about the substantive or procedural problems surrounding the crime of rape without confronting questions about the society's sexual attitudes and its (asserted) domination by the male. The reaction of the criminal law to corruption in government teaches a good deal about our politics. Of course, one does not need to be a lawyer or a law student to learn about or react intelligently to issues of that kind; in their current form, they are more the stuff of newspapers than of casebooks. Studied within the framework of criminal law and brought into focus by actual cases and rules, they may display aspects of a larger and more persistent social reality.

Other doctrines of the criminal law which are not so unsettled are equally illuminating. In 1887, the Supreme Court of Indiana referred to "the tendency of the American mind" to approve a person who "stands his ground" against an attack, even if he has to kill his attacker.[7] For the most part, the law of self-defense has respected that tendency, despite increasing concern about the violence of American life and the fact that "standing one's ground" may have little meaning, or a special meaning, in the conditions of compacted urban life. The legal doctrines that regulate the use of force to defend oneself or others, to defend one's property or habitation, to prevent a felony or to capture a felon, provide a field day for those who like intricate analytic problems. (Combined with all the varieties of homicide, they appear regularly on examinations in criminal law.) They are also, more importantly, expressions of attitudes that lie deep within the society, which have significance far beyond their application in particular cases.

Not so long ago, the distinctions among larceny, embezzlement, and false pretenses, which were the classic forms of theft in English and American common law, provided another fertile field for the display of analytic prowess. Since the history of the law's development was a progressive plugging of holes through which inventive rogues had slipped with their ill—but not yet illegally—gotten gains, it is not surprising that the distinctions among the various crimes became exceedingly narrow. Comparatively recently, using a pattern developed in the Model Penal Code, state legislatures have combined the historical crimes into a single crime of theft. That itself is instructive. It is not without interest that the law treats alike a physical taking, a fraudulent transaction, and a breach of trust, so long as the common element of a deprivation of property is involved. And, of course, the original problem of distinguishing permissible and impermissible appropriations of another's property has not been solved; it has only shifted. The intellectual richness of criminal law is displayed in the connections it allows us to make between a fifteenth-century puzzlement about whether a carrier who kept goods that he had promised to deliver elsewhere was a thief or just a very crooked fellow,[8] and our uncertainty now whether a seller's exaggerated claims for his goods are only "puffing," part of the commercial relationship, or violate that relationship and should be prohibited.

It would misrepresent most courses in criminal law to suggest that substantive criminal law is really, or mainly, a window onto the whole social order. It is first of all a complex body of legal doctrine, general awareness of which is part of a lawyer's professional equipment. It is also, however, a source of more general insights, which in turn makes the doctrine more comprehensible and meaningful.

Before about 1960, "crimes" was much the largest part of first-year courses in criminal law. At the end of the course there might have been a few weeks of discussion about some procedural issues involving constitutional law and federalism: due process, search and seizure, self-incrimination, a bit about habeas corpus and federal review of state convictions, and not much more. That is no longer true. One way or another many law schools now allot a substantial share of the first-year course, often half or more, to the criminal process. Almost certainly, the main explanation for the change is the Supreme Court's active concern for this area starting in the 1960s. In a series of well-known decisions during that decade, the Court made what has frequently been called a revolution in criminal procedure. Since about 1970, with another majority on the Court, there has been something of a counterrevolution. While these changes have taken place, our attention has been fixed permanently, I think, and properly so on the means that the state uses to establish guilt in a particular case.

Law schools generally consider the large issues of constitutional law the most important to include in a first-year course. For a number of reasons, not least the courts' willingness to step in where legislatures have declined to tread, many of the most important aspects of criminal procedure have constitutional overtones and underpinnings. Discussions of criminal procedure tend to be organized around a few central phrases of the Constitution, which may, falsely, suggest that what is at stake is a peculiar kind of textual exegesis. In this country we commonly debate large questions of political and social organization in constitutional terms, but it is not simply the meaning of a text that we seek.

The most comprehensive of the constitutional clauses affecting criminal process is the Due Process Clause in the Fifth and Fourteenth Amendments: no person shall be deprived of "life, liberty, or property, without due process of law." During the 1960s the Supreme Court made most of the provisions of the Bill of Rights that previously had been applicable only to federal prosecutions applicable also to state prosecutions by "incorporating" their content into the Due Process Clause of the Fourteenth Amendment.[9] The debate over "incorporation" suggested three ranges of significance that the notion of due process of law might have. The narrowest construction of the Due Process Clause would require only that a criminal conviction be based on a legal process established according to the forms of law, without specification of its content. Even so limited a reading would impose restraints on arbitrary government action, but it would give the broadest scope to legislative and executive authority. Another possible construction, defended primarily (though not always consistently) by Justice Black,[10] is that the Due Process Clause mandates a particular criminal process, defined by constitutional provisions not all of which are equally fundamental. So not only large principles, like those of the Fourth Amendment, but also much more particular requirements, like indictment by a grand jury, would be part of due process. A third view, which has prevailed, is that due process of law embodies basic principles of justice and "ordered liberty" (including those contained in the Bill of Rights), which endure but the detailed specification of which may change in changing circumstances. As they study the leading cases that construe any of the important constitutional provisions, students should not only examine the particular doctrine but also try to acquire a sense of the process as a whole to which the doctrine contributes and of the values it affirms.

Among the constitutional principles that are part of due process are the Fourth Amendment's prohibition of unreasonable searches and seizures and the Fifth Amendment's privilege against compulsory self-incrimination. Both provisions have been important mostly in criminal cases, although they are not so limited: they restrict the government's power whatever its purpose. The Fourth Amendment limits the occasions when our privacy in private places can be interrupted. It assures us opportunities to be alone or with others unobserved by the government and to extend our personality by impressing it on places or things without exposing ourselves to the world. The privilege against self-incrimination gives a narrower protection absolutely. Unlike the Fourth Amendment, which allows the government to search and seize in some circumstances, the Fifth Amendment prohibits the government altogether from compelling us to incriminate ourselves. We may confess freely; but, the Amendment declares, there is no necessity of government so great that a man should be made to admit his guilt against his will.

It is a measure of the strength of these constitutional provisions that we take them so much for granted. They are not, after all, self-evident or unremarkable. Even if the basic principles are admitted, as they have not always been even in this country, their particular applications in the context of a criminal proceeding have been the subject of continuing disgreement, among the Justices of the Supreme Court as well as in the lower courts, the legislatures, and among people generally.[11] The changing equilibrium that is reached is a product of the same choice between individual autonomy and social order that affects our conclusions about criminal responsibility. Respect for a private domain bids us proceed cautiously to accomplish the state's purpose even when we are convinced that the purpose is a good one.

Other provisions of the Bill of Rights, principally in the Sixth

Amendment, deal directly with a criminal prosecution. The right of the defendant "to have the assistance of counsel for his defense" is the lynchpin of our "adversary system." In 1963, the Supreme Court held that no person could be convicted of a felony without having had the aid of counsel, paid for by the state if the defendant was indigent.[12] For nine years, the Court avoided the question whether the same rule applied to prosecutions for misdemeanors; finally, in 1972 the Court held that it did if the consequence of conviction was imprisonment.[13]

These cases and others in which an indigent defendant has claimed that the quality of criminal justice depends on wealth raise a central issue for a system like ours, which depends heavily on private initiative and effort. So long as defendants are permitted to retain counsel and other services privately, the possibility that the process and even the result will be affected by the defendant's wealth cannot be avoided. On the other hand, reliance on the private bar helps to preserve important values. Not least of them is the assurance that the administration of criminal justice will regularly be challenged by persons who are not themselves part of an administrative bureaucracy.

The conflict between what is most just in a particular case and a procedure which, if followed generally, will be most just and decent arises repeatedly in the criminal process. One may, for example, believe that it is unwise or unjust for a criminal fortuitously to escape conviction because evidence of his guilt is suppressed. Nevertheless, suppression of evidence obtained in violation of constitutional rights, whatever its defects, may improve the administration of justice generally enough to justify deliberately letting off some criminals while others guilty of the same crime are convicted. Similarly, the principal justification for the practice of plea-bargaining almost certainly is simply our inability to preserve other features of the criminal process, including most obviously the elaborate trial by jury, without it.

Some aspects of the criminal process, like the abuses of bail and the incredible delay that attends most prosecutions for a serious crime, are criticized by everyone. Often, the criticisms are acknowledged and dismissed on the ground that anything better would be too costly. But that explanation is rarely adequate; we are not, after all, without some choice about what we shall spend and how we shall spend it, even if we cannot spend as much as ideally we should like. Students' understanding of the criminal process will be greater, and their criticisms will be more effective, if they search out and evaluate the assumptions on which our practices depend.

Like teachers of other first-year courses, teachers of Criminal Law usually feel—and make their students feel—harried to cover just the material that seems indispensable. The solution, which teachers work out differently, has to be a careful selection of what is "most indispensable," most suggestive of the large themes and exemplary of what is omitted, and most challenging for students and teachers both. Because the course in the first year is their only work in criminal law for many students, teachers may choose to present as well as they can a view of the whole field. Although that allows too little time to study many issues deeply, it may be the best way to introduce as many students as possible to areas of interest to which they can return in advanced courses at law school or later on.

Students may be particularly troubled by the omission of much material dealing directly with crime as a social phenomenon. The doctrines of the law may seem abstract and remote from current problems of social disorder: urban violence and street crime, narcotics, organized crime, white-collar crime, political corruption, police-community relations, and others. To deal with such matters seriously, at a level beyond reporting of current events and impressionistic accounts of one's own experiences, requires a range and depth of knowledge and understanding that cut across the social sciences and professions. The methodology of most first-year classes, which emphasizes analytic skills, does not easily accommodate the need to present large amounts of general theory and detailed information. Most teachers, therefore, have thought it best to leave such study to elective courses or seminars later in law school or sometimes elsewhere in the university.

Another kind of omission may also be puzzling. Rules of criminal procedure, especially as they are embodied in constitutional rules, often appear—accurately—to take little account of the actual institutions for which they prescribe: police departments as part of the complex bureaucratic and political structure of a city, courts, especially the low-level courts that dispose summarily of huge numbers of minor criminal cases, jails and prisons. Having their own professional careers in mind, students may want to learn more than rules alone tell them about the actual practice of criminal law. There is not a simple justification for these omissions beyond the obvious fact that time is limited. Rules and principles need to be tested concretely and their practical implications—or lack of implication—understood. So far as such considerations affect our understanding of the rules of law or furnish the basis for criticizing them, they are appropriately part of a first-year course, to be fitted somehow into the available time along with everything else. Beyond that, perhaps all that can be said is that it has generally seemed sound in the first year to emphasize the lawyer's unique professional competence, his or her command of the law. From that common center students are usually able to pursue their diverse interests effectively afterward.

It is a constant phenomenon of legal education that students arrive with an interest in criminal law and leave without it. Would-be criminal lawyers are many; criminal lawyers are few. The lack of a larger criminal-defense bar is perhaps to be regretted, although it is a small part of the community's general need for legal services. It does not seem to me, however, that legal education is responsible for the lack. A criminal practice is not usually as rewarding in the ordinary ways as a corporate practice or a general practice on a smaller scale. It has its rewards, among them ones that a general practice does not offer equally. Teachers of criminal law, and sometimes students, lament the "second-class status" of criminal law in the curriculum. If it is indeed second-class, which I think is now rarely the case, that is a reflection of much more general circumstances in the society. The value of criminal law in the curriculum is not measured by the number of criminal lawyers who emerge. It is not an important subject only for students who may be interested in criminal practice. Criminal law is an expression of the community's basic values in a form that lawyers especially need to understand.

(1984)

In the seven years since the first edition of this book was published, the directions of the criminal law that were evident then have become more pronounced and have had large and important effects. The "hard line" toward criminals and crime has continued and carried the procedural "counterrevolution" of the seventies into the eighties. Doctrines favorable to a criminal defendant that were declared less than a generation ago have been limited and sometimes abandoned. Pronouncements that were originally cast as broad statements of principle have been recast as narrow and rather technical rules. Perhaps the most vivid example of this change is the fate of the "exclusionary rule," which provides generally that evidence obtained in violation of a defendant's constitutional rights is not admissible against her at trial. After 1961, when the Supreme Court applied the rule to state criminal prosecutions,[14] it was for some years treated as a broad statement of constitutional law. In the seventies, the Court continued to apply it, but declined several times to extend it and sometimes described it as a judicially fashioned rule protective of constitutional law rather than a part of that law itself.[15] In the 1982 Term, the Court explicitly undertook to reconsider the exclusionary rule and suggested, as several Justices had already done individually, that it might be limited to the more extreme cases of constitutional violation.[16] In the end, the Court declined to answer the question it had itself posed,[17] an indication of how difficult and contentious the question is. The executive and legislative branches of the government have also considered proposals to limit the exclusionary rule. The issue is likely to remain before us and not be definitively settled soon.

Angry and frustrated by an apparent increase in violent crime and a sense of personal insecurity, the public has demanded that more stringent measures be taken. The legislatures have generally responded in the only way they can, by increasing the penalties for crime. It is an open question whether stiffer sentencing has a significant deterrent effect; but the effect on our prisons is beyond question. Throughout the country, prisons are desperately overcrowded. Prisoners are subjected to conditions that all abhor but not all agree should be ameliorated. Their amelioration would require either a drastic reduction in the prison population or a vast expenditure of public funds, neither of which is a practical likelihood in the near future. The debate over capital punishment has continued. Most states have responded to the Supreme Court's restrictions on the use of the death penalty with new legislation designed to meet the restrictions. In consequence, the United States has seemed to go contrary to a trend against capital punishment elsewhere in the world.

More particular developments similarly reflect general social circumstances. There has been increasing awareness of kinds of activity that statistically threaten harm indirectly to many persons: the creation of environmental hazards, the manufacture and distribution of products with hidden safety defects, the promotion and sale of goods harmful to health. There has been increasing concern about unethical conduct or corruption of public officials. So far, the criminal law has intervened erratically and, on the whole, ineffectively, in the face of such problems. It has proved far easier to condemn practices abstractly than to make the concrete, particular distinctions without which condemnation by the criminal law is impossible. One may conclude that there are other values that society wants to protect, openly or not, which contend with the values of life, safety, and health when the risks are uncertain and diffuse.

Persistent efforts, mostly by women's groups, to reduce the crime of rape seem to have had some, but limited success. Part of the difficulty has been the broad range of conduct, from a brutal aggression against a stranger to an assault on someone thought to be willing, that may be characterized as rape. Part also has been genuine perplexity about the implications of rapidly changing patterns of sexual activity. Probably the major part, however, has been the law's failure to change its practices at all dramatically, unless the community is strongly united behind the change. For all the protestations about the crime of rape, the attitudes that would induce such change have not been felt by enough persons.

Students in law school may find that they have to make the specific connections between criminal law and social and economic conditions mostly for themselves. A semester or a year course in criminal law cannot hope to do more than show that there are such connections and explore a few examples. Recent developments in the law display vividly its interaction with the social forces that shape our lives generally. Whether one believes that the current direction of the law is a just and appropriate response to wrong, harmful conduct or that it is unjustly harsh and ought to be changed, the connections between the criminal law and other constituents of the social order are unmistakable and inescapable.

(1990)

Since I last brought this essay up-to-date, in 1984, the criminal law has continued in the same direction that it was taking then. Public concern about crime and determination to "get tough" with criminals have remained high. The predictable results have been still harsher criminal penalties and a continuing shift of criminal procedure away from rules that are perceived to be unduly favorable to the defendant. The "revolution" in criminal procedure in the 1960s (and also, therefore, the "counterrevolution" of the 1970s) now appear to have been less dramatic events than they seemed at the time, although the most fundamental aspects of the Warren Court's decisions in this area have become a permanent part of our jurisprudence.

Whether getting tougher has any general effect on the amount of crime is conjectural at best. The assumed connection is based on the proposition that people will engage in criminal activities less if the "cost" of them goes up. Even if it is true that that sort of economic calculation is much of a factor in the decision to commit ordinary crimes—which is itself far from obvious—so many other factors besides the possible sentence enter into the calculation that merely increasing the sentence seems likely to make little difference. Most significant among those factors are the improbability of being apprehended, convicted, and finally sent to prison and the long delay between crime and punishment on the occasions when punishment is indeed imposed. For the present, all that is certain is that more persons are sent to prison, for longer periods, than was the case in the past. Wanting a response to crime, we may feel satisfaction that criminals are incarcerated, whatever the further effects may be; but we ought not regard an increase in the prison population as self-evidently a good thing.

There is continuing disagreement about particular aspects of criminal procedure, which is evidenced most obviously by the large number of dissenting opinions in the Supreme Court reports. Probably, however, there is less disagreement than previously about the larger issues. Although some conservatives, on and off the bench, believe that decisions like *Mapp*[18] and *Miranda*[19] should be overruled, and some liberals believe that they have been dangerously eroded already, the current controversies are about matters of detail more than general principle. Even at that level one discerns the conflict between individual liberty and social order that the criminal law has to resolve one way or another.

Recent discussions about crime and criminal law have been dominated by the explosive growth of the illegal narcotics industry. Not only the drug traffic itself but also other drug-related crimes, not infrequently including homicide, have strained the capacity of every aspect of law enforcement: police, prosecutors, and prisons alike. There is much talk about a "war on drugs"; but it remains mostly talk and, so far as criminal process is concerned, within our constitutional system must remain so. The problem lies deeper than the threat of a criminal sanction can reach; and the solution will have to go deeper as well.

NOTES

1. See Commonwealth v. Feinberg, 433 Pa. 558, 253 A.2d 636 (1969).

2. 214 F.2d 862, 94 U.S. App. D.C. 228.

3. M' Naghten's Case, 10 Cl. & F. 200, 8 Eng. Rep. 718 (H.L. 1843).

4. See, for example, the series of cases which followed Durham in the District of Columbia: Carter v. United States, 252 F.2d 608 (D.C. Cir. 1957); Blocker v. United States, 288 F.2d 853 (D.C. Cir. 1961); Campbell v. United States, 307 F.2d 597 (D.C. Cir. 1962); McDonald v. United States 312 F.2d 847 (D.C. Cir. 1962); Washington v. United States, 390 F.2d 444 (D.C. Cir. 1967); and finally Brawner v. United States, 471 F.2d 969 (D.C. Cir. 1972), in which the history of the Durham rule is reviewed.

5. Model Penal Code § 4.01 (Proposed Official Draft 1962).

6. *Liberty, Equality, Fraternity*, 151 (R.J. White, ed., 1967).

7. Runyan v. State, 57 Ind. 80, 84 (1887), quoted in Beard v. United States, 158 U.S. 550, 561–62 (1895).

8. See Anon. v. The Sheriff of London (The Carrier's Case), Y. B. Pasch., 13 Edw. 4 pl. 5 (1473), 64 Selden Society 30 (1948).

9. Stages in the debate over incorporation in the Supreme Court can be noted in the various opinions in, for example: Palko v. Connecticut, 302 U.S. 319 (1937); Adamson v. California, 332 U.S. 46 (1947); Rochin v. California, 342 U.S. 165 (1952); Duncan v. Louisiana, 391 U.S. 145 (1968); Johnson v. Louisiana, 406 U.S. 356 (1972); and Apodaca v. Oregon, 406 U.S. 404 (1972).

10. For example, Adamson v. California, 332 U.S. 46, 68 (1947) (dissenting opinion), with which compare Katz v. United States 389 U.S. 347, 364 (1967) (dissenting opinion), and Williams v. Florida, 399 U.S. 78, 106 (1970) (concurring and dissenting opinion).

11. For a suggestion of the range of disagreement about the meaning of the Fourth Amendment, see, for example, Coolidge v. New Hampshire, 403 U.S. 443 (1971); and the Fifth Amendment, Miranda v. Arizona, 384 U.S. 436 (1966).

12. Gideon v. Wainwright, 372 U.S. 335.

13. Argersinger v. Hamlin, 407 U.S. 25.

14. Mapp v. Ohio, 367 U.S. 643 (1961).

15. United States v. Janis, 428 U.S. 433 (1976); United States v. Calandra, 414 U.S. 338 (1974).

16. Illinois v. Gates, 459 U.S. 1028 (1982) (case restored to calendar for reargument).

17. Illinois v. Gates, 462 U.S. 213 (1983). (The Court subsequently considered the question again and concluded that evidence obtained in a search conducted pursuant to an invalid warrant need not be excluded if the officers conducting the search were acting in good faith and had a reasonable belief that the warrant was valid. United States v. Leon, 468 U.S. 897 (1984); Massachusetts v. Sheppard, 468 U.S. 981 (1984).)

18. Mapp v. Ohio, 367 U.S. 643 (1961) (the exclusionary rule).

19. Miranda v. Arizona, 384 U.S. 436 (1966) (police interrogation).

CHAPTER 13

Property

Curtis J. Berger
COLUMBIA UNIVERSITY

Before you begin Property, try to clean out the attic of your mind. You are likely to find there several common misbeliefs that will clutter up your entry into the course. At the moment you may well believe that property is wealth; property is private; property is static; property is dull. None of this is necessarily true.

To begin: Property law deals with items of wealth, such as land, or buildings, or Swiss watches; but Property is not wealth itself. Let me illustrate that distinction.

Sharman was hired to clean out a pool on Water Company's land. While so engaged, he found two gold rings. When the rings' owner failed to claim them, both Sharman and the Water Company insisted that the rings were rightfully theirs. To whom did the rings belong: the workman or the landowner?

For many of you the celebrated case of *South Staffordshire Water Co. v. Sharman*—where these facts appear—will help to initiate your study of Property. The case concerns jewelry and, incidently, land, two of the myriad forms of wealth, but the holding establishes a right as to that wealth (the water company has the right that the rings stay with it) and a correlative duty related to that wealth (the workman owes the duty not to remove the rings). As you will soon see, Property is a series of rights and duties pertaining to wealth. To define those rights and duties—as well as various other sets of interests—is the task of the legal system. That system mediates among the competing claims to wealth that landowners, finders, tenants, and all others in our society constantly assert. Out of this competition for wealth have evolved the relational interests—that is, rights and duties, powers and liabilities, etc.—which define the institution we call Property.

Nor is Property necessarily private. For the public oversees the use of wealth in ways that may sharply limit the powers or the privileges that individuals can enjoy. Let me give several illustrations: X dies, leaving her entire wealth to her favorite charity; the law intrudes, giving to XH, X's surviving spouse, the right to take a share of the estate despite X's last will. Or consider this: Y owns a paper factory whose air-polluting emissions threaten the well-being of all nearby residents; the law intrudes and requires Y to end the pollution or pay a staggering fine. And finally: Z owns an apartment house: the law intrudes and places a ceiling on the rental that Z may charge, and prohibits Z from refusing to rent to blacks, or Jews, or unmarried couples simply because he does not want them as tenants. These illustrations suggest that in our own society, which extols the privatism of property, the rights of private enjoyment of wealth are far less absolute than one might expect. To thoughtful observers this should not be surprising, or even unduly alarming. In a society of finite resources—whether land, or clean air, or investment capital—accommodation is necessary. Otherwise the rewards would go always to the swift, the strong, and the mean.

Sometimes the public takes privately held land away from the owner in order to widen a highway or build a school or renew a neighborhood. On these occasions the public exercises its power of eminent domain, as to which the Constitution requires that the landowner be paid just compensation for his loss and that the taking serve a public purpose. But mostly the law serves the public interest by regulating how the landowner may manage his wealth and to whom he may dispose of it, as the above illustrations show. Regulation, too, must satisfy the Constitution, which bars government from depriving anyone of property without due process of law. The requirements of due process, which you will discuss more fully in other courses, protect the landowner against arbitrary procedures, unfairness, senseless measures, and regulation that fails to serve the general welfare. The key phrase is *general welfare*, for it manifests a limitation not only upon the government but

also, impliedly, upon the individual. Private ownership must serve
not only the individual but also society at large.

Nor is Property static, even though much of its learning is
centuries old. Thus you will discuss estates in land, which trace
their roots to feudal society, and title by adverse possession, which
draws on a statute of James I, and covenants real, which at one
time dealt with such exotica as a nobleman's right to have Vespers
sung at his manor house. One need not be an antiquarian to gain
some pleasure from discovering the sources of our legal system or
from understanding the chain of tradition that links one generation
to another. Yet we live in a society where zoning, fair housing
laws, environmental controls, and equal rights for women—to give
only a few examples—are all impressing their stamp upon the
institution of Property, moving with a dynamism that is often
exhilarating and, for both the teacher and student of Property,
hard to stay abreast of.

You would be mistaken, however, in believing that property law
is an unguided missile, or that the rules that govern how property
rights evolve have totally changed or lost their thrust. Remember
the key phrase *general welfare* and our premise that property
interests must serve that welfare. This stewardship exists no less
today than it did seven hundred ago, when English courts first
sought to prevent noble landowners from turning their estates into
vast dynastic holdings. What does change, however, from one era
to another, sometimes imperceptibly, sometimes radically, is each
generation's perception of the general welfare. One cannot find
that phrase defined anywhere. A society must state its values; it
must apply them to an ever-changing mass of economic, social,
political, and psychological variables; competing claimants must
receive a hearing. Eventually a consensus will emerge as to how—in
each instance—the general welfare shall best be served. In our
system both legislatures and courts help to formulate that consensus.

Have we convinced you already that Property need not be dull?
At times highly technical! At times even arcane! But mostly enormously stimulating! You will need to learn some new vocabulary.
Phrases such as *fee tail, equitable servitude,* and *tenancy-by-the-
entirety* do not come with your mother's milk. Language is hard for
most of us, yet once you have assimilated Property terms and the
rules they embody, Property will unfold before you in endless and

colorful patterns. And as you struggle with the language it will often be helpful to remember the circumstances in which the language grew, to understand that common-law courts were not inventing a vocabulary in order to plague twentieth-century law students but were responding to immediate controversies over the use or disposition of wealth and—in their response—seeking to promote the general welfare as they perceived it.

In many schools Property is a year-long first-year course. Elsewhere Property arrives—somewhat compressed—in the second semester. Where Property begins earlier, you are more likely to spend several weeks discussing cases on wild animals and a succeeding group of cases on finders, bailments, and gifts—so-called personal-property topics, which once introduced all students to their study of Property. In the ceaseless struggle for curriculum attention, personal property has become a frequent casualty. And few of you will study personal property with the lavish care it once received.

But whether your instructor starts off with foxes, or water rights, or rental apartments, you will be asked to consider how property rights are formed and what values they serve. The process and the policy are as important to your understanding of Property as is the technical apparatus. In whatever way your instructor begins his or her particular course, you will almost certainly receive that message.

The Topics You Will Encounter

After the opening weeks, Property courses travel in a half dozen different directions. Yet many topics appear in nearly every course. I will relate what I teach, because most of my colleagues work much of this (and perhaps much more) into their instruction. Each topic is briefly described below.

Estates in Land

The common law divides all ownership into present and future rights to enjoyment. For example, you have a two-year lease on your apartment. You are said to have a term-of-years (the present estate) and your landlord is said to have a reversion (the future estate). This part of the course catalogs present and future interests and the legal consequences that flow from calling something a determinable fee, or a vested remainder, or some other estate.

Concurrent Interests

Wealth is often owned by two or more persons simultaneously. For example, a husband and wife buy their house jointly. The law gives them several ways to take title and, depending upon their choice, various legal and economic relationships ensue. Concurrent interests is the generic term for the various cotenancy forms. The condominium is the newest example of cotenancy ownership.

Adverse Possession

A and B are neighbors. A builds a garage that encroaches on B's land for a distance of eight inches. A and B are unaware of the encroachment. Ten years later B discovers the error. What are B's rights? The answer to this and related questions concerns the doctrine of adverse possession, one of the oldest, yet pragmatically most useful, areas of property law. Be prepared for a few surprises.

Marital Rights in Property

Not so long ago this seemed a relatively minor part of the course. Dower and courtesy, where most of our attention lay, were archaic, fast-disappearing devices for securing the economic well-being of a surviving spouse. However, the new wave of female self-consciousness has forced a harder look at the property institutions that govern marriage itself and in particular the quite different arrangements of the common-law and the civil-law (community property) systems. You may well hear, for the first time, about the advent of "equitable" distribution, which seeks to bridge some of these differences.

Landlord and Tenant

Most students approach this part of the course with hearty biases, born of long-suffering years as tenants. Here you will find a seething cauldron of law reform. The doctrine of *caveat tenant* is doing badly, yet where should the law head? An open, flexible mind will be valuable. Although the problems of landlord and tenant are urgently real, the solutions, given the economics of housing, are tantalizingly difficult.

Easements

A owns a lot across which the B Utility Company has permission to run a power line. We call B's interest an easement. Easements are a frequently used device for sharing the use of land. Easements also appear as common driveways, pipelines, railroad rights-of-way, agreements for unobstructed sunlight (solar easements). This part of the course discusses how easements (and their siblings, licenses and profits) are formed and enforced, and how they are terminated.

Real Covenants and Equitable Servitudes

Many students find this material the most difficult to handle, largely because of its highly technical, somewhat mystifying aspect. Let me illustrate the problem. A and B, neighboring landowners, each promise to share the upkeep costs of the common driveway that both use. A later sells his lot to A', who refuses to honor the promise made by A. Does B have any recourse against A'? Or against A?

The answers may seem self-evident if you were to apply your knowledge of contracts. But the A←→B mutual promises concern land, and, as you will learn, property law and contract law do not always lead to the same result. The answers, in fact, require an elaborate factual and legal analysis. Moreover, the answers have more than academic importance, because the use of covenants and equitable servitudes certainly has grown, particularly with the advent of condominiums and home associations, whose members live in a regime governed closely by sets of interdependent promises.

Here, largely through the efforts of the American Law Institute in restating the law of servitudes, you should expect some significant clarification in the coming years. As the Institute's work unfolds, servitudes will be at Property's cutting edge.

Land Use Regulation

Not so long ago, only advanced Property courses dealt with zoning and various other forms of public land-use control. Today virtually all basic courses do so—some quite extensively. The limits of zoning, environmental protection, landmark preservation, and measures to control or shape aesthetics, adult uses, community growth, housing costs, and household composition present some of the knottiest and most intriguing questions you will meet in law school, as well as some of the most far-reaching in their importance to our daily lives.

Eminent Domain

Eminent domain offers the community another tool to advance its land-use plan. It allows the government or other authorized body to acquire private property for a public purpose in exchange for just compensation. The problems here partly parallel those you will meet under regulation: for example, does the "public-purpose" requirement prevent a city from condemning eleven hundred homes to provide a site for a privately owned automobile assembly plant—cf. *Poletown Neighborhood Council v. City of Detroit*? Eminent domain also involves "just compensation," and you will grapple with that term to see what it includes and what it does not. Finally you will consider when the community may pursue its land-use goals through regulation, which restricts the landowner but does not pay her for economic loss, and when the community must turn to condemnation, which compensates the landowner for her losses. No question in Property is harder than that, as the Supreme Court rediscovers whenever it returns to this issue.

Conveyances

A conveyance is a transfer (usually of real estate) from one party to another. This is the realm of deeds, recording acts, covenants of title, mortgages, title insurance, contracts of sale, escrows, and brokers. Many first-year courses stress this material, preparing students who may not take an advanced property course to handle a simple real-estate closing should they ever have to do so.

The Economic Analysis of Property

Although not taught as a discrete topic, the economics of property law offers a further dimension for analyzing ordinary doctrine, one that can often be quite useful. Concepts like the Coase Theorem, transaction costs, externalities, and Pareto optimality help to illuminate many of the issues that arise in your study of such disparate areas of property law as nuisance, servitudes, and eminent domain. Financial analysis and present-value calculation can also strengthen your grasp of the problems that the modern property lawyer might expect to face.

The agenda above, although extensive, is still not inclusive. I have not discussed such other topics as nuisance, lateral support, waste, fixtures, water rights, racial discrimination, rent control, homelessness, the jurisprudence of property, intellectual property, Indian claims, the Rule against Perpetuities, the Statute of Uses—some of which you may very well study. Most Property teachers would like to teach everything in the field and wish they had more than the four to six hours that the curriculum makers have given them.

Advanced Courses in Property

Those of you who do advanced work in Property (and I hope most of you will) should find that the basic course offers a firm grounding for the work that follows. I have charted below the succession of courses Columbia Law School offers. It typifies the curriculum of many schools. You can see how widely Property ranges.

Donative Transfers	Commercial Transactions	Resource Allocation
Trusts and Estates	Real Estate Transactions	Environmental Law
Taxation of Wealth	Partnership Taxation	Urban Development
	Seminar in Adv. Real	Controls
	Estate Transactions	Housing and Urban
Trust	Seminar in	Development
Administration	Condominiums,	Seminar in
	Cooperatives, and Home	Environmental
Seminar in Estate	Owners Associations	Litigation
Planning and	Community Development	Seminar in Land-use
Administration	Clinic	Regulation and
		Development

How to Read and Brief a Case in Property

Appellate court opinions share a common organization whether the issues deal with property, torts, or some other legal field. Any system for briefing cases that has worked well for you elsewhere should also work in Property. However, let me make a few suggestions that may enhance your ability to prepare for and follow a Property class discussion.

Law students tend to pay less attention to a case's factual pattern than they ought to, believing mistakenly that the legal holding or conclusion can stand on its own bottom, quite apart from the facts that led to the decision. In Property, I believe that fact slighting is especially risky; often the outcome depends on whose interpretation of the facts the court prefers. Accordingly, whenever I prepare a case for discussion, I carefully chart its facts, and sometimes much of a class hour centers on a factual analysis. Three factual patterns frequently recur in Property decisions. They involve (a) family trees, (b) chains of title, and (c) descriptions. Let me illustrate from actual cases each of these factual patterns. The examples will be most useful if you can look at the cited cases beforehand.

Family Tree

Baker v. Weedon, 262 So. 2d 641 (Miss. 1972) is a dispute about the power of a life tenant to sell a farm property and reinvest the proceeds over the objections of the contingent remaindermen. In preparing for class, I find it useful to prepare the following "family tree." One can better feel the antagonisms here by noting that John Weedon's third wife, the life tenant Anna, was only seventeen years old when she married John, who was then fifty-five.

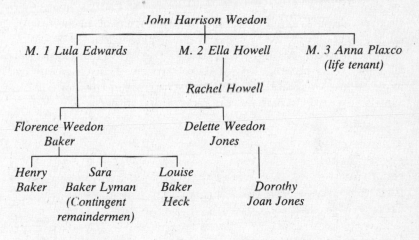

John Harrison Weedon

M. 1 *Lula Edwards*   M. 2 *Ella Howell*   M. 3 *Anna Plaxco*
(life tenant)

Rachel Howell

Florence Weedon Baker   *Delette Weedon Jones*

Henry Baker   *Sara Baker Lyman (Contingent remaindermen)*   *Louise Baker Heck*   *Dorothy Joan Jones*

Chain of Title

Chains of title are useful devices in many contexts, as illustrated in *Sanborn v. McLean*, 233 Mich. 227, 206 N.W. 496 (1925). The issue there was whether the plaintiffs could enforce a set of tract restrictions against the present owners of Lot 86. My chain of title appears below:

1891	McLaughlins	Subdivision	Green Lawn (98 lots)
12/28/1892	McLaughlins → X (Restrictions against nonresidential structures)	Deed	Lots 37–41, 58–62
9/7/1893	McLaughlins → Y (Deed silent as to restrictions)	Deed	Lot 86

?	X → plaintiffs	Deed	Lots 37–41, 58–62
1911	Y → defendants	Deed	Lot 86
	(Deed silent as to		
	restrictions)		

The chain of title shows that the plaintiffs' claim derives from the rights that X acquired in 1892.

Description

Property disputes often center on the ownership of an interest in land. It is good practice to map out the dispute whenever possible. *Van Sandt v. Royster*, 148 Kan. 495, 83 P.2d 698 (1938) concerns whether, years before, two lot owners received an easement by implication to operate a sewer line across a third owner's land. This is how I would map out the facts in that dispute.

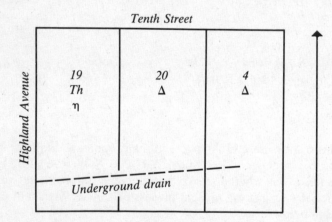

Conclusion

I have only two more thoughts that may aid your understanding of property decisions. You have probably heard each of them already. First, approach every case with a policy cast of mind. Ask what value choices led to the court's decision. Often those choices have been obscured by a highly technical analysis, and the careful reader must look behind the doctrine to ferret out what the judges were really thinking. Second, approach every case with a touch of the skeptic. This advice is related to the first. Judges often write their decisions with a self-assurance and certainty that belies the difficulty they may have had with the case. Look for the faulty logic, the twisting of doctrine, the dodging of precedent, the fudging of hard questions. Your powers of criticism will improve as you become sensitive to the policies that underlie the result.

Most of you should find this unnecessary, but let me suggest several one-volume treatises written especially for students in the basic Property course. They are *Preface to Estates in Land and Future Interests* by Thomas F. Bergin and Paul G. Haskell (Foundation Press, 2d ed., 1984); *Principles of the Law of Property* by John Cribbett (Foundation Press, 3d ed., 1989); the student edition of *Powell on Real Property*, edited by Patrick Rohan (Matthew Bender, 1968); and *The Law of Property* by Roger A. Cunningham, William B. Stoebuck and Dale A. Whitman (West Publishing, 1984). I am also impressed by the late Ray Andrew Brown's treatise *The Law of Personal Property*, edited by Walter B. Raushenbush (Callaghan & Co., 3d ed., 1975).

It will surprise me if Property is not one of your first year's most intellectually challenging and rewarding experiences.

Good luck as you venture forth.

CHAPTER 14

Torts

Jeffrey O'Connell
UNIVERSITY OF VIRGINIA

"Automobile accidents, falls in stores, fights, bursting water mains, bad food processing, swindling, slanders, and many other unpleasant events touch off tort litigation."[1]

As a result of incidents like these, the injured party tries to recover damages for his losses from the person he considers responsible. He therefore often makes a claim—perhaps ultimately resulting in a lawsuit—to recover those damages. By "damages" we mean compensation for the loss he suffered, which may include his medical bills, his loss of wages, the repair bill for his automobile, as well as compensation for his pain and suffering, as difficult as it is to translate these psychic reactions into dollars and cents.

The most spectacular part of tort claims work is, of course, work in the courtroom—actually trying a suit arising out of a tort, whether it be an automobile accident, an amputation from the use of a power lawn mower, or lung cancer from exposure to asbestos. It is a mistake, however, to concentrate exclusively on this role of the lawyer as the advocate in court actually trying a case. For every hour in court, many more may be spent studying the law applicable to the case and attempting to ascertain the facts—what actually happened. Indeed, even the prospect of getting to court in any given case is remote, since more than 95 percent of tort cases are settled prior to trial.

Law schools have not traditionally done much in teaching law students how to dig out facts. The facts as developed in a trial come neatly packaged in the opinions of appellate courts—opinions

222

which so largely constitute the stuff of law study—and consequently the facts in law study are often taken for granted. This is very misleading. Fact-finding by the lawyer is an important and difficult job. Accidents usually happen quickly, and they lead to traumatic events such as an automobile smashup. These events then have to be filtered through the memory of individuals, perhaps months or even years later. Memories may be bad, witnesses may be so inarticulate that they cannot readily express what happened, or witnesses may have moved away so that they are unavailable to tell what happened. In addition, of course, most people tend to find themselves blameless and someone else blameworthy after an accident, so there will often be diametrically opposing versions of what happened. The result is that for most good trial lawyers the hours spent preparing the case by interviewing witnesses and examining, say, damaged machinery may be far more important than even the time spent examining the law applicable to the case.

But unlike studying legal rules and legal doctrine, the ability to ferret out facts is not nearly so teachable. It is not so much intellectual and theoretical as particularized and practical. As a result, law schools—being institutions of learning—understandably concentrate on the more intellectual and theoretical task of formulating and analyzing legal rules.

In this connection, legal doctrine is much misunderstood. It is not composed of an exhaustive set of rules, capable of precise statement, against which one can lay varied and complicated fact situations and thereby obtain a ready answer to what is the "law" governing the facts. Karl Llewelyn, a great legal thinker, expressed it this way: "If the law of the state be seen as in first essence not a 'code,' nor a body of Rules but as in first essence a going institution, it opens itself up at once to inquiry by the nontechnician."[2] Harold Berman, a professor of law at Harvard, has stated that law must be defined "in terms of a set of actions and ideas, instead of in terms of a set of rules."[3]

Granted, then, that the law is more than a set of rules and that it is a growing institution, surely we can be more specific in defining it. To the lawyer, whose job it is to advise clients, the law might be defined as what the courts do in particular cases. In the words of Oliver Wendell Holmes, "The prophecies of what the courts will do in fact, and nothing more pretentious, are what I mean by law."[4]

That is all very well, but how can a lawyer rationally know or predict what the courts will do with the facts of a given case? Here enters the subject of legal reasoning.

When a case is decided by a court, it is possible to state "the law" of the case in terms merely of what the court actually did in that case, that is, a statement that defendant Smith must pay plaintiff Jones for the damage caused when Smith was negligent in failing to apply her brakes in time and so drove into Jones's vehicle while it was stopped at a red light. But such a statement accords us little help in deciding another case, especially when the facts are somewhat varied, as where a defendant applies her brakes in time but the brakes are defective because of an unforeseeable malfunction in the braking system.[5] Thus, we examine a decision of a court, not simply as an adjudication of a past dispute, but as "precedent" in aiding us to decide future disputes that are similar or analogous.

Let's examine more closely the process by which a lawyer prophesies what the courts will do on the basis of an earlier case or earlier cases, similar or analogous to his or her new problem.

Start from the premise that there are at least four levels (not always distinct) from which a party may be judged as to his responsibility when he causes injury to another.

1. Traditionally a defendant is held liable only when he negligently injures the plaintiff (as where he negligently drives his automobile into the plaintiff or where, as a manufacturer, he negligently fails to inspect his goods for quality before marketing them).

2. In an expansion of rule 1, courts have held concerning manufacturered products that regardless of how carefully manufacturers inspect goods they are liable for a breach of contract (or warranty) to the immediate party to whom they sell the goods if that party is injured by goods that were defective when manufactured.

3. As a further expansion of rules 1 and 2, courts have held that regardless of how carefully they inspected their goods, manufacturers may be liable (under the rule of so-called "strict products liability") to whoever was injured by their defective goods—not just the party to whom they sold the goods.

4. As a further expansion of rules 1, 2, and 3, courts and legislatures have decreed that in some extraordinary instances, regardless of whether the defendant was negligent or whether his goods were even defective, he must pay anyone injured by his activity. (This is the rule for those engaged in extrahazardous activity such as blasting. It is the rule under workers' compensation statutes, which make the employer liable for employee injuries even though it was the employee rather than the employer who was careless and there was no defect in any industrial machinery. It is also the rule for making the motorist liable for injuries to her passenger or a pedestrian, under so-called *no-fault* auto laws, regardless of who was or was not negligent and whether or not the car was in a defective condition.)

In the case of *Greenman* v. *Yuba Power Products, Inc.,* a case found in many torts casebooks, the following occurred:

Plaintiff [sued] . . . for damages against . . . the manufacturer of a Shopsmith, a combination power tool that could be used as a saw, drill, and wood lathe. He saw a Shopsmith demonstrated by . . . [a] retailer and studied a brochure prepared by the manufacturer. He decided he wanted a Shopsmith for his home workshop, and his wife bought and gave him one for Christmas in 1955. In 1957 he bought the necessary attachments to use the Shopsmith as a lathe for turning a large piece of wood he wished to make into a chalice. After he had worked on the piece of wood several times without difficulty, it suddenly flew out of the machine and struck him on the forehead, inflicting serious injuries. . . .

. . . Plaintiff introduced [at the trial] substantial evidence that his injuries were caused by defective design and construction of the Shopsmith. His expert witnesses testified that inadequate set screws were used to hold parts of the machine together so that normal vibration caused the tailstock of the lathe to move away from the piece of wood being turned permitting it to fly out of the lathe. . . .[6]

In 1962, the California Supreme Court held in this case that when a product is proved defective, a manufacturer is liable for damages under a new tort theory regardless of the fact that the manufacturer had not been negligent. Proof that the product was defective was enough to impose liability on the maker of the product, whereas, formerly, liability was imposed only when the defendant was proved to have been careless or guilty of a breach of contract. But except for cases of product liability, the rule that liability is imposed only where there is negligence continued—and continues—to be the normal rule.

In the same year, in the case of *Goldberg* v. *Kollsman Instrument Corp.*, also found in many casebooks, the New York Court of Appeals, basing its decision on the legal doctrine enunciated in the Greenman case, also held, under this new rule of strict liability, that if a product was proved defective a manufacturer was liable for damages regardless of the fact that it had not been negligent. The Goldberg case arose from the crash of a Lockheed aircraft near LaGuardia Airport in New York City. Plaintiff's daughter was a fare-paying passenger on the fatal Chicago–New York flight and was killed in the accident. Her parents brought the suit for damages resulting from the death. The Court of Appeals (the highest court in New York State) held that if, as alleged, the altimeter on the aircraft turned out to be defective and thus caused the crash, that fact alone would be enough to cause Lockheed to be liable for the death regardless of the fact that neither Lockheed nor the manufacturer of the altimeter, Kollsman Instrument Corporation, had been in any way negligent.

In both states, then, the highest courts indicated that the law had not only moved beyond rule 1 above (liability only for negligence) to rule 2 (liability for breach of contract—or warranty—to the purchaser or airline passenger) but arguably to rule 3 (strict liability), which would mean that manufacturers were liable regardless of negligence not only to the immediate purchaser but to *anyone* injured by the defective product—including, say, a bystander.

Assume that a few months later in New York a GM car with a defective driveshaft goes off the road and injures a pedestrian. The unanswered question (the answer to which a lawyer must predict) is: Can the pedestrian sue GM and recover for her damages regardless of her inability to prove that GM was negligent in the way the car was manufactured, based on the precedent of the Goldberg case (which in turn relied on the Greenman case)?

On first blush, one might think so. But when GM is sued in such

a case it might defend on the ground that the new doctrine of strict
tort liability still applies only for the benefit of people who had
contracted to buy manufactured goods or a plane ride on the
manufactured item, and not to bystanders such as pedestrians, as
seen in the following quote:

> . . . Early expansion of liability beyond only for negligence for
> injuries from manufactured goods was grounded on the law gov-
> erning the sale of goods. The theory seems to have been that any
> special right to be paid for injuries caused by a product was
> granted only to the purchaser and his immediate family—the "con-
> sumer." As [Professor Harry] Kalven [of the University of Chi-
> cago Law School] points out, the new strict . . . product liability
> was "closely linked with the rhetoric of consumer protection,"
> stemming from a kind of sales warranty concerning the safety of
> the goods in the transfer from the seller to the buyer; [liability
> based on breach of warranty, as opposed to negligence] . . . was
> applied first and foremost to food products. But most food pur-
> chases are consumed by the purchaser and his family and injuries
> to bystanders by food products are quite rare. So the hunch of
> many lawyers was that [strict] . . . liability would not be extended
> by the courts in their case-by-case rulings to protect bystanders, as
> distinguished from purchasers. In other words, given the rationale
> for justifying the extension of special [strict] . . . protection to
> purchasers, refusing to protect bystanders would have seemed to
> present a logical stopping place for the new [strict] . . . product
> liability.
>
> As a corollary, if the bystander were to be protected under such
> [strict] . . . liability, a new rationale would seem necessary for
> applying such broad . . . liability to all product injuries but not to
> other kinds of injuries. [Dean William] Prosser [of the University
> of California Law School] has expressed it best: "Bystanders and
> other nonusers . . . present a fundamental question of policy. If
> the philosophy of strict liability is that all injured plaintiffs are to
> be compensated by holding the suppliers of products to strict
> liability for all the harm they do in the world, and expecting them
> to insure against the liability and pass the cost onto society by
> adding it to the price, then there is no reason whatever to distin-
> guish the pedestrian hit by an automobile with bad brakes, from
> the injured driver of the car. [But i]f the supplier is be held liable
> because of his representation [to the purchaser] of safety in market-
> ing the goods, then the pedestrian stands on quite a different

footing. He is not the man the supplier has sought to reach, and no implied representation [or warranty] has been made to him that the product is safe for his use; nor has he relied upon any assurance of safety whatever. He has only been there when the accident happened; and in this he differs from no other plaintiff."[7]

In addition to such general considerations, and as an illustration of the technical detail with which cases must be read, counsel for GM would rely on language from the opinion in the Goldberg case which at least arguably limits the precedent to the narrow view that bystanders are *not* protected by the new products liability. In the second sentence of his opinion, Chief Judge Charles Desmond of the New York Court of Appeals states the issue to be decided in the case in the following terms: "The question now to be answered is: does a manufacturer's implied warranty of fitness of his product for its contemplated use run in favor of all intended *users,* despite lack of [a] . . . contract?"[8] Similarly, at the end of the next-to-last paragraph of his opinion, Desmond states that "Adequate protection is provided for the *passengers* by [making liable] . . . the airplane manufacturer which put into the market the completed aircraft."[9] Counsel might also point to language in the Greenman case, relied on by the New York court in Goldberg, which similarly suggests an exclusion of bystanders, as opposed to users, from the benefits of the new strict products liability. At the end of the next-to-last substantive paragraph in that opinion, Mr. Justice Traynor of the California Supreme Court stated, "To establish the manufacturer's liability it was sufficient that plaintiff proved that he was injured while *using* the Shopsmith in a way it was intended to be used. . . ."[10] As [then] Professor [now Judge] Robert E. Keeton of the Harvard Law School suggested at the time,[11] all this language from these cases does not necessarily suggest that bystanders would be excluded from the new strict products liability but it certainly doesn't sweepingly include bystanders or other *nonusers.* And given the fact that Goldberg and Greenman represented a very significant extension of liability, such caution in the language employed might be hugely significant.

But the important thing for beginning law students to note is how important these distinctions are in practice. In the bargaining over how much the case of the pedestrian is worth, how much of a discount, if any, will plaintiff's lawyer be inclined to take in collecting for the plaintiff's damages, based on the defendant's determination to resist the application of strict liability to bystanders? Even if plaintiff's counsel is successful in convincing a trial court that the new rule extends to bystanders, note that the defense counsel has a basis of appeal—which at least means more delay in the payment of losses to a plaintiff, who may be in desperate need of funds to pay for medical expenses and to replace wage losses. If, then, the plaintiff has suffered $40,000 in losses, is the likelihood of either the trial or appellate court not extending the new rule to bystanders—or in the delay of getting the matter settled—worth, say, taking only $30,000 in settlement? Only lawyers on both sides, knowledgeable about the holdings of cases and the bases and trend of holdings, can accurately appraise how successful will be an attempt to extend precedent such as that established in the Greenman and Goldberg cases. Thus it is that case holdings—and the language contained in court opinions—are not only important in a theoretical sense of knowing the law but are intensely practical tools in negotiating settlements as well as in litigating cases. (On the issue of extending strict liability to bystanders, gradually—but only gradually, case by case and with eddies in various jurisdictions— bystanders *were* accorded the same protection as purchasers following product injuries.)

Such use of tort doctrine or legal precedent is the part of the law that your first-year course in torts—and indeed most courses—will focus on. And, as suggested earlier, that is appropriate because such use of legal doctrine is the most intellectually disciplined aspect of the law and therefore most appropriate for intellectual and scholarly institutions such as law schools.

But in addition to tort doctrine, the world of tort law has two other tiers—one a lower tier and the other an overarching upper tier. The lower tier is the intensely pragmatic world of tort law in practice, which will often skew even the most practical use of scholarly tort rules and doctrines in bargaining over settlements or in litigation. Because so much accident law deals with personal-injury victims, tort trials become very emotional, as well as intellectual, affairs. The flavor of this emotional side of the battle of wits—quite apart from the technical use of tort doctrine in negotiating and litigating cases—is perhaps conveyed by the following few paragraphs:

> Whatever the circumstances of an accident, the lawyers for the contending parties, in our adversary system of laws, will arrive in court prepared to present, as theatrically as a judge will tolerate, the "best" case for their clients. Extraneous matters are introduced into proceedings to sway jury verdicts. Indeed, lawyers try during the empaneling of juries to select persons who, by dint of certain stereotypes, are likely to be more—or less—inclined to find in favor of one party or the other. A plaintiff's lawyer might prefer jurors who are young, or Jewish, or black, or who work in the blue-collar jobs, and who are presumed to be generous in their impulses toward the injured. The lawyer representing the doctor accused of malpractice is likely to want on the jury retired persons living on fixed incomes and "tight with a buck," middle-management types, or a highly diverse group liable to squabble and unlikely to grant a large award.
>
> Once a trial is underway the plaintiff and the defendant, each in his own way, will try to win the sympathies of jurors with irrelevancies. The blind plaintiff might be encouraged to come to court with his seeing-eye dog and to dab at his eyes with a handkerchief. The corporation's lawyers might dress shabbily and play the rube and sit in court next to a "goat"—[an] . . . official of the sued company [such as a foreman] who, it is heavily implied, will personally suffer an adverse verdict [whereas in fact an insurance company or other corporation will almost always pay any verdict].[12]

At the other extreme, the upper tier of the tort world concerns the interrelationship of tort law with all the many schemes of society for alleviating distress—accident and health insurance as well as life insurance, sick pay, and programs of governmentally mandated and/or administered social insurance, such as workers' compensation or social security. To what extent does the existence of this other world of recompense impinge on the world of tort law and its insurance? For example, if health insurance has already covered the plaintiff's medical bills, must the person committing a tort—the *tortfeasor,* as he is called—nonetheless pay for medical bills all over again? (Generally speaking, the answer has been yes, but statutes sometimes change this.) Closely allied with such questions are the questions of reforming tort law itself in an attempt to shape it more in accord with insurance and even social-insurance principles in the form of so-called no-fault laws. Under no-fault auto laws, each motorist is required to insure himself (and his passengers and pedestrians injured by him) for out-of-pocket losses (medical expense and wage loss but not for pain and suffering) regardless of who is at fault in the accident or even whether there was a defect in a product. In return, each motorist (now assured of payment of his losses by his own insurance company) is required to waive—at least to a certain extent—any claim against the other driver based on the latter's fault. In other words; in return for being assured payment of his out-of-pocket loss to at least a modest extent, the motorist must waive to a corollary extent his right to be paid based on fault for all his out-of-pocket losses, plus pain and suffering.

Increasingly, too, economics as a discipline is being injected into tort doctrine and thinking, as notions of strict tort liability for injuries from manufactured products are extended to more and more injury victims and as no-fault auto insurance is in effect (in fifteen jurisdictions as of 1990), and generally as more and more thinking is done about abandoning traditional forms of tort law—whether based on negligence or product defect under strict products liability—in favor of more insurance- and social-insurance-oriented programs. New Zealand has scrapped all tort law for personal injury in favor of paying everyone modest damages from government-run social insurance on the happening of any accident. What system of compensation best achieves deterrence and optimal resource allocation? The flavor of much of this "economic" thinking is perhaps conveyed by the following paragraphs:

> Even if we could cover all losses from all injuries under social security or general health insurance [as is being attempted in New Zealand], economists specializing in loss allocation, such as Professor Guido Calabresi of the Yale Law School, tell us it would be unwise to have all injuries from whatever cause paid out of a big, undifferentiated pool of "insurance" such as social security. Rather, they argue, a given activity or industry should be made to pay for the particular losses it causes. Otherwise, the argument goes, there is less incentive to keep that activity or industry safe. Isn't your incentive to produce a safer product greatly lessened, it is asked, if persons injured by your product are paid exclusively from social

security funded by assessments that make no distinctions between relatively safe products (like pillows) and unsafe ones (like power tools). For Calabresi, what might be termed *market deterrence* is the best way for accident law to combine payment for loss with a reduction of accidents and accident costs.

Professor Leonard Ross [then of the Columbia Law School] . . . best summarized Calabresi's thesis: "[Market] . . . deterrence operates by placing the costs of accidents on the activities which cause them; for example, by making power lawn mower manufacturers liable for all [personal injury] damage[s] caused by malfunctions of their mowers. . . . In theory, mower prices would then rise and sales fall; some families would be induced to shift to manual mowers; the total amount of power mowing would be reduced; and the level of accidents would abate. Moreover, manufacturers might become choosy about customers, raising prices to noninstitutional buyers or perhaps simply to obvious schlemiels. Finally, they would have an incentive to redesign mowers to improve safety features. A variety of market forces would be set in motion to lower the total loss through accidents."[13]

Because of the interaction of these different but interrelated tiers, no subject in the law school curriculum is more intense a prism than is torts. And it is a colorfully controversial prism (given the battles, for example, over whether no-fault insurance should be legislatively instituted)—a prism of many fascinating disciplines: law, insurance, economics, politics, psychology, and ultimately jurisprudence and philosophy (who really deserves what?).

Especially in recent years, controversy swirls around tort law. As tort law expands, proponents of the expansion (such as Ralph Nader and many personal-injury lawyers) urge that this is a helpful development, curbing the excesses of businesses and health-care providers who often ignore safety in traditional areas of injury as well as burgeoning new areas, such as the adverse affects from toxic substances. Others argue that overly expansive tort law gives rise to unmanageable new burdens on businesses and health-care providers, causing reputable manufacturers to cease innovating and even producing such essential products as vaccines, and obstetricians to give up their practices. And so the battle rages in the courts and legislatures.

Most law students are intellectuals—people gifted in their appre-

ciation and use of ideas and books. Were they not, they wouldn't
have achieved sufficient scholarly success to get into intensely
competitive law schools today. But note that law students are
intellectuals with a difference. Confident of their intellectual ability and desirous of a profession which gives bent to their bookish
nature, most of them nonetheless do not want careers as "professional intellectuals"—as academics, if you will. They desire the
bookish *and* the pragmatic—hence law school. Most of you are not
at all sure at first if you want to be lawyers; most likely you are not
sure what you want to be. (Someone once defined a law student as
a bright young person who can't stand the sight of blood.) But
most of you will end up as lawyers. You will get hooked on the law
(or at least won't find anything else as attractive). Torts will give
you as good an insight as you can get to many different facets of
law—the intensely practical and the ultimately theoretical, with all
the stops between.

As I have emphasized, Torts—like most courses, especially first-
year courses—focuses on legal rules and doctrines. However, I'd
like to make several points, perhaps not directly related to torts,
but of interest. Learning to *do*, rather than just to analyze and
compare, is something law schools haven't bothered much with.
Clinical training (a kind of internship with, say, a social-welfare
agency or legal defender's office) is available in most law schools,
but the trouble with such training, in my view, is that often it has
very little intellectual content—landlord-and-tenant and bill-collection
disputes, and so on. One is at the mercy of the often very human,
but intellectually humdrum, needs of clients, coupled with the
often endless frustrations of trying to meet classes while trying to
adapt to schedules of courts and agencies and to appointments
with clients and others. This is not to denigrate such clients or their
problems, but it is to assert that to the extent one is interested in
learning law in an intellectually exciting milieu—the reason we
have made law schools part of great educational institutions—clinical
experience can be frustrating. So take part in clinical work if you
choose, but don't expect (although you may be lucky) to find it
very broadening intellectually. How to *do* (as opposed to study
and listen) in law school and yet to do so in an intellectually
rigorous and controlled milieu? How to *do*, in other words, and

yet retain the advantages of learning within the efficient confines of an educational institution, with its structured schedule and careful supervision? There are two routes open in most law schools which I think you should try to take advantage of. First, take a course in trial practice, if at all possible. Learning to try a case is somewhat like learning to swim or ride a bike. Reading all the books on how to do it cannot replace actually trying it—actually examining or cross-examining a witness, getting documents admitted into evidence, making or responding to objections to testimony. A trial practice course can give you that experience, and once you have done some of it, like learning to ride a bike or learning to swim, you never really lose it (though of course you can get awfully rusty). And even if you never try a case again, having done it you are always a much better lawyer, because so much legal work looks to the possibility of what might happen if everything breaks down (the contract is broken or the will or tax return challenged) and ultimate resort is had to litigation. A trial practice course, granted it only simulates trial work, is thereby conducted on law school schedules with fascinating cases and with careful critiques by judges and professors, and is an ideal way to be first exposed to trial work.

The other means of *doing* (keep in mind that law students by definition have spent a long time in school and, at least after the first year in law school, often find more study and listening rather boring) in a controlled, disciplined intellectual milieu is drafting instruments—whether drafting statutes, regulations, wills, contracts, pleadings, or other documents. This too must be done to be really appreciated. Even more than trial work, this work is done by almost every lawyer sooner or later. Drafting combines in an almost unique way broad, creative planning with exhaustive, exhausting technical execution. Take a course if at all possible that entails some drafting. Here too you will work with fascinating problems, provided by the simulated reality of a law school setting, with close professional, professorial supervision.

Another interesting aspect of torts not covered directly in the text above is its joinder with the insurance industry. Almost all tort settlements or judgments are paid by insurance companies (or companies that through one device or another arrange to insure themselves). The casualty insurance industry, tied often to legal liability as the determinant of its payouts, offers unique opportunities for lawyers. Perhaps, then, more than any other industry, insurance offers the lawyer an unusual advantage in that the insurance industry is so peculiarly tied to legal criteria in its operations. Thus a lawyer's expertise is recognized as a real plus for technical as well as general intellectual reasons and for the purposes of line responsibility as well as staff duties. Among the additional advantages to lawyers in the casualty insurance industry are:

1. The industry has long been considered by knowledgeable observers as lacking talent (with many individual exceptions, of course), so that a bright, able person can make his/or her mark and have influence there more readily, and earlier, I would venture, than in a field more crowded with talent (such as big-city law firms, labor relations, banking, etc.).

2. The insurance industry is heavily regulated, as well as constantly subject to further legislative intervention, so that a lawyer's knowledge and understanding of legislation and government are put to a special use, in dealing both with legislatures and with insurance regulators.

3. The insurance industry not only writes policies that are payable based on the determination of legal liability—essentially legal questions—but also generates many other technical legal problems, including drafting and interpretation of all kinds of insurance contracts, including life, health, fire, and so on. Thus a lawyer's technical skills are much more in demand and applicable in the insurance industry than in most industries, even those that are also closely tied with the law, such as banking or labor relations.

4. On the other hand, if a lawyer eventually discovers his talent lies even more in, say, administration, personnel, investments, or other opportunities afforded by sizable corporations, he can switch to such endeavors without leaving the industry or even the company he knows and has advanced in.

5. Finally, insurance is, as suggested in the text, a uniquely important activity (that's one of the main reasons it's regulated so closely), touching on the basic human issues of risk and security. Everything in our socioeconomic legal life comes

together in insurance to make it a vital activity of pervasive importance in our society. To be a part of such an activity is to be very much in the center of things.

Of course there are disadvantages to insurance as a career. Salaries are relatively low. As H. J. Maidenberg, a consumer columnist for the *New York Times*, has written, "Secondary management salaries in the traditionally low-paying insurance field are set either to repel aggressive, bright executives or to force many in the industry to leave."[14] (But one can more quickly move nearer to the top where a more than comfortable income can be earned.) And any regulated industry can be frustrating. "Let's face it," says a member of the New York Insurance Commissioner's staff, "this is a hothouse industry, just like the railroads. Nearly every time it wants to make a move it has to get approval from us. This is not the sort of atmosphere which bright young [people] . . . thrive in."[15] (But, as suggested, a lawyer is better able to deal professionally and advantageously with the frustrations of regulation than probably anyone else.) Ultimately the disadvantages explain why there is a relative vacuum of talent. The industry is plagued by "inept and stodgy management"—what one Wall Street investment banker described as "dinosaur clubs disguised as top management, who do not have the constitution to change."[16] But as a vice-president of a major concern said to me recently, "I like to market where there is a vacuum of sellers." Not a bad idea for you at least to think about marketing your talent where there is such a vacuum. So when the time comes to think about a career, don't overlook, as too many law graduates do, the insurance industry.

NOTES

1. C. Morris, *Torts* (1953).
2. As quoted in H. Berman, *The Nature and Functions of Law,* 9 (1958).
3. *Ibid.*
4. O. W. Holmes, "The Path of the Law," 10 *Harvard Law Review* 461 (1897).
5. F. Cooper, *Living the Law,* 9 (1958).
6. Greenman v. Yuba Power Products, Inc., 59 Cal. 2d 57, 59–60, 27 Cal. Rptr. 697, 698–99, 377 P.2d 897, 898–99 (1962)
7. J. O'Connell, *Ending Insult to Injury: No-Fault Insurance for Products and Services,* 60–61, quoting from Kalven, "Tort Law—Tort Watch," 34 *Journal of the American Trial Lawyers Association* 1, 46 (1972), and Prosser, "The Fall of the Citadel (Strict Liability to the Consumer)," 50 *Minnesota Law Review* 791, 819–20 (1966).
8. Goldberg, v. Kollsman Instrument Co., 12 N.Y. 2d 432, at 434–35, 191 N.E.2d 81 (1963). Emphasis supplied.
9. *Idem* at 12 N.Y. 2d at 437, 191 N.E.2d at 83. Emphasis supplied.
10. Greenman v. Yuba Power Products, Inc., 59 Cal. 2d 57, 64, 27 Cal. Rptr. 697, 701, 377 P.2d 897, 901 (1962). Emphasis supplied.
11. At a continuing legal education session at Harvard Law School, Summer 1964.
12. Sanford, book review of J. O'Connell, *Ending Insult to Injury: No-Fault Insurance for Products and Services* (1975), in the *New York Times,* Aug. 10, 1975, Section 7, p. 4. For some material describing the workaday world of tort law in practice, see the collection of pieces by various authors in J. O'Connell and R. Henderson, *Tort Law, No-Fault & Beyond,* Ch. 2 (1975).
13. J. O'Connell, note 7 *supra,* at 76–77, citing G. Calabresi, *The Costs of Accidents: A Legal and Economic Analysis,* 26 (1970), and Ross, book review of *idem,* 84 *Harvard Law Review* 1322, 1323 (1971). For a discussion of the discipline of economics as applied to tort law, see R. Posner, *Economic Analysis of the Law,* Ch. 6 (3rd ed., 1986). For a general discussion of the interaction of tort law and insurance, together with discussions of the future interrelationship of both, see the collection of pieces by various authors in J. O'Connell and R. Henderson, *Tort Law, No-Fault & Beyond,* Ch. 5 (1975).
14. *The New York Times,* June 2, 1968, Section 3 (Business and Finance), p. 1, col. 8.
15. P. Hellman, "Your Policy Is Hereby Cancelled," *New York Times,* Nov. 8, 1970, Section 6 (Magazine), pp. 32, 126.
16. *New York Times,* June 2, 1968, Section 3 (Business and Finance), p. 1.

CHAPTER 15

Constitutional Law

Paul Bender
ARIZONA STATE UNIVERSITY

Most first-year law school courses explore subjects that may seem
unfamiliar to incoming law students. Almost every beginning law
student, however, probably knows and cares something about constitutional law. "Clear and present danger," "separate but equal,"
"one person, one vote," "the power to tax involves the power to
destroy," "separation of church and state," "checks and balances,"
"*Miranda* warnings"—these phrases from constitutional jurisprudence have some meaning for most Americans, whether or not
they have ever set foot in a courtroom, law office, or law school.
We all know something about our constitutional rights as Americans, and we also have some sense of what it means to have a
"federal" governmental system with "separation of powers." We
learn some constitutional law in high school civics or history classes,
and many have taken constitutional law in college political science
courses. The U.S. Supreme Court—the primary expositor of constitutional rules—is a familiar institution. Supreme Court Justices
are well-known figures; we pay attention when Court vacancies are
filled; and we know something about major constitutional law
decisions such as the *Bakke* case and the abortion cases, and about
important doctrinal trends concerning levels of judicial "activism,"
and whether the Supreme Court is becoming more or less "liberal"
or "conservative."

Constitutional law, moreover, is definitely "relevant." It is difficult these days to read a newspaper or hear a television newscast
without encountering a reference to a live constitutional law con-

troversy, even when no specific Supreme Court decision or appointment is making headlines. The crime problem, police brutality, the death penalty, racism, affirmative action, women's liberation, the right to abortion, states' rights, welfare rights, presidential powers, school prayers (and countless other current political and social questions as well) are all issues that touch directly or indirectly upon matters of constitutional law. Torts, contracts, real property, and civil procedure may seem like alien and hostile territory to new law students, but constitutional law should seem familiar, important, and interesting.

There is good reason, I think, for widespread interest in constitutional law. Constitutional rules are important in ways that other legal rules are not. Rules of constitutional law are, in fact, actually on a level *above* other rules of law, for one of their main functions is to set limits on the other rules—limits that cannot be removed by presidents, governors, legislatures, or simple democratic majorities, but only through a long, difficult, and rarely invoked constitutional amendment process. In James Madison's words, the Constitution not only enables "the government to control the governed," it also obliges it "to control itself." Constitutional rules place limits upon every conceivable area of federal or local governmental operations: the regulation of business; the control of the environment; the systems of taxation; the control of crime; the promotion of morality; foreign affairs; raising armies; landlord and tenant law; public welfare assistance—everything. Constitutional rules are also of special interest because they reflect, or are responsible for (usually both), some of the most important aspects of American life today—the things that make life in the United States different from that in other places: the pervasiveness of the role of the federal government, the official tolerance of dissent, and the strong value placed upon nondiscriminatory treatment, to name three.

Constitutional law is not only different from other law in terms of its level of importance but it is also (as, perhaps, befits its importance) a difficult and controversial subject. The Supreme Court's decisions on constitutional questions are constantly and sharply criticized by public officials, politicians, the press, and the law reviews (to say nothing of law professors, who *never* seem to be satisfied). Constitutional issues—especially those that are frequently litigated—have that maddening quality of rarely being able to be answered in absolute terms. The essence of most constitutional rules is, rather, that governmental decisions and actions must be fair and reasonable in light of all the legitimate competing interests and constitutional values. "Balancing" judgments like these pervade the law. In the constitutional area, however, they often concern matters of national political significance, where feelings run high, where the quality of life for many people may hang in the balance, where perfectly plausible arguments can often be made on either side of the case, and where ultimate decisions must flow from general principles and be rationally and logically justified in the limelight of national publicity. Moreover, the courts are often required, if they are going to live up to their constitutional responsibilities, to disagree flatly with the opinion of the majority of Americans on questions of wide concern—sometimes even with the opinion of a very large majority in some areas of the country. These are not ideal conditions for making law, and it has been exceptionally difficult to develop meaningful and satisfactory general principles in many important areas. Even academics, who can study issues at leisure and with the benefit of hindsight, are often unable to come up with widely acceptable and principled solutions, so intractable are some of the problems that constitutional law must solve.

Because constitutional law concerns the legitimacy of other law and official behavior, constitutional rules also frequently contain subtleties that legal rules in other areas may lack. Although the courts have, from the beginning of the nation, asserted the power to decide upon the constitutionality of the actions of the other branches of government, they have not been so brash as to pay no deference whatever to the views of those other branches. Total deference obviously cannot be paid, for that would cancel the judicial power to decide constitutional questions. So, substantive constitutional rules (difficult enough to apply in and of themselves) are often overlaid with other rules about how much and what kind of deference is to be given the views of other bodies in the decisional process, and on how the quality and quantity of deference should vary according to the nature of the constitutional issue involved, the branch of government that has acted, and whether the critical issue is one of fact, speculation, or value judgment.

Constitutional decisions thus often turn upon preliminary determinations about the governmental action involved is presumptively valid or presumptively invalid, on whether it needs to be shown merely that government *might* have been acting properly or whether it must be shown instead that, in fact, the government action was justified, and on who should resolve disputed issues of fact and judgment. The process of factoring in all these variables, while preserving the proper respect for underlying constitutional values, is a formidable intellectual feat.

It should be clear, from what has been said thus far, that although you may already be familiar with constitutional law issues from a historical or social perspective, the treatment of these issues in law school is likely to be quite different from what you have experienced in college or in your general reading or discussions about history and government. Supreme Court decisions (almost all of the cases you will read in Constitutional Law will be U.S. Supreme Court opinions) will be approached in law school, not primarily from their place in the politics of the time (although that aspect will by no means be ignored), but in terms of their precise holdings, their consistency with other cases, their fidelity to the constitutional text and implicit constitutional values, their potential significance for future cases, their logic, and so on. You will be encouraged in law school to be critical of these decisions—to think about whether the Court was right or wrong, to consider whether alternative solutions would have been preferable, to try to devise arguments for limiting the significance of some decisions and for expanding the significance of others. Although the text of the Constitution remains relatively stable (witness the recent defeat of the Equal Rights Amendment), constitutional law is constantly evolving and changing through the process of judicial interpretation. As a lawyer—and perhaps as a future scholar or judge—you can have an effect on this process, both as it affects particular litigation in which you may be involved and as it affects general issues, such as the development of the right of privacy, the application of constitutional rights to prisoners and mental patients, or the allocation of power between state and federal governments. Constitutional Law courses try to give you the tools to do this job as effectively as possible.

Few, if any, lawyers practice constitutional law as such, in the way that lawyers practice criminal law, tax law, securities law, welfare law, labor law, or medical malpractice law. Constitutional issues can come up anywhere. Why, then, have a separate course in constitutional law? Since the Constitution affects so many different areas, why not teach the Constitution as it affects antitrust law in the antitrust course, the Constitution as it affects taxation in the tax course, and so forth? This is actually done in law school to some extent. You will probably pay some passing attention to constitutional rules and limits in many courses, and some subjects— such as criminal procedure and family law—have a heavy constitutional content. But many constitutional principles have more or less the same substance as they cut across the various subject-matter areas where they are relevant. Thus the same basic Commerce Clause principles govern federal power to regulate both labor unions and securities transactions. Similar due process principles govern state procedures to revoke eligibility for welfare and to suspend a student from school for alleged misbehavior. Racial and gender discrimination are subject to similar judicial scrutiny whether contained in laws about family relationships or a code governing commercial transactions. It makes sense to study these general principles in depth in one course rather than several.

Why, then, don't we at least have separate courses in free speech, in equal protection, or in the federal foreign affairs power? Surely, these are different topics. Most law schools do, indeed, have upper-level courses that concentrate intensively on these or other topics, but law schools believe that all students should have some understanding of a range of important constitutional issues, and a single basic Constitutional Law course is a convenient gathering place.

There are other reasons for offering a single basic course. A number of pervasive constitutional themes apply to many different constitutional issues, and it is these that the basic course is ordinarily designed to emphasize. One of these themes has already been mentioned. It concerns the level of deference that ought to be shown by courts to decisions made by the other branches of government. Should we have an "active" Court, willing (even anxious) to impose its values on the nation through constitutional interpretation, or one that construes its prerogatives strictly? A related theme concerns the proper modes of constitutional interpretation. To what extent should the meaning of the Constitution (the provisions of which are often extremely general) be derived from the text itself? To what extent are the unwritten understandings of the Framers at the time of adoption controlling? To what extent should the Constitution change or grow in meaning to meet evolving conditions and societal values? Another pervasive theme—that of "federalism"—involves the division of governing responsibility between federal and state legislatures and between federal and state courts. A very large theme in the area of individual rights relates to whether different levels of protection should be afforded to different constitutional rights. Are some rights more essential or important than others—leading perhaps to less judicial deference or stronger standards of required governmental justification when these rights are infringed?

The basic Constitutional Law course is likely to consist of three main parts: (1) justiciability, that is, the power of courts to decide constitutional questions; (2) the affirmative constitutional powers of the federal government and the preclusive effect of those powers on state prerogatives; and (3) the constitutional rights of individuals. The most traditional basic courses take these topics in the order given, and if topics are omitted, they are likely to be individual rights topics. Some of these are covered in optional or advanced courses. Somewhat less traditional courses do justiciability issues briefly at the outset (deferring the details either to later in the course or to an advanced course), try to get through affirmative federal powers fairly quickly (and in considerably less detail than in the traditional courses), and reserve at least minimally adequate time for individual rights. Recently, some courses have given clear preeminence to individual rights subjects, in recognition, perhaps, of the fact that most live constitutional issues today are individual rights issues. Individual rights principles also arise with increasing frequency in other courses, making increased attention in the basic course appropriate.

Whatever the order of study, it is wise to remember throughout the course that every case challenging governmental action under the U.S. Constitution potentially raises three questions, each of which roughly corresponds to one of the three main parts of the course: (1) Is the constitutional question justiciable—that is, can a court decide it? (2) If the federal government is responsible for the challenged action, did the Constitution give the branch of government that acted affirmative authority to act as it did; if state or local action is involved, was that action "preempted" by the grant of affirmative power to the federal government? (3) Is the challenged action prohibited because it is in conflict with constitutional provisions protecting individual rights?

The specific subjects covered in the basic Constitutional Law course vary among schools, among teachers in the same school, and even from year to year with the same teacher. What follows is designed as a basic orientation in the topics most frequently encountered.

Justiciability

Virtually every basic course begins with the grandparent of all constitutional cases, *Marbury* v. *Madison*. *Marbury* was decided by the Supreme Court in 1803 in an opinion by Chief Justice Marshall who, as you probably know, played a large part in developing the basic postulates of our constitutional jurisprudence. *Marbury* is important primarily because it establishes the single most essential feature of American constitutional law as we know it, namely, that in exercising their jurisdiction the courts have the power to determine the constitutionality of the actions of the other branches of government. The Court in *Marbury* held an act of Congress unconstitutional—and therefore void and without effect—although the statute had been duly enacted by the legislature and approved by the President. This judicial role is not explicitly provided for by the constitutional text, so *Marbury* also introduces another basic feature of U.S. constitutional law—that the words used in the constitutional document cannot be used as a reliable mechanical guide to its meaning. The courts, that is, not only apply the Constitution to what the other branches do, they also must decide what the Constitution means, even in its most fundamental aspects (such as whether and to what extent courts are to sit in judgment on the other branches).

Although *Marbury* unquestionably remains "good law" in its

broadest outlines, you will nevertheless be asked to direct your attention to the question whether it was correctly decided (*should* the courts have the power that Marshall gave them?) and also to direct your attention to the pervading question of what it means to say that a constitutional rule is "correct" (does "correctness" imply consistency with the constitutional text, with the "intent" of all or some of the Framers as revealed in the constitutional debates and other contemporary evidence such as the Federalist Papers, with the enlightened views of modern Justices, with the evolving values and conditions of American life, with all or some of the above, and so on?). It may also be pointed out to you that *Marbury* contains an interesting irony, for the law held unconstitutional in that case was one that actually gave the Supreme Court power to entertain a certain category of cases. Thus, the Court in *Marbury* diminished its power in one respect in order to assume an even larger general power to sit in judgment on whether Congress acts constitutionally. This aspect of *Marbury* also shows that even the federal courts (like the other branches of the federal government) only have the powers that the Constitution (as judicially interpreted) gives them.

With all of this (and more!) to be extrapolated from the case, the discussion of *Marbury* v. *Madison* can occupy a substantial amount of class time. Some courses will drop justiciability questions at this point; others will get into the vast array of intertwined doctrines that have grown up since *Marbury* and that moderate and limit the power of the federal courts to decide constitutional questions. According to these rules, constitutional questions must be raised in "actual" controversies between "adversary" parties; the controversies must be "ripe" and not "moot"; parties must have "standing"; the Constitution must not explicitly commit the particular decision to a nonjudicial body, and so on. A main theme to look for here, if you get into the details of justiciability, is the recurrent question of whether these various limits on the federal courts' jurisdiction over constitutional controversies are self-imposed or "prudential," on the one hand, or mandated by the Constitution, on the other. If the limits are self-imposed by the courts, to what extent can they be removed by legislation? On the other hand, to what extent can Congress, if it wishes, limit or eliminate the jurisdiction of courts—even perhaps the Supreme Court—over cases raising constitutional issues? (If it can contract that jurisdiction to zero, what has become of *Marbury* v. *Madison*?)

Affirmative Federal Powers

This topic has two main parts. The first, the subject of federalism, concerns the division of responsibilities and prerogatives between the central federal government, on the one hand, and the states (and the local governmental units that function under the states), on the other. The second part concerns the division of responsibilities among the three branches of the federal government—the question of "separation of powers." Many basic courses will deal thoroughly only with federalism issues, leaving separation of powers topics to advanced courses.

The basic postulate in the area of federalism is that, although state governments are governments of general or residual power—that is, they are constitutionally able to do anything that is not prohibited to them by the Constitution—the federal government is one of "delegated" powers. As such, it has only those powers assigned to it by the Constitution. For example, if Congress were to pass a federal statute prescribing the procedures, conditions, and grounds for marriage and divorce within the United States, the first constitutional question would be whether the Constitution gives the Congress power to regulate those subjects. Just because governments generally regulate marriage and divorce does not mean that our *federal* government can. The theory of our federal constitutional system is that the tasks of general government are primarily to be performed by the states; the federal government has only those powers that were ceded to it by the sovereign states through their adherence to the Constitution.

Many of these federal powers are listed in Article I, Section 8 of the Constitution. The most well-known, perhaps, is the power to regulate interstate and foreign commerce (Art. I, §8, clause 3), but there are also other significant affirmative federal powers, such as the powers to tax and spend, the war and foreign relations powers, the power to establish lower federal courts, and the powers to "enforce" constitutional individual rights provisions, such as the Due Process and Equal Protection Clauses of the Fourteenth Amendment. (This is, by the way, as good a time as any to suggest very strongly that you *read* the Constitution, straight through, and several times, before starting the basic Constitutional Law course, or indeed before starting to study law at all. Even with the amendments, the whole document runs only fifteen or so printed pages. It is a mistake to start picking apart the various clauses without a sense of the whole, and you may be amazed at how many insights into meaning you can gain by such a perusal, especially if you read critically, and with an eye out for how each provision relates to the others, and to what you know about how our governmental system actually works in practice).

Although the *theory* of federalism is that general government comes from the states, rather than from Washington, we all know that, in actuality, much (although not nearly all) government in America today has a federal source. What you will learn in this part of the basic course is how the present importance of federal law came about. The central constitutional language here is the famous "necessary and proper" clause at the end of Article I, Section 8 of the Constitution, a clause giving Congress the power to do all things "necessary and proper" to effectuate its limited list of enumerated powers. Once again Chief Justice Marshall wrote the landmark decision in a case called *McCulloch* v. *Maryland*. The Court held there that "necessary and proper" does not mean *necessary* (i.e., essential) and proper, but rather *appropriate* and proper, and that great deference must be paid by the courts to congressional judgments of appropriateness. Much of the broad use of federal power today is based on this concept. In recent years there have been glimmerings of interest in the Supreme Court (currently more "states' rights" oriented than at any time in the recent past) in perhaps creating some meaningful limits upon federal regulatory powers—limits that have not seemed to exist since the New Deal days of the 1930s and 1940s.

A second branch of the study of federalism has to do with the negative implications for the states of the existence or exercise of federal power. Are there areas (foreign affairs might be one) which are *exclusively* federal, which the states simply cannot regulate under any circumstances? Are there other areas where the states may act so long as the federal government remains silent, but where the exercise of federal power ousts the states? This is the subject of "preemption," constitutional and statutory, and it implicates another famous piece of constitutional text, the so-called Supremacy Clause of Article VI.

Individual Rights

At the law school where I have taught, Constitutional Law is a required course in the second semester of the first year, and individual rights topics constitute the major part of the course's content. Individual rights cases provide the bulk of modern constitutional litigation, largely as the result of the considerable attention paid to individual rights guarantees by the Supreme Court during the 1950s and 1960s (the so-called Warren Court era). Unlike principles relating to justiciability and affirmative federal powers, individual rights principles today ordinarily place identical or closely similar limitations on both federal and state governments. Individual rights issues often seem more accessible and understandable than the relatively abstract subjects of federalism and justiciability. At the same time, these individual rights questions, such as abortion rights, the right to express hateful opinions in public, the constitutionality of racial quotas in affirmative action programs, and the constitutionality of school prayers, also often involve enormously strident and partisan political and philosophical controversies.

Classroom consideration of individual rights is likely to begin with some historical and theoretical orientation. You will learn (perhaps to your surprise) that the original U.S. Constitution of 1789 contained few guarantees of individual rights, and that even the famous Bill of Rights, adopted in amendment form in 1791 shortly after the basic Constitution was adopted, limited only the *federal* government. The Bill of Rights' First Amendment, for example, provides only that "*Congress* shall make no law . . . abridging the freedom of speech." Yet most individual rights problems today involve challenges to state or local, rather than to federal, action. The revolutionary events in the area of individual rights were the Civil War and the subsequent enactment of the Fourteenth Amendment. That amendment, adopted in 1868, brought a broad range of state action affecting private rights directly under federal constitutional scrutiny for the first time. Today the Fourteenth Amendment imposes broad equal protection principles on the states, applies most of the provisions of the 1791 Bill of Rights to the states, and also has some independent substantive significance (it is, for example, primarily responsible for the modern constitutional right of individual privacy). Before the Fourteenth Amendment the states could, so far as the federal constitution was concerned, forbid free speech or religion; deprive persons of life, liberty, or property without due process of law; or blatantly deny them the equal protection of the laws, the latter practice, of course, being the factor which, more than any other, caused the Civil War. (Remember, however, that there were and are *state* constitutions and some of these may have imposed, and still may impose, limitations on state and local government in addition to the limitations contained in the U.S. Constitution. Although the basic Constitutional Law course is not often concerned with these state constitutional rights, they have become increasingly important in recent years as the Supreme Court, with its present relatively conservative majority, has slowed, and in some areas even reversed, the development of individual rights principles under the U.S. Constitution. Some state courts have used state constitutions to protect individual rights that the U.S. Supreme Court has refused to recognize under the federal constitution.)

The three individual rights subjects most frequently encountered in the basic Constitutional Law course are due process rights (which include some rights of "privacy"), the right to equal protection, and rights of free speech and association. You may also study other rights, such as those connected with religion and the right to travel. Most basic constitutional courses give little or no coverage to the rights of defendants in criminal cases, leaving that subject for courses in criminal law or procedure. In studying U.S. constitutional rights you will find that they are not often in the nature of affirmative entitlements, but rather are negative *limitations* on what governments may do. Affirmative rights to welfare, medical care, or education are not constitutional rights in the United States. Rights we do have—such as the First Amendment right of political speech—are also essentially negative in character. Thus there is no federal constitutional right to the financial resources necessary to own a newspaper or a television station. What the right to free speech means is that the federal government cannot, except under certain conditions, restrict or prohibit us from using the resources we have to say what we wish.

Another essential quality of most federal constitutional rights (the right to be free from slavery or involuntary servitude is an exception) is that they are rights only as against governmental or governmentally related interferences. They do not usually apply as against purely private action. You do not have a constitutional right to prevent a private citizen from stopping you from speaking. Having said this, I should also tell you that the courts have been quite imaginative at times in finding governmental characteristics in some formally private action, so that the governmental action requirement is not always as serious a limitation on the breadth of constitutional rights as it might be. What acts constitute "governmental" action for constitutional purposes is a topic studied in most basic courses. The principles behind the law in this area are harder to find than in most other areas of an already difficult subject. In thinking about the character of constitutional rights, it is also useful to bear in mind that there are statutory rights as well as constitutional ones. Although you may not have a federal *constitutional* right to be free from private interference with speech or private racial or gender discrimination, you may have a federal or state *statutory* or common law right against such private behavior.

Issues regarding the substantive content of the various individual rights are inherently of enormous interest to most students, and are so varied that I cannot possibly attempt a complete summary here. You will undoubtedly enjoy exploring, among other things, the meaning of constitutional "privacy," the question of which governmental discriminations or classifications ought to be constitutionally prohibited, and the question of whether obscene or vulgar speech can legitimately be censored or limited. You may find it useful to notice that the constitutional law of individual rights is largely a law of required government justifications. U.S. individual constitutional rights are rarely absolute in character; to recognize a right to free speech, religion, or privacy is really to say that a certain level of justification is necessary in order to permit the government to interfere with activities in these areas. According to how strong a justification is needed, only that strong, and no stronger, is the constitutional right.

One of the main themes running through the individual rights area of constitutional law is that of different levels of rights. On one level are strong rights which, when they apply, require a "compelling" or similar need to support governmental invasion. On a lower level are much weaker rights which require only that government act rationally for legitimate purposes. A vital question with respect to emerging rights, such as the right to privacy and the right to be free from gender discrimination, is whether they are to be relatively strong or relatively weak rights. The text of the Constitution is often of little help in making these decisions. Speech and religion rights are strong rights, vis-à-vis both state and federal governments. Rights of "privacy" (such as the right to obtain an abortion) seem to be strong rights as well. Rights against racial discrimination are also strong, but gender discrimination seems to have been given an intermediate status. Property, contract, and business rights have been weakly protected in recent years. A primary general topic in the area of individual rights is that of the legitimacy and coherence of these different levels of rights.

Constitutional law is a wonderful subject. It affords a chance to apply principles and logic to some of the most important and interesting issues that face society. Using these principles, lawyers can have an enormous impact upon American life, and get a great deal of personal satisfaction as well. What more could you ask of a law school course?

CHAPTER 16

Legal Writing

James Boyd White
UNIVERSITY OF MICHIGAN

Perhaps no aspect of legal life is more important, yet more widely misunderstood, than legal writing. Law firms and law schools alike are all too ready to regard legal writing as a technique of expression that one should somehow pick up on one's own, or be taught by overworked graduate-student fellows. Excellence in legal writing is often reduced to "clarity," as though the only thing one did as a lawyer was to express one's ideas more or less precisely. But in fact lawyers use language to achieve the widest range of professional purposes, to manage the widest range of professional relations. As we shall see below, "clarity" is not the only virtue of such expression. Indeed sometimes it is not a virtue at all.

Full competence at writing law is impossible except as a part of a more general competence at expression, which itself can exist only as part of a whole education of the mind. Law school, and the law more generally, can contribute much to such an education, including to its expressive aspects, but only if that is seen as one of its purposes. This means that one's understanding and mastery of legal writing depends in the first instance on a question of attitude: Is it to be regarded as a formal technique, learned from trained craftsmen, or is it seen as an aspect, indeed perhaps as the center, of a whole professional life and education?

It may be hard for you even to imagine that legal writing could be regarded as interesting or important. As a prospective law student what you are likely to know, after all, is that the law has its own special terms and locutions (which seem to be a kind of jargon) and that legal documents are often outrageously complex and obscure. (Think, for example, of the unintelligibility of the tax laws or your insurance policies.) About this seemingly dreadful language you may have conflicting feelings of irritation, fascination, and fear. As a citizen you are vexed: Why can't lawyers and legislators and judges be compelled to speak a plain language that will make sense to the rest of us? As a future lawyer, however, you may feel some excitement at the prospect of being initiated into these mysteries and of acquiring an ability—that of speaking and understanding the private language of the cult—which is denied to others. In our world this prospect may be especially alluring, because the language of the cult is to such a large degree also the language of power. (It is in part because the law makes no sense of an ordinary kind to ordinary people that we can make our living as its interpreters.) But there may be fear too: fear that as you learn this language your own mind and character will be stamped by it; that as you become one to whom this language is second nature you will become a stereotype of a kind of lawyer you cannot admire.

This fear is in some sense perfectly realistic. In law school you will be so busy trying to master the ways of talking that make up the culture of law that you will hardly be able to stop to imagine what it all sounds like to someone else. By your Christmas vacation you will already be on the other side of the line that separates you from the layman you will then once have been. The language that now seems foreign and obscure will have become natural to you. Its practices and structures will be a part of your mind. What that will mean to you is a real question; the major purpose of this chapter is to help you envisage and think about the range of possibilities.

In most schools "legal writing" is the subject of formal, if narrowly conceived, instruction. You will probably find that your own law school offers some training in the forms of legal expression, usually as part of a course in legal research or bibliography. You will perhaps be asked to abstract (or brief) a case; to write a memorandum summarizing the law as it is reflected in a series of a half-dozen cases you are given to read; to write a longer memorandum, or perhaps two, for which original research is required; and to write a brief and present oral argument in a hypothetical case (usually on appeal). If your course is especially intensive, you may be asked as well to draft a statute or set of regulations or a contract, or to prepare discovery requests or pleadings. But you may find this training somewhat disquieting, for it may often seem to be a training in forms of expression that are rigid, mechanical, or dead; to allow no room for the work of the individual mind or the expression of the individual imagination. Much of the talk you will hear about legal writing will assume that in each case there is a perfect or ideal version of the form in question—the memo or the brief—which it is your object to try to approximate, almost as if it were a Platonic form. In an ideal class, it may seem, all papers would be identical.

You gradually come to realize that the bulk of your active life will be given to speaking and writing in the forms of the law, and the question is what this will mean for yourself and your mind. Will I become molded to these modes of speech, my mind cast into these ideal forms? Is my life to consist of learning by imitation? You can imagine yourself becoming a caricature of a lawyer, a figure from a Dickens novel perhaps, or the proper butt of lawyer jokes, and wonder what you have got yourself into.

I hope these apprehensions will prove unfounded for you, that you will find the law offers you the occasions and means for a life that is free and self-expressive. But these fears are natural and to some degree realistic. One does learn these forms in part by imitation, and they do have a force of their own that is difficult to control. Some lawyers and some firms do seem to try to approximate an ideal determined by others, to lead a life of imitation with very little room for the values, imagination, and inner strengths of the individual. Other lawyers, by contrast, seem to lead lives that are deeply self-confident and self-expressive, not imitative of others but largely self-determined. They mold their language and its forms, and to some degree thus their world, as autonomous and adult minds. Different lawyers find (or make) very different answers to the question, "What are the expressive possibilities of the profession I have chosen?"

These differences naturally show up in one's writing and other expressions. Attention to one's writing—to the way one has composed this memo, or brief, or letter, or phone conversation—is in my view the best way to subject this process to control. Learning to write well can be the central focus of an education, including a legal education.

But how is this to be done? To ask what makes good legal writing is necessarily to raise the larger question, what makes good writing, and on that point our expectations, our training, and our language of criticism are likely to be rather defective. Many of the rules we have learned, for example, although in a sense correct in themselves—be specific, be clear, use the active voice when possible, avoid adjectives, watch out for waste and redundancy, and so forth—are of rather little use, and may actually be harmful, for they imply a view of writing as a technique or a set of tools, like crescent wrenches, to be maintained and polished, rather than as an aspect of thought and mind. If the student adopts this view, her attention will be directed to the wrong place: to compliance with rules of elegant composition rather than to her own difficulties with thought and expression. Much teaching of writing implies that one can divorce form from substance, that one can be a "good writer," for purposes of a particular course, with nothing to say. It is thus quite common to find in law school and college alike papers that are praised for being "perfect" from a technical point of view, but are substantively empty, devoid of thought or life. (It is not only in law school that writing is learned by imitating a voice and style.) Such writing is in a sense more disturbing than real illiteracy, for such writers are likely to think that they write well, and to have a great deal of ego invested in the value of what they have so painstakingly learned.

I think you can best begin to think about legal writing by abandoning the idea that it is a technique or a skill and instead conceive of "legal writing" as including all legal thought and expression. By "all legal expression," I mean not only briefs and contracts and securities registration statements and the like, but letters to other lawyers and to clients, interviews with clients and witnesses, negotiating sessions with opposing lawyers, arguments to a jury or judge, telephone calls to the other side, and so forth. In all of these contexts you are talking as a lawyer, and you should be thinking about how to do it well. In doing this I believe you will find it helpful to think about the ways in which you already know how to manage social relations in language, to make yourself clear, to ask a question, to tell a story, and so forth. If you can draw on and render explicit your already substantial competences, you will find that they can serve both as a source of capacity and as a standard of judgment.

To expand your conception of legal writing in this way may lead to the modification of some of the standards by which you naturally want to evaluate writing itself. Take, for example, the nostrum, referred to above, that good writing is writing that conveys an idea precisely and efficiently to one's audience. In some contexts a lawyer may not wish to convey an idea at all, or may wish to do so with deliberate ambiguity. The point of her expression may not be communication of anything substantive, but the display of power over language or over the law, or the performance of a social gesture: to indicate an openness to compromise, for example, or a determination to fight.

To think well about legal writing, that is, one should abandon the metaphor that the "function" of expression is to "communicate information or ideas" (although that is of course sometimes part of it) and attend as well to the other things that are involved when one writes or speaks as a lawyer. How are we to do this? We can start with a simple but neglected point, that all legal speech (as opposed to some policy discussions, philosophical explanations, etc.) takes place in a defined social context, populated by actual human beings with needs and motives and concerns of their own. Good legal writing requires constant recognition of the fact that it is located in a specific social and cultural context. The first questions for the lawyer may therefore be: In whose interest am I acting? To whom am I speaking? What relationship do I wish to establish with each of these people? You will speak rather differently to a jury or an opposing lawyer, to a judge or a witness; and in every instance what you say will be largely determined by the needs and wishes of the person for whom you speak—though what those needs and wishes are, and how far they are limited by the law and by your own ethical requirements, will be a topic of serious conversation between you and your client.

It is not enough to ask what your audience "wants to know," for your object may not be to inform him at all, but to engage in some other social practice. "What do I want the effect of this expression to be?" is a better way to frame the question. In talking with a client, for example, you will frequently be in the position of drawing his attention to aspects of his situation that he wishes to deny: weaknesses in his legal position or his evidence. In talking with another lawyer a constant concern is the question of saving face: You must present your alternatives in such a way as to make them seem sensible from her point of view, not a kind of defeat. And in every case you must be as aware as possible of the character, motives, and circumstances of the person to whom you speak.

A second question, to some degree determined by your answer to the first, is: "In what voice do I wish to speak to this person? Who shall I be in my expressions to him or her?" Or course you are not a chameleon, and the range open to you is limited by the range of actual versions of yourself that are comfortable for you. To play a role you cannot perform would be disastrous from a practical as well as an ethical point of view. But we all have different modes of being, and the question is which of these shall we be: the "all business" voice, brusque and efficient; the relaxed and sympathetic voice; the scholarly lawyer voice; the impassioned advocate voice; and so on. To put it this way may sound manipulative and artificial, but in ordinary life we all have a wide range of voices at our command, among which we make choices all the time, more or less unconsciously. This same process continues in the law, and is in fact an important aspect of legal thought and expression. The more you can make it conscious and controlled, the better for you and your client.

The usual mistake is not to appear woodenly the same in every context, but to vary the voice and role in a crude and obvious way. This badly damages one's effectiveness as well as one's character. Think, for example, of the cross-examining lawyer who speaks in syrupy tones, adopting an obviously false demeanor of sympathy with the witness, and how little he achieves of what he wants. The voice you use will be effective only if it is authentic to you; this aspect of writing and expression accordingly requires a good deal of introspection and a good deal of self-knowledge, and ultimately a good deal of self-creation, for good or for ill. To the extent you can make a voice of your own, or a range of voices, you will find that you have avoided becoming a "stereotyped lawyer." You will have learned to work as an independent mind in your own way.

In sum, you can best approach the practice of legal writing if you see it as part of the larger field of legal expression; if you consider expression as continuous with substance; and "substance" as the set of aims you have in the situation as a whole. This view in fact fits with the way law school itself works, for what one learns in law school is not a set of rules, or even rules and principles and policies, but a whole way of thinking and talking; a language, in fact, if that term is defined broadly enough to include all those practices that make up the culture of law. "Legal writing" is thus the center of what you learn: how to read and understand the literature of law—the cases, statutes, books, and general understandings that are our common heritage; and how to make compositions of one's own, oral and written, out of that material. These compositions are never merely attempts to define or communicate an idea, but always involve the construction and management of a social reality. Whenever you speak you make a character for yourself, for your audience, and a relation between you; and how you do these things is determined in part by the identity of the person for whom you speak, and the purposes or aims that you share. Similarly, these compositions are never merely routine repetitions, or ought not be, for they are always argumentative reconstitutions of the world and the culture: they always say, or imply, that this is what counts, and how it counts; and that what is left out can be disregarded. In this process every word and phrase makes a contribution, constructive or destructive. Good legal writing is therefore always rewriting, asking just what it means that this word is used just here, or that phrase or sentence. Everything may count.

What are the possibilities of this field of discourse for one who has mastered its materials? If you think for a moment about the occasions on which, and the audiences to which, a lawyer will speak, you will see that the possibilities of expression present a challenge worthy of any mind.

For example, whenever a lawyer speaks she both tells a story and claims a meaning for it. This means that the challenges of storytelling itself are constantly present in the work, and it is hard to imagine a fact more full of promise than that. This is easy to forget because there is a pressure in the law, especially in law school, to reduce all stories to mere theoretical outlines, examples that illustrate rules. But in the real world stories do not happen that way. They have all the complexity and mystery of genuine human events. The best way to see this may be to imagine that you are in your office when a client walks in and tells you his story. What do you do? Simply tell him what legal conclusions flow from the facts he has presented? Of course not: His story is incomplete, fuzzy, and fragmentary, and you ask him questions over and over, constantly seeking more facts until you have a sense of his story as a whole. Notice how creative and instinctive a process this is. Where is the story to begin for example: with the accident itself, at the party before the accident, when the driver took his fourth drink, with the quarrel that afternoon that made him depressed and frustrated, with the experiences in earlier life that had made him turn to oral pleasures for consolation, or where? Your choice of beginning point has large implications for who the actors in your story will be and what their conduct will mean. Similar questions can be asked about how and where the story ends, and what line is run between the points. What do you include and why? To tell a story is to start out on a process the end of which can never be foreseen. One cannot know at the beginning all that will ultimately belong to the narrative, or what its set of meanings will be.

A legal dispute can in fact be defined as a narrative competition: Each side tells the story as well as it can from its own point of view, with its own actors, causes, and antecedents, its own characterizations of result, its own as yet missing ending, with the hope of prevailing over the other, either directly, by forcing a capitulation or compromise, or indirectly, by persuading a trier of fact to accept this story as the authoritative one. A part of the lawyer's art is telling the story in such a way that the desired ending, rather than the other one, seems to be the natural and fitting conclusion to the tale. This requires a narrative art in its own way equal to that of the novelist, especially where the materials of your story are not invented by you but determined by what has happened in the world and where your version will be challenged at every stage by another.

In claiming a meaning for the story that you tell, you must make use of the existing body of cases, statutes, understandings, and rules of law that we call the law, which exists, before you organize it into argument, simply as raw material for you and your adversary, full of obscurity and contradiction and uncertainty. In making your argument you revive and reorganize—you reconstitute—this cultural inheritance, creating a new version of it in competition with another mind. Your task is to make your version seem, indeed to make it be, more natural and appropriate. In every legal case, in every legal conversation, you are one who remakes your culture, in an improved form, and offers it to others for their use. At every turn you thus address the tensions between past and present, between what others have said and thought and what you say and think, between the particular and the general, between fact and fiction, between the authority of "the law" and what seems right to "us." You create the moment at which these things can be connected in a composition that preserves and transforms your culture. And in every case the ultimate question addressed by your audience, and to which, therefore, you speak, is one of justice: What is the best language of justice? What is the best justice in this case? The intellectual possibilities of this sort of writing know no limits.

To return to the apprehensions about legal writing with which we began, let me suggest that the great opportunity of the law is not that one can learn to manipulate forms, but that one can acquire a voice of one's own, as a lawyer and as a mind; not a bureaucratic voice but a real voice. This is what we expect of judges and can demand of ourselves. In this sense training in legal writing can be an education in autonomy and responsibility, if you choose to make it so. It should be obvious that if you are to "write well" in the sense defined in this chapter, you must do more than imitate the forms and styles and moves of others: You must think through each case, each moment of speech, and make your own decision about how to speak. The responsibility is yours alone.

BIBLIOGRAPHICAL NOTE

The standard work on plain and direct writing is W. Strunk and E. B. White, *The Elements of Style* (3d ed. MacMillan, 1979). The precepts of this book are well applied to legal writing in R. Wydick, *Plain English for Lawyers* (Carolina Academic Press, 1979). For views of writing as a process see W. E. Coles, Jr., *Composing: Writing as a Self-Creating Process* (Hayden, 1974) and W. Stafford, *Writing the Australian Crawl* (Univ. of Michigan Press, 1977). For fuller statement of my own views see J. White, *The Legal Imagination* (Little Brown, 1973); "The Invisible Discourse of the Law," 54 *Colorado Law Review* 143 (1983), J. White, *Heracles's Bow,* Chapter 4 (1986).

PART FOUR

Special Courses and Course Selection

CHAPTER 17

Planning a Three-year Course Program

Robert A. Gorman
UNIVERSITY OF PENNSYLVANIA

For most law students, the first year of law school is a refreshing, challenging, and mind-expanding experience. The student learns about the development and operation of lawmaking institutions, particularly courts, and about basic concepts that order the lawyer's way of looking at society, such as causation, ownership, fault, and remedies. Perhaps most significant is the student's exposure to the lawyer's analytic method, which questions the unsupported generalization, assesses the breadth of a legal principle, examines the pertinence of particular facts.

The second and third years of law school, pushing even further into the study of legal institutions, substantive principles, and lawyering skills, can be just as challenging, just as rewarding. But the burden of wisely shaping a program in the second and third years lies almost exclusively with the individual student. Although not too long ago, many law schools required a number of courses after the first year, most have moved away from such requirements and have sought to maximize student free choice in course selection. This development is probably attributable to a number of factors: an appreciation that law school graduates will engage in varied careers, so that there is less confidence that there is subject matter of pervasive significance for all; a realization that much knowledge conveyed in second- and third-year courses is, if not quickly forgotten after law school, quickly rendered obsolete by social change; and a submission to widely expressed student objections to regimentation and paternalism.

This "electivization" of the second and third years of law school gives the student an opportunity to fashion a course program that is constructive, challenging, lasting in its intellectual and professional significance and, quite simply, enjoyable. But a random or undirected selection of upper-level courses may result instead in only modest progress beyond the lessons of the first year, and may generate restlessness and apathy. The following suggestions are designed to help the student to steer the right course. Many of the suggestions require that the student become familiar with the quality and method of teaching, and the subject matter covered, in particular courses. Don't hesitate to interrogate your classmates, "older" students, your faculty adviser (if you have one), your dean's office, or the instructor in the course. Although course catalogs are useful sources of such information, they are quite often incomplete, erroneous, or unduly optimistic.

To give some perspective to the balance of this chapter, there follows a list of all the suggestions that will be developed:

1. No one course, or group of courses, is indispensable.
2. Comply with any requirements of your law school, and of the bar of the state in which you will likely practice.
3. Certain elective courses are strongly recommended.
4. Certain elective courses are of general utility.
5. Students should seriously consider taking courses that give "perspective" to the study of law, more particularly Jurisprudence, Comparative Law, or Legal History.
6. Be aware of the opportunities for interdisciplinary study.
7. Take courses that train in, and generalize about, different lawyering skills. Well-designed "clinical" courses can be of great educational value.
8. Participation in a seminar is often valuable (and sometimes required).
9. A third-year program of specialization or concentration would be advisable for most law students.
10. Select the best teachers and best "minds."
11. Enjoy!

1. No One Course, or Group of Courses, Is Indispensable.

It is simply not true that a second- or third-year student must take some particular elective course(s) in order to flourish at the bar or in life generally. What law students learn about most in law school is how to learn. You learn—in any event, your instructors attempt to teach—the capacity to master on your own new doctrine in strange areas of the law, a capacity that is indispensable in a fast-changing world. Lawyers must be able to deal, after some study and reflection, with novel issues in such disparate areas as copyright, environmental law, and workmen's compensation. Law school equips the student to use the available research tools and to employ a critical intelligence.

This is not meant to imply that law school courses are indifferent to matters of substantive knowledge. What these courses can leave with the student—long after the black-letter details have been forgotten or rendered obsolete—is an impression of broad super-structure: the major issues in a field of law, the overall policies that compete for application, the broad responses of our legal system, the general tools of analysis. The problem in trademark or zoning that confronts an attorney in practice can be fitted into such a broad superstructure, and thus can be handled more quickly and with some greater sense of sophistication and interrelation, if a course has been taken in law school. But even without that course, a lawyer can usually function effectively after putting in a few extra hours, reading an additional text or two, or chatting with a colleague.

2. Comply With Any Requirements of Your Law School, and of the Bar of the State in Which You Will Likely Practice.

One obvious limitation upon your freedom in course selection will be the requirements of your law school. Some of the more common requirements are courses in professional responsibility and (where not already required in the first year) Constitutional Law, Civil Procedure, or Criminal Law. These will be well publicized in your course catalog. Somewhat more difficult to identify are the course requirements imposed by some state bars. Many students may be uncertain as to where they will practice law. Moreover, some state bars require that students take a number of specified courses (especially professional responsibility and practice courses), because of a concern about the "competence" of young attorneys. A convenient way to discover such requirements is to consult a book revised frequently by the American Bar Association titled *Comprehensive Guide to Bar Admission Requirements*; a copy should be available in your library or in the dean's office.

3. Certain Elective Courses Are Strongly Recommended.

Although most law schools have abandoned second-year course requirements, many have chosen to articulate a "strong recommendation" that certain courses (generally the ones formerly required) be taken before graduation. The objective is to continue the work of the first year in exposing the student to a broad range of subject matter which most lawyers are likely to encounter in their professional life and which in addition can serve as stepping stones to other advanced law courses. What follows is one person's strong recommendations, buttressed by a perception that a number of law faculties appear to concur overall. Again, neglecting to take *all* of those courses will not destroy one's capacity to function effectively as a lawyer. But neglecting to take *any* can deprive the student of a general appreciation of the role that law plays in many aspects of our society and can unduly confine the vision of a lawyer (whether practitioner, legislator, judge, or journalist) as to basic concepts and issues in much of his or her professional endeavors.

A list of strong recommendations (arranged alphabetically) follows.

(a) *Commercial Law.* Persons from all walks of life are constantly trafficking in goods, services, and intangible interests. Large corporations and the individual consumer must be aware of the means afforded by law to facilitate those transactions, to allocate the risks of the marketplace, and to protect the disadvantaged. A basic course that studies the Uniform Commercial Code will explore these issues and will also provide an opportunity to learn about statutory interpretation.

(b) *Constitutional Law.* Many law schools do not require Constitutional Law to be taken by first-year students. But the course must be strongly recommended as an elective, for reasons set forth in Chapter 14 of this book.

(c) *Corporations (or Business Associations).* A preponderance of the nation's commercial activity is done through business associations such as corporations. The lawyer should be aware of how such associations are structured and how they function. The course also studies how law shapes the relationship between those who "own" the business (in a corporation, the shareholders) and those who "run" it (the directors and officers); more broadly, it studies how the law limits the discretion and assures the accountability of persons with business power.

(d) *Estates, Trusts, and Wills (or Gratuitous Transfers, or Transmission of Wealth).* Death and taxes are certain, and all mortals must cope with the legal rules regulating the holding and transfer of property, real and personal. Unlike some areas of the law where intuition can go far, the rules governing the transmission of wealth are largely "artificial," shaped by history and by allied principles of tax law (income, estate, and gift). They are thus not easy to master "on one's own."

(e) *Evidence.* This course is not merely for the fledgling litigator. Even the office-based lawyer who seeks to avoid litigation and who will never enter the courtroom must know about prospective problems of proof and documentation when giving advice on transactions or putting together a contract, a corporation, a will, or whatever.

(f) *Income Taxation*. The federal tax system is a pervasive influence in the life of individuals and business entities, and helps to shape an extremely large share of society's transactions. It also represents a force for the allocation of wealth in our society, and should therefore be understood by enlightened citizens. (Another good reason for taking a basic course on federal income taxation is that the complexity of the subject matter renders it too difficult to "pick up" after law school.)

(g) *Professional Responsibility*. Almost all students attending law school will seek admission to the bar and will engage in the profession of the law, most likely with a private law firm or with a single business client; some will serve with an agency of government at the federal, state, or local level. Prospective lawyers should have an appreciation of the role of the profession in society and issues relating to the delivery of legal services. They should also be sensitized to the ethical dilemmas and larger societal responsibilities of the practicing attorney. The practice of law continues to change at a rapid pace, and the limits imposed by law and ethics have become increasingly complex. Many schools require students to take a course relating to professional responsibility, but even if that is not the case at your school, such a course is strongly recommended.

4. Certain Elective Courses Are of General Utility.

Whatever disagreement there may be about the desirability of taking the courses just listed, there is considerably greater disagreement on the importance of most other elective courses. What follows is simply one person's perception of other courses that commend themselves for serious consideration as having general utility for lawyers. (Again, the listing is alphabetical.) These courses should not, however, stand in the way of your following the other suggestions made below.

(a) *Accounting*. Most lawyers will probably be asked on several occasions in their professional lives—on matters as diverse as corporations, wills, and divorce—to scrutinize a balance sheet, or indeed simply to draft or interpret a contract that invokes accounting concepts. A course dealing with the rudiments of accounting will provide a basic understanding, an ability to ask questions, an appreciation of the judgments and conventions that shape these documents, and an opportunity to overcome the fear of technical terminology.

(b) *Administrative Law.* Much of our law is made or enforced by administrative agencies, and it is important to understand their procedures and powers, and their relationship to the courts and to the legislature. These issues *may* be considered in a particular substantive course, for example, Labor Law or Environmental Law or Communications Law; in that event, a systematic course in Administrative Law would be less useful. But because many such substantive courses focus principally upon the rules of law in the particular field, it may be that the only opportunity to reflect on broader "institutional" issues will be found in the course generally named Administrative Law.

(c) *Regulated Industries (Antitrust or Business Regulation).* The interests of the consumer in securing goods and services of high quality and at a fair price may be protected either by assuring competition in the marketplace through the law of antitrust, or by imposing direct restrictions in noncompetitive industries (such as the public utility). Such forms of regulation are pervasive in our society and affect many clients that an attorney will represent (whether a producer or a consumer). A course that considers the relevant policy choices and statutory approaches can provide general insights for the student—and this is true even (or especially) in a period of government deregulation.

(d) It is strongly recommended that the student take a course which explores the major modern-day social and legal issue of inequality in the distribution of wealth and resources, or stated somewhat more simply, the law's response to the problems of the economically disadvantaged. The enlightened lawyer, simply as citizen, should be sensitized to these issues. Moreover, as a practitioner or as a counselor to social, political or governmental groups, the lawyer may be directly affected by (or may be influencial in shaping) such legal matters. Relevant courses can likely be found labeled Welfare Law, or Urban Legal Problems, or Race and Gender Discrimination or Poverty and the Law.

At first glance, it might appear as though almost all of the courses listed above as strongly recommended and as generally useful are concerned with the problems of the rich and powerful rather than those of the needy or oppressed. In my judgment, that is a false appearance. The laws dealing with business associations, commercial transactions, taxation, administrative law, wills, and the like are tools which must be mastered by lawyers serving persons from all segments of society. It may be, however, that the focus of the cases or problems studied in many of these courses is that of the wealthy, when a number of the same principles could be taught as well in the special context of the less privileged. The student can legitimately ask the instructor whether the course will include materials of the latter kind; instructors should be sensitized, if they are not already, to such student interest.

5. Students Should Seriously Consider Taking Courses That Give "Perspective" to the Study of Law, More Particularly Jurisprudence, Comparative Law, or Legal History.

Law students can become so preoccupied with mastering the rules of disparate substantive fields that they pay little attention to the overarching themes of law and legal development. To study these themes can give perspective to and insights in other courses, and— not an insignificant virtue—can provide a welcome respite from the conventional diet of judicial opinions and case analysis.

Jurisprudence courses generally invite a discussion of the objectives of governing society by law; they may also explore a wide range of emerging philosophical views about the role of judges, legal interpretation, and the like, issues of direct significance to the more "traditional" curriculum. Legal history can impart both an understanding of the interaction among law, society, and politics, and, more pragmatically, an understanding of many of the doctrines of our own modern law. The same is true of Comparative Law, which shows how common problems are addressed in other societies and thereby forces us to challenge many of our own fundamental assumptions. Another course that can be said to fall within this class of "perspective" courses is International Law, which invites us to think about the extent to which law—which domestically regulates the relationship between individuals or between individuals and the state—can be used to regulate the relations between sovereign states.

6. Be Aware of the Opportunities for Interdisciplinary Study.

More students are coming to law schools with an interest and proficiency in some other discipline; indeed, it is not unusual to find a number of your classmates with advanced degrees in the arts or sciences. At the same time, law schools have come to acknowledge the importance of examining law within the context of other academic disciplines. Research is being done across disciplinary lines, and courses in "Law and . . ." have sprouted with vigor, the most frequent conjunctives being economics, anthropology, psychiatry, sociology, and statistics. Courses that explore the contribution of economic analysis to legal topics are becoming particularly well represented in the curriculum; such courses have become increasingly important for purposes of understanding not only the proliferating law-and-economics scholarship in law journals and casebooks but also the increasingly evident examples of economic analysis in judicial opinions.

Interdisciplinary courses may be team-taught by a law-trained instructor and one trained exclusively in the other discipline, or alone by one or the other. A well-taught course of this kind can not only provide a change of pace in the law school routine but can also be most valuable to the student. It can provide tools for advanced work in various legal subjects, such as antitrust or government regulation, corporate finance, family law, or antidiscrimination law. Perhaps more important, it can break down the suspicion the lawyer may have of persons with a different training, perspective, or disciplinary language, and can demonstrate both the contributions and the limitations of interdisciplinary discourse.

A word of warning is in order, however. The student considering enrolling in such a course should ascertain whether it is essentially an intensive dose of the other discipline—which the student will be expected on his or her own to incorporate into other law school subjects—or is instead a course which directly considers the implications of the other discipline *for the law*. (If the course is taught exclusively by a nonlawyer, this should tip off the student that the course is likely to follow the former pattern.) The former kind of course—an introduction to the other discipline in isolation— may be appealing to some, but others may find it technical or "irrelevant"; yet others, who have studied that discipline previously, may find such a course duplicative and time-wasting.

Courses relating to the law can also usually be taken outside the law school. Most law schools permit cross-registration in other university departments, subject to limitations upon the amount of course credits that can be accumulated elsewhere and subject also quite frequently to a demonstration that the desired course bears some direct relevance to law study. Moreover, a substantial number of law schools have developed joint degree programs with departments of arts and sciences, the objectives being both to shorten the time necessary to earn the J.D. and the M.A. or Ph.D. degrees (by "cross-crediting" several courses) and also to encourage discourse between the two disciplines. The most desirable joint degree programs are those that truly meld the two disciplines, with courses jointly planned and jointly taught and with major written work jointly supervised. Some students, anticipating just such "jointness," have been disappointed with joint degree programs which do little more than "cut and paste" wholly independent courses in the law school with wholly independent courses elsewhere. But even in such situations, the imaginative and tenacious student may well be able, in his or her own individual program planning, successfully to integrate work in the two disciplines.

7. Take Courses That Train in, and Generalize About, Different Lawyering Skills. Well-Designed Clinical Courses Can Be of Great Educational Value.

At perhaps the other end of the pedagogical spectrum from the interdisciplinary and perspective courses are courses that focus upon sharpening the skills used by the lawyer in practice. A good part of law school—some people would argue too large a part—is devoted to case analysis, that is, the critical appraisal of appellate decisions and the reasoned extensions of judge-made rules to new hypothetical situations. Lawyers do such things during their professional life, and these analytical skills are undoubtedly useful in a broad range of lawyering endeavors. But lawyers also draft documents, plan transactions, gather facts, counsel, and otherwise deal with and relate to individual human beings. The second- and third-year student should make an effort to take courses that invite the use of such skills and that reflect upon their function in the lawyer's professional life.

It is, for example, most important for the student to learn how to discern the goals that a client has in mind—whether in the creation or operation of a business, the transmission of property in a will, or the preparation of legislation—and how to achieve these goals through creative planning and clear and effective language. Lawyers have to gather information from laymen, and convey it to them, while being both probing and sympathetic, concise and patient. Many graduates have been heard to comment upon the failure of their law school training to sensitize them to these kinds of professional activities. Although these skills will be sharpened in real-life situations after law school, it is perhaps only law school that will afford an opportunity to generalize from these situations and to consider, in converse with others, how these skills can be improved and what their impact will be upon the lawyer, the client, and the profession.

Many courses dealing with these issues "simulate" the lawyer-client situation through prepared case records or videotapes. Other "clinical" courses afford the student the opportunity to learn while actually serving real clients, just as would a licensed professional.

When properly administered, clinical courses can afford an invaluable learning experience. A student who deals with the real needs of real persons must translate the abstractions of the classroom into practical application; new skills are learned, new motivations develop, a fresh and hard-nosed perspective is brought with the student back into the classroom. The student will have to reflect on the lawyer-client relationship, and often to address difficult problems of professional ethics and responsibility.

The student is well advised to determine in advance the extent of close and thoughtful supervision that is available from the faculty or "field" supervisor. If the instructor leaves the student largely to his or her own devices, possibly doing work that soon becomes routine or repetitive, this will not provide a sound educational experience. The student should seek not simply exposure to "real-world" matters, which will come soon enough during summers and after graduation. Rather, the student should attempt to assure that his or her clinical work is done within a supervised and reflective framework, and that the work-study opportunities within the course or program are varied and of educational value.

8. Participation in a Seminar Is Often Valuable (and Sometimes Required).

Perhaps all that can be said with any confidence about seminars is that they are small. Most observers would agree that this is a virtue. Many law school classes are rather large and impersonal, and the seminar provides the welcome opportunity to meet one's instructor and classmates at close range, in a setting which brings together self-selected and interested students who tend to participate more actively in the less forbidding seminar setting. Beyond that, seminars come in all styles and shapes. Some are conducted very much as the usual Socratic case-based course. Some have the students preparing and exchanging papers for mutual evaluation and criticism. Some hardly meet at all, with the faculty member according what is in effect individual supervision to student paper-writers. Others may be centered around exercises in planning transactions and/or drafting documents. Some schools require that a seminar be taken, or that a lengthy paper be written (whether in or out of a formal seminar).

More generally, the student should be on the alert for supervised writing opportunities. Words are the lawyer's main tool and law school may be the last opportunity for sustained attention to matters of language, style, communication, and persuasiveness.

Although the seminar format has much going for it, it is doubtful that there is a consensus among upper-level students regarding the relative merits of seminars and large classes. But a well-taught seminar can be far more exciting than even the well-taught large class, in view of the motivation and sophistication of the students and the opportunities for extended and spirited exchanges across the seminar table. The primary determinants—apart from the students—are the quality of the teacher (some who are not highly regarded in the large class may be outstanding in a seminar setting) and the format of the seminar meetings.

9. A Third-Year Program of Specialization or Concentration Would Be Advisable for Most Law Students.

Most law schools offer a significant enough number of elective courses for second- and third-year students that a law student can graduate having taken a complete diet of introductory courses in various fields, but having done little or no "advanced" work in any one of them. Surely, a student who wishes to learn a little bit about a lot of things is not necessarily choosing courses unwisely. But many students would benefit from a more intensive concentration of effort in one or two substantive fields of law. Specialization or concentration permits the student to use most of the second year to develop a familiarity with basic principles in a number of substantive areas of the law, and to use most of the third year to create a different kind of course program, one that will be more challenging and will give a sense of progression in law study.

To do advanced work in a particular field means that the student will not simply learn more about the law of that field but, more important (because detailed learning is often quickly forgotten), the student will be able in a systematic way to examine related issues from several different perspectives—through the application of other disciplines, such as economics or psychology; through exercises in draftsmanship; through clinical activities servicing clients or working in government agencies; through legal history and law reform. The purpose of concentration of this kind is not so much training for a particular professional career in a single field but rather the development of a sophisticated capacity to address legal problems in depth, a capacity that is likely to be transferrable to other fields of law beyond the one focused upon in law school.

As an example, one might consider a program of advanced work in employment law. The student interested in this area, after taking the basic course on labor law in the second year, might find it possible in the third year to take some advanced substantive course, such as Employment Discrimination, Public Sector Labor Law, Rights of Non-Union Workers, or Labor Arbitration; a course or seminar that would explore problems of negotiating and drafting (for example, a course dealing with the collective bargaining agreement); a course in the economics or history department of the university dealing with labor economics or labor history; and a clinical placement with a labor union or with a local office of some government agency regulating labor relations. As another example, a student could, after taking the basic course in federal income taxation, take advanced courses in taxation of corporations and in business planning; take advanced courses within or without the law school in such areas as finance, accounting, or economics; or participate in a study dealing with the reform of the tax laws, which would call into play some principles of economics and some skill in legislative drafting.

Realism demands an acknowledgment that not many law schools offer such a richly varied curriculum, at least in a substantial number of substantive fields of law. Even so, students should be aware of the attractions of such specialized programs and should be encouraged to scrutinize their course catalogs—both inside and outside the law school—to see what opportunities of this kind are present. Many law schools do in fact offer a sufficient number of elective courses such that one can find several courses "clustering" around a common subject matter. Although a perfunctory examination of a course catalog will likely indicate what advanced courses cluster about a single general subject, that will be done here for the reader's convenience. (You should be warned, however, that course titles are merely labels that are not always fully descriptive of the contents; what one gets out of the course may depend far more upon the teacher than upon the syllabus. The course labels that follow are meant simply to be suggestive of a range of subject matter commonly taught thereunder.)

Administration of Justice: Evidence; Criminal Procedure; Administrative Law; Constitutional Law; Federal Courts; Conflict of Laws; Trial Practice; Remedies.

Commercial Law; Accounting: Sales or Secured Transactions; Creditors' Rights; Bankruptcy; Negotiable Instruments; Antitrust or Regulated Industries; International Business Transactions.

Constitutional Law: Civil and Political Rights; Race and/or Gender Discrimination; Federal Courts; Prisoners' Rights; Rights of Juveniles; Criminal Procedure; Education Law; Poverty Law.

Corporate Law: Accounting; Corporate Finance; Securities Regulation; Corporate Reorganization; Business Planning; Taxation of Corporations; Bankruptcy; Antitrust or Regulated Industries; Multinational Corporations.

Criminal Law: Constitutional Law; Criminal Procedure; Evidence; Prisoners' Rights; Rights of Juveniles; Law & Psychiatry; Criminology.

Employment Law: Labor Law; Workers' Rights; Labor Arbitration; Public Sector Labor Law; Equal Employment Opportunity (Employment Discrimination); Internal Union Affairs; Collective Bargaining.

International Law: Public International Law; International Organizations; International Trade or Business Transactions; Multinational Corporations; Foreign Relations Law; courses in comparative law.

Public Law: Constitutional Law; Administrative Law; Education Law; Environmental Law; State and Local Government (Municipal Law); Labor Law; Antitrust or Government Regulation; Patent, Trademark and/or Copyright; Consumer Protection; Food and Drug Law; Communications Law; Transportation Law; Poverty Law; Family Law; Health Law. (Most of those courses also fall within a somewhat narrower category which might be labeled "Urban Problems.")

Real Estate: Land Use; Estates in Land; Zoning; Real Estate Transactions; Landlord-Tenant Law; Real Estate Financing; Environmental Law.

Taxation: Taxation of Individuals; Corporate Taxation; Corporate Finance; Business Planning; Estate and Gift Taxation; Estate Planning; State and Local Taxation; Accounting; Tax Policy and Public Finance.

Wealth Transmission: Trusts and Estates; Wills; Estate and Gift Taxation; Fiduciary (Trust) Administration; Estate Planning.

10. Select the Best Teachers and the Best "Minds."

Every law school has one or a number of particularly gifted teachers. A thoughtful and stimulating teacher can make it exciting to learn about the complexities of subject matter that the student might think in advance will be dreadfully dull. An outstanding teacher can convey a great deal about the law and about lawyering regardless of the course; he or she can give insights into how to read cases, how to draft and read documents or legislation, how to deal candidly and effectively with questions or with stress, how to resolve complex personal or transactional dilemmas, how to explore challenging policy questions, and how to approach problems of professional responsibility. The student would be well advised, in planning a course program, to select the gifted teacher in addition to selecting the interesting subject matter. The same injunction applies to the choice of a teacher who—regardless of pedagogical skills—possesses a deep and probing mind, or is *the* authority or a recognized innovator in a field of legal study. That kind of mind is worth seeing in action, as a stimulus and as an exemplar. The student can easily learn, by word of mouth or through student questionnaires and published evaluations, who are the stimulating teachers and rewarding minds. This suggestion is perhaps as important as any that has been set forth above. A faculty member who gets high marks on qualities such as "made me think hard" or "pushed the students for deeper reflection"—even if that teacher is not terribly popular—is likely to impart training and ideas that will have a lasting impact.

11. Enjoy!

This injunction, reserved for last, is probably the most important. Training for the practice of law can, if the student lets it, become a grim enterprise—but it surely need not be. It is true that much is at stake in your law school performance, for it starts you on the way to a professional career. But it is also the last time most lawyers will have the opportunity to go to school, to select courses and teachers of interest, to view law in a larger context, to work on problems in a reflective atmosphere, free of the time constraints imposed by client needs or economic considerations. After law school, most of your intellectual direction will be beyond your control. The message should be clear: Consider not merely the courses you think you *need* but the courses and teachers you think you would enjoy. Law school can provide a "liberal arts" education even though the law may be a somewhat more confined "art" than was studied as an undergraduate. Admiralty may give the scent of the sea; Copyright will touch upon the creative and performing arts; Jurisprudence invokes philosophy and Comparative Law history and sociology; Trial Practice can give the pleasures and disappointments of courtroom combat; Conflict of Laws can cut across all subject matter and across state lines in intricate and lively fact situations. There may be few enough opportunities in later life to partake of the "romance" of the law, and the opportunities in law school should therefore not be overlooked.

CHAPTER 18

Legal Ethics

Geoffrey C. Hazard, Jr.
YALE UNIVERSITY

Legal ethics is, or should be, a subject of intense concern and careful examination in law school and afterward. Unfortunately the subject sometimes is not given very deep attention in law school, and tends to disappear from consciousness after graduation until perhaps an ethical crisis suddenly looms. Ethics—deciding what one should do in a morally difficult situation—should be "practiced" in hypothetical terms while in law school and thereafter, so that one is intellectually and psychologically ready when a crisis arises, as inevitably it will.

Legal ethics can be considered from two perspectives. The first is the set of legal rules that governs a lawyer's conduct. These rules are in form and substance like any other body of law, such as the traffic law or corporation law, in that they prescribe legal rights, powers, and duties in the performance of a lawyer's professional functions. The legal profession can be regarded as a regulated "industry" in which these rules are the governing regulations.

The second perspective is the lawyer's own subjective assessment of his or her conduct in practicing law. From this view point the legal rules and their interpretation and enforcement are only part of the relevant reality. Another part is the lawyer's personal set of values and personal knowledge of what is going on. These personal values and perceptions may be at odds with the legal rules and the "objective" facts, and the discrepancy can be a source of great personal distress, and sometimes serious professional and legal risk. Part of legal education is becoming aware of, and learning to cope with, this conflict of values.

Sources of the Law of Professional Responsibility

The legal rules governing the practice of law are generally known as the law of professional responsibility. This body of law has two main sources. One is the common law—accumulated decisional law—governing the lawyer's relationship with the client, with the courts, and with third persons. Under the common law a lawyer is a special kind of agent who acts for a client, the principal. As agent, the lawyer has the authority to act for the client within the scope of the representation and has a fiduciary duty to protect the client's interests within that sphere. The lawyer, as officer of the court, has authority in matters of trial technique and tactics to decide how the representation should be carried out; and has similar implied authority as to means of representation in out-of-court matters, such as negotiation. Subject to these qualifications, however, the lawyer is obliged to defer to the client's choice of objectives; for example, whether to settle rather than going to trial and whether to accept terms of a contract proposed by an opposite negotiating party.

A special common law evidentiary rule protects the client-lawyer relationship. This is the attorney-client privilege, according to which information communicated by the client to the attorney in furtherance of obtaining legal advice and assistance is protected from disclosure in court. In recent years this privilege has been augmented by the attorney's work-product privilege, which similarly protects information developed by the attorney from sources other than the client. A corollary duty is that the lawyer must maintain confidentiality of information about the client.

The lawyer has other common law obligations to the client. The lawyer is required to use reasonable care in carrying out the representation and is prohibited from using his or her position to the disadvantage of the client. For example, a lawyer may not engage in a business transaction with the client unless the transaction is fair to the client when considered from an independent viewpoint. Common law also obliges a lawyer to refrain from assisting a client in committing a legal wrong against a third party. A lawyer who, for example, assists a client in effectuating a fraud can be held civilly liable as a co-tortfeasor. If the conduct is also a crime, the lawyer can be criminally liable.

Also as a matter of common law, a lawyer has obligations to the court in connection with representation of a client. Lawyers are required to be truthful in representations made to the court on the basis of their own knowledge. The advocate has a further duty to refrain from committing fraud on the court, particularly to refrain from offering evidence the lawyer knows to be false.

Alongside this body of common law are rules of professional responsibility in the form of legislation. Originally, these rules were admonitory ethical precepts rather than legal obligations. The precepts were promulgated as such by the bar, notably the Canons of Legal Ethics of the American Bar Association, issued in 1908. The precepts covered much of the same ground as the common law, but also contained some loftier prescriptions. Thus, Canon 15 stated, "the office of attorney does not permit, much less does it demand of him for any client, violation of law or any manner of fraud or chicane. He must obey his own conscience and not that of his client." The Canons were considered guidelines, but were often relied on by courts and professional disciplinary authorities as definitive by the ABA Code of Professional Responsibility, which was subsequently adopted in most of the states, sometimes with significant amendment.

The Code of Professional Responsibility has three levels of norms. The first are very general propositions, called Canons. Illustrative are Canon 4, which provides that "A lawyer should preserve the confidences and secrets of a client," and Canon 7, which provides that "A lawyer should represent a client zealously within the bounds of the law." The second level of norms is called Ethical Considerations. Some of these are descriptive or explanatory, but others are in obligatory form. For example, Ethical Consideration 6-6 states that "A lawyer should not seek, by contract or other means, to limit his individual liability to his client." The third norm level in the Code are the Disciplinary Rules, often referred to as the "black letter" rules. These are in the form of legislative prohibitions and are intended to be binding as such. For example DR 5-101(A) provides that:

> Except with the consent of his client after full disclosure, a lawyer shall not accept employment if the exercise of his professional judgment on behalf of his client will be or reasonably may be affected by his own financial, business, property, or personal interest.

Because the Code was adopted in almost all jurisdictions, and because it contains obligatory Disciplinary Rules, the Code has had the force of law. The relationship between the Code and the common law, in defining a lawyer's professional obligations, is an intricate question. The Disciplinary Rules clearly constitute obligations that may be enforced by the mechanism of professional discipline, including the procedure of investigation and trial for violation, with the potential sanctions of reprimand, suspension, and disbarment. In considering matters of professional discipline, however, the courts have often drawn on the preexisting common law to deal with matters omitted from the Code. For example, the Code does not explicitly prohibit acting contrary to the interests of a former client, but the courts have applied such a rule where the lawyer represents a second client in the same matter. On the other hand, the Code undertakes to confine its operation to disciplinary liability and thereby to be inoperative in matters of professional malpractice. Notwithstanding this attempted self-limitation, the Code has been used by the courts as a basis for determining whether civil liability arises. For example, DR 5-101(A), concerning a conflict of interest, has been treated as defining the lawyer's common law duty of loyalty to a client, the violation of which gives rise to malpractice liability.

The Code regulates not only a lawyer's professional functions but also other aspects of the practice of law. Thus, as originally promulgated, the Code virtually prohibited advertising and also prohibited most forms of professional association between a lawyer and anyone not a lawyer. The rules on advertising have now largely been abrogated by Supreme Court decisions, but the prohibitions on professional association still stand. The Code also establishes auxiliary duties, such as the obligation to report violations of the Code and to cooperate in investigations concerning such violations.

In 1983, the American Bar Association adopted a revised set of professional rules, called the Model Rules of Professional Conduct. The Model Rules, like the Code, have no direct legal force of their own. However, they have been adopted in about half the states as a replacement for the Code of Professional Responsibility. When so adopted in a state, the Rules are legally binding on the lawyers in that state. Several factors sustained the revision.

Primarily the three-level system of the Code proved very confusing, for courts and disciplinary authorities often invoked the Canons or the Ethical Considerations as rules on an equal footing with the Disciplinary Rules. In addition, the Code was legally obsolete on the subject of advertising and silent on such matters as the relative obligations of lawyers in a firm when the firm confronts an ethical problem. The deliberations over the Model Rules generated a great deal of controversy, within and without the legal profession. The Rules still leave some key problems unresolved, particularly a lawyer's duty upon discovering that a client is engaged in fraud. However, the debate has impelled the profession to make serious analysis of its ethical obligations to an extent never previously experienced.

The Central Ethical Problems

Although the law of professional responsibility engages diverse subjects, the central problems are relatively few, if exquisitely difficult. These are the problems of competence; of confidentiality, particularly where the client is engaged in legally wrongful conduct; of conflict of interest in representation of multiple clients; and of responsibility on the part of client and lawyer where the client is an organization and where the legal service is rendered by a firm.

The rule regarding competence is easily stated, but its application is a matter of nearly infinite variation. The rule, as stated in the Code, DR 6-101(A), is that "A lawyer shall not handle a legal matter which he knows or should know that he is not competent to handle, without associating with him a lawyer who is competent to handle it." The counterpart common law rule is that lawyers must use reasonable care and competence in performing their services, the standard being the care and competence of reasonably competent practitioners under similar circumstances. Obviously the definition is verbally circular and has meaning only by empirical reference to going practice. But going practice covers a wide range, not only between general practitioners and specialists, between seasoned lawyers and those newly admitted, between firms of various types, but also between individual lawyers and firms that outwardly resemble each other. Thus, although the rule sounds as though there is a uniform standard of competence, in fact there are great variations.

Compliance with the rule of competence is very difficult to define at the boundary. The legal sanctions against incompetence consequently are weak, although competition for clientele induces lawyers to take on matters that should be referred to others. The result is pervasive marginal competence of low visibility, a chronic problem of practice in law, as in other professions. Marginal technical competence also affects lawyers' responsiveness to other ethical obligations. Misrepresentations by lawyers to their clients, for example, often are attempts to cover or rationalize blunders; many instances of conflict of interest arise because the lawyer has not anticipated the intersection of multiple representations. In any case, a key ethical question for lawyers is whether they have the skill required to handle the matters they are in fact handling. This question obviously can be very difficult for lawyers newly admitted to practice, because they lack experience in assessing the relative complexity of a matter.

The rule of confidentiality is fundamental to the lawyer's function. Clients confide matters that could be embarrassing, damaging, or even fatal; they properly expect that their confidences will be protected not only against deliberate exploitation but also against careless leak. As a general principle, a lawyer should not discuss a client's affairs with anyone, except in the course of the representation and for the purposes of fulfilling the client's purposes. As stated in Model Rule 1.6, with limited exceptions, "A lawyer shall not reveal information relating to representation of a client unless the client consents after consultation, except for disclosures that are impliedly authorized in order to carry out the representation." This principle of confidentiality is supported by the attorney-client privilege, which prohibits courts or other official agencies from interrogating a lawyer about client confidences. The supporting rationale of the principle of confidentiality is twofold. First, with regard to prospective transactions, confidentiality promotes full disclosure, which in turn provides opportunity for the lawyer to guide the transaction within the bounds of the law.

Second, with regard to litigation, confidentiality permits preparation for trial without the risk of giving away the case.

The rule of confidentiality, however, has narrow but crucial exceptions. Essentially these exceptions aim to prevent a client from exploiting the lawyer, and thereby the system of legal representation, in order to further criminal or fraudulent purposes. In general terms the "crime-fraud" exceptions have been recognized virtually since the establishment of the confidentiality rule itself. The interminably controversial question is exactly how to define the scope of the exceptions. The present Code permits a lawyer to disclose client confidence where necessary to prevent crime; for example, in calling the police where the client is setting out upon murder or assault. The Code provisions concerning prevention of fraud, however, are quite ambiguous. Literally, the provisions in most states require that a lawyer prevent a client's consummation of fraud, yet in a few states the rule can be interpreted to prohibit a lawyer from making such a disclosure. Most lawyers probably understand the rule to mean that they have the discretion, but not a duty, to prevent fraud by a client, and such is the effect of the provisions of the Model Rules of Professional Conduct. In any event, a lawyer may have strong incentive to prevent a client from carrying out a fraud in which the lawyer's services have been involved. In such a situation, even if the lawyer had no knowledge that the transaction was fraudulent, there is a chance that he or she may be accused of complicity, and perhaps found civilly or criminally responsible.

A related problem is the question of client perjury in litigation. A lawyer may not assist a client in devising false evidence. But what if the client nevertheless intentionally lies in giving testimony? The issue has been bitterly debated in recent years. Some have argued that the duty of loyalty and confidentiality precludes the lawyer from revealing his client's perjury. The argument has much force, especially in a criminal case, where it can be said that the defendant's legal obligation to tell the truth is merely formal. However, the common law and the old Canons pretty clearly gave precedence to the lawyer's duty to the court, requiring that if the client in a civil or criminal case refused to recant the perjury, then the lawyer must advise the tribunal that false evidence had been submitted. The present Code is somewhat ambiguous but is most accurately read as affirming that requirement. Model Rule 3.3, adopted after much controversy, is in accord, as is a leading decision by the Supreme court of the United States, *Nix v. Whiteside*. Needless to say, carrying out that duty is perhaps the most onerous responsibility a lawyer can have.

The principle of loyalty to client implies that a lawyer may not pursue commitments that are at a variance with a client's interest. The prohibition on conflicts of interest applies, first of all, to relationships between the lawyer and client. In addition to the general rule of fair dealing with a client, referred to earlier, several specifications have evolved for the client's protection. Some of these are advisory under the Code, but under the Model Rules they are obligatory. Thus the Model Rules require that the fee arrangement preferably be in writing; they prohibit lawyers from making themselves the beneficiary of a will they have drafted; they require disclosure to the client where the lawyer's fee is being paid by a third person; and so on.

Conflict-of-interest rules also govern the circumstances under which a lawyer may represent two or more clients in the same matter, or represent clients successively. The general principle is that a lawyer may not undertake representation that will be directly adverse to an existing client unless that client consents after disclosure. Furthermore, a lawyer who has represented one client in a matter may not later represent another client in the same matter, if the interests of the two clients are adverse and if they have not consented to the representation. Related rules govern situations where a lawyer moves from one firm to another, or between private practice and government service.

Although the general principles regarding conflict of interest are clear enough, in practice there are infinite variations where application of the principles often involves close calls. So far as possible, a lawyer is safest in proceeding on the proposition that if a client believes there is a conflict, then there is a conflict. Compliance with conflict of interest requirements in a busy practice requires constant vigilance and readiness to consult the affected clients when conflict situations arise.

Traditionally the rules of ethics visualized the situation of an individual lawyer giving advice and assistance to an individual client. In modern practice, however, most lawyers practice in groups—firms, law departments of corporations, government agencies, and so on—and most legal service, measured in dollar value if not in the number of separate client-lawyer relationships, is rendered to business, government, and nonprofit organizations. On both sides of the modern client-lawyer relationship, therefore, there is a group exercising collective authority and responsibility. Neither the Canons nor the Code of Professional Responsibility addressed the problems arising from this circumstance, although common law decisions had engaged a few aspects of it. The Model Rules formulate rules in very general terms, looking to future evolution.

As for a law firm or law department, the Model Rules require its partners or managers to establish systems for achieving conformity to ethical requirements and require a lawyer with direct supervisory responsibility to take action when a violation can be corrected. There is a similar responsibility for the work of the paralegal staff. Correlatively, a junior lawyer is entitled to rely on a "supervisory lawyer's reasonable resolution of an arguable question of professional duty." In effect, these rules give limited effect to the hierarchical order of a firm or legal department. Whatever the rules, however, very difficult questions of responsibility obviously can arise whenever knowledge and opportunity to act are diffused among a group of people, as they are in a firm or law department.

For the organizational client, such as a business corporation, the Model Rules recognize correlative problems presented by its hierarchical structure of authority. They provide that the lawyer must consider whether to "go over the head" of the employee or officer with whom the lawyer usually deals where a proposed course of action poses a substantial legal risk to the organization. As Irangate reminds us, such an upward referral can involve serious controversy within the client organization and between the members of its staff and its lawyers. Yet there is no escaping the possibility of conflict over the handling of risky legal situations, just as there is no such escape in a lawyer's representation of individual clients. Some framework for dealing with the problem is therefore necessary, and that is as far as the Model Rules go.

A Lawyer's Personal Value

From the foregoing analysis it should be evident that understanding and application of the legal rules of ethics involve an important element of personal judgment as to right and wrong, and as to what is really going on in the transactions that a lawyer handles. Not all ethical problems fall in gray areas, to be sure, and much of law practice involves only a remote possibility of encountering serious ethical dilemmas. Yet the rules, even those that are relatively specific, are uncertain at the margin, and in some areas confer on the lawyer a substantial range of professional discretion. Thus a lawyer is free to decline proffered representation, except when appointed to representation by a court or practically compelled by the force of client expectation; having undertaken a representation, a lawyer has considerable discretion in how it shall be carried out. In short, although a lawyer is formally an agent or instrument—a "mouthpiece," as it is impolitely put—in fact a lawyer has a good deal of moral autonomy, certainly in how he or she goes about accomplishing professional tasks.

The lawyer's tasks, however, are often morally ambiguous or even repugnant. Thus, although it is deeply satisfying to achieve acquittal of an innocent client, the satisfactions are remote and diminished when the lawyer knows the client is guilty. (Many lawyers escape this moral burden by asserting that they never know whether their client is right or wrong, a willful cognitive dissonance that is implausible but understandable.) In less dramatic terms, a lawyer necessarily handles many grubby matters for greedy clients, absorbing in the process deep understanding if not great admiration of the typical limits of human virtue. Despite these ethical difficulties, however, the moral satisfactions of practicing law can be great. It takes some kind of personal moral philosophy to perform the lawyer's function over time, and every lawyer has one whether he or she is aware of it or not. For the law student the task of developing such a philosophy can start at once.

CHAPTER 19

Clinical Studies in Law

Gary Bellow
HARVARD UNIVERSITY

Clinical programs, in a variety of institutional forms, exist today in over 80 percent of America's law schools. In some, law schools run their own clinics, with students handling cases (usually for indigent clients) and taking related courses or seminars. In others, students receive credit for their involvement in specialized projects supervised by faculty members, are "farmed out" for clinical work in local agencies and institutions, or participate in elaborate simulations of practice experience.[1] Whatever the form, clinical programs have brought major changes in legal education in the past fifteen years.[2]

They have also brought a great deal of controversy. In virtually every school, whether clinical programs are offered or not, there has been heated debate about the nature, cost, and goals of clinical instruction and the role of practice-related activities in law study. What follows is a brief description of the issues and insights that this controversy has generated.

I. The Structural Roots of the Debate:
The Bifurcated Nature of a Lawyer's Education

Since its beginnings, the American law school has never purported to produce graduates competent to practice law. Legal education has always been seen as *part* of a process of professional training.

Law schools introduce future members of the bar to basic concepts and doctrines in a variety of substantive fields, the rudimentary skills needed for legal research and case analysis, and the operative norms and values of legal professionalism. Knowledge of the day-to-day workings of the legal system, elaboration of the ideas and practices dominant in particular legal fields, and development of the skills needed to actually serve clients[3] are left to the practicing profession. In large firms this involves some form of tutelage from partners and associates, the incremental introduction of responsibility for cases, and a good deal of imitation, trial and error, and self-instruction. In smaller firms, or among single practitioners, reliance on self-teaching is more central, although, particularly in small communities, it is supplemented by guidance from more experienced attorneys, judges, and colleagues going through a similar learning process. Over time (estimated at somewhere between six to eight years) this process is expected to change the neophyte law graduate into the pragmatic, competent professional.

Whether it does or not, there is no doubt about the general support this allocation of educational responsibility in law enjoys in both the academy and the bar. This may be, as Dan Lortie has argued, the consequence of the increased status and income (relative to their parents) of most lawyers and the socializing effects of learning "on the job."[4] Few people who feel relatively successful challenge the only route to that success that they've known.

More likely, however, the existing educational system in law enjoys much of its support because of the benefits it confers on those with power in the profession to change it. Affiliation with higher education has, for a century, limited access to law study to the more upwardly mobile (and often least rebellious) members of the population, while enhancing the profession's claims that law study and practice are relatively apolitical activities properly controlled by the profession itself. These have long been considered desirable goals by the elite segments of the profession,[5] and, when stated in somewhat different form, by most law teachers. When one reflects on the close fit between the skills and knowledge emphasized in law school and the entry-level job in the larger corporate firm, the stated preference of many such firms for molding their future partners, the enormous financial success of the law school as an institution, the status and discretionary time available under the existing system to law professors, and the rule-making and rule-reforming roles to which this time is put (with the eager approval of the judiciary), it is not hard to understand the considerable staying power of the status quo in legal education.

What is less clear is whether—looked at from the perspective of the profession and public as a whole—the status quo can be justified. As many clinicians have pointed out, it is very doubtful that the public is well served by a system that leaves so much of a lawyer's education to chance. It is, of course, true that all lawyers learn to practice from practice. What is not true is that what they learn will be uniform or necessarily consistent with what one would consider even minimally adequate professional practice. The bulk of law graduates do not get jobs with institutions or firms which have the time, resources, talent, or inclination to develop systematically their knowledge and skills. In most instances, the new lawyer is simply introduced to the "way we do things here" and is expected to act accordingly. If the "way we do things here" incorporates high standards, systematic consideration of alternatives, adequate models, and appropriate ethical norms, the young lawyer may well learn what is worth learning. If the opposite is the case, the young lawyer will learn the opposite. In either case, the judgments and actions involved will be too complex, and too easy to explain away[6] to depend very much on the client to monitor performance. The client, like the law school, will have to hope for the best.

It is equally doubtful that such a sharp separation of law-on-the-books from law-in-practice makes sense, even in terms of the well-accepted research and scholarly goals of most legal educators. The bifurcation of legal education means that, in general, law schools are filled with teachers who know very little about the day-to-day operation of the legal system or whose knowledge is anecdotal or highly personal at best. There is no tradition in legal education of systematic empirical research into the way law and lawyers actually function, and no patterns of regular involvement by legal academics either with practitioners or legal institutions. This explains, I believe, why so much discussion of legal doctrine and policy in the law school classroom ignores the mediating and sometimes nullifying effects of their real-world application, why so little attention is paid to the effects of class and race on the ordinary person's experience of the legal system, and why there is so little reference to the realities of lawyer behavior and decision making in law school discourse.

The "professional" law schools' graduates often leave their schooling with assumptions about and descriptions of the law world that, from my own observations, seem grossly incomplete or simply wrong. The "research" law schools conduct parse doctrine, policy and (more recently) their philosophical underpinnings on the basis of models that bear far too little resemblance to the realities on which they build. The introduction into law study of empirical work in the last twenty years from economics, political analysis, and sociology is surely salutary. But very little of this focuses directly on legal insititutions and legal culture. These remain essentially unexamined by what appears to be a modern variant of scholasticism. Without overstating the virtues of empirical inquiry, it is hard to justify so little of it in an academic institution.

Finally, there is the question of the impact of this approach on the quality and character of the profession itself. If law graduates, in fact, learn to practice on the job, with few opportunities for critical reflection on what and how they are learning, and if their law school experience offers them very little help in sorting through the value choices, moral implications, and alternative possibilities necessarily implicated in doing the "law job,"[7] from where will the impetus for change, or, at least, self-criticism and evaluation within the profession come? One would assume that the most desirable relationship between a practicing profession and its academic institutions would involve a good deal of tension and interdependence, the practitioners providing insight and information from their experience, the academicians providing overview and critique, and both committed to a dialogue designed to enhance each other's capacity to change and learn. The isolation of law teacher and lawyer from each other avoids the conflict and the potential growth offered by such interchanges. Combined with an often uncritical pragmatism that pervades legal culture, the separation of law study from law practice may make both legal education and professional activity much less reflective, informed, and self-critical than it might otherwise be. It may also account for some of the moral obtuseness displayed by so many members of the Bar. Moral sensibility is obviously not simply a function of character or knowledge. It is nurtured and developed by constantly examining and publicly justifying the consequences of one's choices. There is little in the current structure of legal education that encourages such an examination.

II. Rethinking the Law School's Role: The Clinician's Perspective

Most clinicians—the men and women in law teaching who identify themselves as clinical teachers—would, I believe, concur with the substance (if not the formulation) of the foregoing critique.[8] Clinicians generally offer the following alternate propositions about the goals and methods of legal education:

1. Legal scholarship and teaching should be much more concerned than it now is with the actual functioning of the legal system and its institutions, particularly the institution of counsel as a law-making, law-enforcing, law-nullifying activity.

2. Such concern should embody a wide range of perspectives and emphases, encouraging attempts to integrate the normative and descriptive, the concrete and the abstract, the reflective and the action-oriented. There should be no sharp distinction between theory and practice in law study. The interplay of choice, action, and generalization in learning should be the primary focal point for gaining an understanding of legal phenomena.

3. Lawyer skills should be approached in the same way, reflecting concerns for developing perfomance competency as well as fostering an understanding of the social relationships and dynamics involved. This approach would include in the curriculum a careful examination of lawyer's relationships with clients, adversaries, and decision makers, and systematic efforts to develop students' interviewing, investigating, research, case analysis, negotiating, and advocacy skills. It also would mean making learning skills themselves—particularly those capacities that enable us to influence and be influenced by others—a central concern of the educational enterprise.

4. Whatever pedagogical approaches are brought to the above

tasks, primary emphasis should be on experienced-based instruction and inquiry. A student functioning in a real-life role (whether in an actual or simulated setting) in which understandings must be used, and insights applied, knows more, learns more, integrates more than a student simply presented with materials and ideas, whether the subject is legal policy and doctrine, lawyering skills, or institutional analysis.[9] Moreover, scholarly understanding of law, lawyers, and the learning process itself is enormously enhanced by drawing on the insights and experiences of students functioning as participant-observers of legal culture. Such a reorientation of teaching methodology would, in no sense, eliminate the central role given to the study of authoritative texts and the extensive secondary literature of the law. But it would—in a curriculum sequenced and structured very differently than the present system—place such study in a considerably altered light.

5. None of the foregoing changes should be accomplished simply by adding an additional "clinical" course to the curriculum in the same way new doctrinally-based subject matters have been added over the years. Nor should "skills training" be introduced into some supplemental program within the second and third year. The perspectives involved in reconnecting law study to practice require far more integration, coordination, and cooperation among faculty and courses than exist in the present system.

6. Finally, all of the above should be informed by what I'll call a moral vision—a normative concern for the fairness, accessibility, and justness of the legal system and its influence on the social order of which it is a part. Notwithstanding the many variations (and conflicts) which such an orientation entails, law and lawyering should not be seen as a neutral, apolitical phenomenon standing above and outside of social conflict. Rather, legal doctrines and institutions should be understood as both expressing and influencing the character of such conflict. Indeed, the posture of the neutrality of lawyer (or judicial) behavior is itself a political position, with causes and consequences. Given this reality, part of the role of all law study and teaching, including clinical studies, is and should be transformative, giving content at every point in time to particular values and visions of social order. What is needed in legal education is not denial of this premise, but a mix of orienta-

tions, capable of giving law training content and direction, while encouraging critique and change.

I realize, of course, that it goes very far to posit agreement among clinicians with so many debatable propositions. But, clinical programs throughout the country reflect variations of and concrete experiments with each of these themes.

Moreover, stating these ideas in this way may illuminate for the reader the depth of the debate over the expansion of clinical study in law and the impact of this controversy on actual programs. Fully embracing the perspectives set out above would require changing the sequence and content of many, many law school courses, enormously increasing the ratio of teachers (whatever their titles) to students, enhancing the access of practitioners to law teaching and, perhaps most important, radically altering the independence and work life of many members of the faculty.[10] There would be many costs, personal and financial. Few law schools have thus far felt the benefits would be worth the price.

III. The Uneasy Present:
Clinical Education in Transition

There are many legitimate questions about clinical pedagogies and aspirations that would have to be satisfactorily answered before changes of the sort discussed here ought to be adopted.[11] However, what is important for a reader trying to understand the law school environment is not the arguments for and against clinical instruction in law but the fact that these arguments go on unresolved.

Responding to the offer of outside seed money from the Ford Foundation and the pressures of student demand for curricular innovation and change, many law schools, in the late sixties and early seventies, added clinical courses and experiences to their course offerings, bringing young men and women, largely from legal service practice into law teaching to develop and implement the programs. Few schools made long-term commitments to this new methodology or to the people hired to teach it, and very rarely did existing faculty undertake responsibilities in the clinical area. The result was a series of mixed signals on the continuation, status, and content of the programs. With the expansion of clinical opportunities in the last decade student interest and satisfaction with clinical experiences rapidly increased, as did the numbers signing up for clinical courses. But at the same time, outside financial support decreased, and hoped-for substitutes (particularly federal legal services funds) did not materialize,[12] and a dollar for dollar substitution of law school funds for outside financial support has been widely resisted by most faculties deeply skeptical of the trade-offs involved. The consequence of these conflicting pressures has been a pattern of changes in programs that shape the character and direction of clinical studies today.

First, the ratio of supervisors and instructors to students is slowly being diluted or redefined to permit larger numbers of students to get credit for clinical work at the same cost. In schools with clinics, lawyer and nonlawyer staff are today often too few in number to handle both client and supervising responsibilities; or, in some instances, caseloads are so restricted that a good deal of the program's potential for teaching students about the workings of the legal system, particularly about "street level" institutions administering law on a day-to-day basis to large numbers of people, is lost. In schools that use outside agencies for supervision of students in fieldwork courses a similar pattern is emerging. Numbers of students have increased without a corresponding increase in the resources devoted to recruiting, training, or compensating supervisory staff. The negative impact of these developments on the quality and intensity of students' clinical experience seems only a matter of time.

Second, there has been a disproportionate increase in the substitution of simulated for fieldwork experience. There is certainly a legitimate issue of cost containment here. Simulation is a relatively cost-effective way to introduce students to the basics of a variety of lawyering tasks and skills, and more elaborate simulations can open up discussion on important questions about institutional and interpersonal relationships in law. It is hard, however, to view simulation as an adequate substitute for the sort of experience and critical discourse that many clinicians wish to generate within the law school. It is also hard to believe that the enormous interest in it is unaffected by its relative low cost and the fact that it can be used entirely within a classroom.

Even used thoughtfully, simulation tends, in my view, to over-simplify the psychological and interpersonal dimensions of lawyer work and to screen out important aspects of the impact of race, gender, and class on the functioning of law and lawyers. Used uncritically, it again heralds skill and craft as the solution to many of the value conflicts lawyers confront and to present idealized versions of the sort of relationships in which law is inevitably embedded. If clinical education is to be a source of new insights into the actual workings of the legal system and a constant re-minder to law students of the need to see the law in operation "from below" as well as "from above," a good deal of actual client contact and real-world exposure is indispensable.

Third, pressures have mounted on clinicians to devote time and energy to more "acceptable" scholarly efforts. These pressures are often inconsistent with the work styles and time demands faced by clinical teachers and are unlikely to tap the academic potential of the field.[13] They have not only deterred new entrants into clinical teaching but have embroiled clinicians in a complex debate over the nuances of status, security, and responsibility in law teaching, which drains energy and attention from the programs themselves. In the absence of a forthright approach to the problems of cost in clinical teaching, whether psychological or financial, the problem of the status and security of clinical teachers, and its impact on their morale and commitment to clinical studies, can only worsen.

Finally, it seems to me that the pressures of cost and continua-tion have begun to diminish some of the critical and experimental tone of many of the early efforts in clinical studies. Courses have become somewhat more routinized, the teaching more patterned, and the willingness to experiment with varying forms of group interaction among students more limited. Similarly the breadth of discussion, both among clinicians and with students, at least as measured by the degree to which these discussions come to grips with the more controversial aspects of the personal and political in lawyer work, seems to have abated somewhat.

All of this may simply reflect a realistic appraisal of what is possible and desirable in clinical teaching, or only a breathing space in the furious amount of innovation in courses and techniques in the early years of the programs. But it also may be that the problems of resources and acceptance conspire here to narrow the risk-taking that this approach to legal education requires. It will be hard to know until and unless these constraints are modified.

IV. Some Concluding Observations

Nothing here should be taken to describe specific programs in particular schools. I have attempted to identify general trends and their relationship to the background debate that, to some degree, affect all clinical programs and courses in law schools today. There are enough exceptions, both within schools and between schools, to counsel considerable caution in taking these general observations too far.

Nor should my focus on the gap between what is and what might be in this field be taken as a reason for students not to participate enthusiastically in the programs that do exist. A student's legal education seems seriously incomplete without careful reflection on the tasks and roles of lawyering, the actual working of legal institutions, and the impact of both on people's, particularly poor people's, lives. Clinical courses and experiences are among the few avenues for such an inquiry in the current school curriculum.

In participating in such programs, however, it is still useful to keep in mind the pressures they are under and the context in which they function. There is no part of the present curriculum so dynamic, so open to change, and so responsive to student initiative, innovation, and interest. The student-teacher relationships they generate, their experimental focus, even their vulnerability, inevitably make clinical studies an enterprise that influences and is influenced by the students who engage in it. Course content, classroom interchanges and, student-teacher and student-student relationships are constantly shaped and reshaped by what students and teachers choose to identify as important and discussable. Both the pedagogy and content of the programs themselves, as well as the law work they do, can be a focus of inquiry in clinical work. It is this possibility—for reflection and participant-initiated change— which creates the uncertainty and radical potential of this newest of innovations in legal education.

NOTES

1. For a discussion of some of the variations that clinical studies can take, see, Report of the Association of American Law School—American Bar Association Committee on guidelines for Clinical Legal Education (1980). In general, these programs combine (1) supervised fieldwork (in which the student has some degree of responsibility for clients or for dealing with real-world legal problems); (2) simulation; (3) group meetings and classes; (4) readings; (5) writing; and (6) evaluation (including grading), in ways that reflect large differences between programs in the degree of commitment, financial and otherwise, of the schools themselves to clinical instruction. The extent of integration between class work and the practice experience, the subject-matter focus of the experience, the status and responsibilities of faculty, and supervisors, the level of involvement of clinical teaching personnel with the remainder of the curriculum all vary enormously.

2. See generally, Reports of the Council on Legal Education for Professional Responsibility (CLEPR) 1969–1979. Changes include new courses, new methods, new teaching roles, new subjects (particularly lawyering skills and tasks), new relationships between courses and between law schools and other institutions in their communities.

3. In contrast to clinical or apprenticeship requirements in other professions (e.g., medicine), a lawyer may be certified to practice law without ever having interviewed a client, negotiated a settlement, drafted a legal document, examined a witness, written and/or argued a motion. Indeed, there is, in most instances, no requirement that the student even have discussed or read about these tasks and what they involve. Bar exams simply test the ability to apply legal knowledge analytically to hypothetical fact situations in a variety of fields.

4. See, Lortie, "From Laymen to Lawmen: Law School Careers and Professional Socialization," 29 *Harvard Educational Review* 352 (1959).

5. The enthusiasm with which leading members of the Bar embraced the model of education pioneered by Christopher Columbus Langdell at Harvard in the late nineteenth century seems to have been directly related to concern for the "ease of access" of immigrant groups into the profession, and a quite explicit desire to press a view of existing legal rules (and the status quo they supported) as products of influences relatively independent of political pressures and processes. The idea that law was a "science" to be studied and taught, like other sciences, in a university setting clearly fits these concerns. See, generally, Jerald S. Auerbach, *Unequal Justice* (New York: Oxford University Press, 1976); for an early challenge, see J. Frank, "Why Not a Clinical Lawyer-School," 81 *University of Pennsylvania Law Review*. 907 (1933).

303

6. For example, what is a client to say when his or her lawyer says: "Look, that's the best way to do it under the circumstances," or "I would not do that. It never works and it makes the judge angry"? The predictions and choices in lawyer work are notoriously hard to evaluate.

7. Indeed, current modes of instruction may exacerbate the profession's insensitivity to the moral and social consequences of lawyer behavior. Consider for example, the impact on a young law student's sense of personal responsibility for his/her actions of sitting through week after week of discussions of cases in which primary emphasis is on making arguments rather than on the justice and consequences of the results involved.

8. See, generally, Barnhizer, "The Clinical Method of Legal Instruction: Its Theory and Implementation," 30 *Journal of Legal Education* 67 (1979); Menkel-Meadow, "The Legacy of Clinical Education: Theories About Lawyering," 29 *Cleveland State Law Review* 555 (1980); Meltsner and Schrag, "Report from a CLEPR Colony," 76 *Columbia Law Review* 581 (1976).

9. The question-and-answer (Socratic) method used so extensively in the first year of law school shares this assumption. The dialogue in class is designed to illuminate and enlarge the case-reading experience done by the student in preparation for the class. Clinical pedagogy differs from first-year teaching primarily by its emphasis on a much broader range of out-of-class tasks and roles, and its concern that students' thinking about these experiences be explicit and self-conscious.

10. Although practices vary among schools, in general, most faculty members teach classes in their area of expertise, minimally coordinate their coverage and approach with their colleagues, and have a good deal of discretionary time for their own interests and scholarly pursuits. Teaching obligations rarely extend beyond nine months a year. Unless clinical faculty is simply added on (a fairly costly proposition), responsibility for linking law study and practice, even in one's field of expertise, would substantially alter these work arrangements, particularly if actual supervision of cases were involved.

11. See, generally, Gee and Jackson, "Bridging the Gap: Legal Education and Lawyer Competency," *Brigham Young University Law Review* 695 (1977); E. Kitch, "Clinical Education and the Law School of the Future" (University of Chicago Law School, Chicago, 1970).

12. Only a few law schools in the country received substantial federal funding for clinical programs. However, many programs placed students with local legal services programs as part of the fieldwork of their clinical courses. The pressures of reduced federal funding on legal services programs since 1980 have drastically limited their continued ability to participate in such programs.

13. The primary issue that is being debated involves the criteria to be applied to evaluate clinical teachers for promotion and tenure. Unfortunately this occurs at a time of general loss of confidence among law teachers about the quality and character of scholarship that should guide tenure decisions, and particular confusion about the sort of scholarly output that is appropriate to clinical work.

CHAPTER 20

Legal Philosophy

Anita L. Allen
GEORGETOWN UNIVERSITY

Legal philosophy plays a vital role in the intellectual life of American law schools. Roscoe Pound's account of why philosophical thinking about law thrives as a scholarly activity and a topic in the classroom seemed to get it right. Legal philosophy persists because of a perceived, paramount interest in rationalizing social change and freedom from oppressive authority.[1]

Typical law schools offer optional courses and seminars in legal philosophy. A few make philosophy instruction part of the required first-year curriculum. It is no secret that constitutional law courses routinely highlight philosophical perspectives on good government and the federal judiciary. But entering students should anticipate exposure to pertinent developments in legal thought in all of their courses—from the *A* of Administrative Procedure to the *Z* of Zoning and Land Use Planning.

General Theories of Law

Three general theories once dominated the discussion of legal philosophy in the United States: natural law, positivism, and realism. These theories, briefly introduced in the pages following, are divergent accounts of the nature of law, legal obligation, and legal justice. They also represent divergent accounts of legal reasoning and adjudication. Although the original versions of the theories have mainly historical value, they are more than relics.

Natural law and positivism survive as major sources of inspiration for contemporary legal theory. Ronald Dworkin, America's best-known legal philosopher, owes a subtle but distinct debt to natural law. The British philosopher John Finnis is noteworthy for a legal theory closely modeled after ancient natural law. Because of the implicit role it plays in Supreme Court decision making, positivism holds special interest as a legal theory. H. L. A. Hart's classic defense of positivism continues to attract critical interest.

The heirs of realism loom large in discussions of legal philosophy in contemporary law schools. In the 1960s, decades after it first emerged as a distinct trend in American thought, legal realism spawned the law and economics movement and critical legal studies. By the 1980s, realism was the distant progenitor of another pair of distinct approaches to understanding law: feminist jurisprudence and critical race theory.

Topical Approaches

Legal philosophy courses offered in law schools often focus on the aforementioned general theories of law. However, instructors sometimes choose to devote their courses to the philosophical analysis of particular law-related topics. For example, legal philosophy courses sometimes have the goal of identifying the philosophical assumptions of the common law.[2] In the area of criminal law, courses assess the moral rationale for prohibition and punishment.[3] Respecting property and tort, courses examine the theories of tort liability and property rights.[4] Courses on the theory of contracts consider whether substantive contract law is held together by a unifying principle, such as the principle of promissory obligation or the proscription against unjust enrichment.[5]

Philosophy of law courses commonly center on the concept of justice. John Rawls's revival of social contract theory remains of interest to law teachers and students, even as feminist and other radical conceptions of justice take hold.[6] Concepts standing for political values—including liberty, equality, neutrality, due process, and fundamental rights—have been the focus of legal philosophy courses. The concepts of privacy and community have earned courses, and so, too, the "isms" critical to an understanding of American law—liberalism, republicanism, federalism, majoritarianism, and racism.

The relationship between law and morality is a centuries-old query. Legal philosophy courses may delve into the relative merits of teleological (consequence-based), deontological (duty-based) and aretaic (virtue-based) ethical perspectives. Courses also consider the plausibility of objectivist theories of moral value. Epistemology, metaphysics, and the philosophy of language occasionally appear in legal philosophy courses to illuminate questions of knowledge, evidence, personhood, and meaning. Finally, legal philosophy courses tackle controversial public-policy concerns. Because the moral stakes are high, abortion, the death penalty, victimless crimes, and preferential treatment are favorite topics.

Finding the Right Course

Law professors have a great deal of flexibility in what they can teach and may vary the content of their legal philosophy courses from one year to the next. To avoid surprise it is always a good idea to find out in advance precisely what a given course or seminar will cover.

Instruction in legal philosophy is also offered under the rubrics of legal theory and jurisprudence. In fact, law schools and textbook writers routinely employ *jurisprudence* (derived from *jurisprudentia*, Latin for the science or knowledge of law) as a synonym for legal philosophy. This usage dates back to the nineteenth century, when theorists often viewed the law as a self-contained system of rules amenable to principled, systematic, and, in that sense, philosophic explication. Now that the view of the law as a formal system has faded, *jurisprudence* is used, along with *legal philosophy* and *legal theory*, to denote philosophic analysis of the conceptual and normative foundations of the law.

However, a word of caution is in order. Courses bearing the jurisprudence label do not always have legal philosophy as their subject matter. *Jurisprudence* has at least three other current uses. First, the term is used to denote substantive areas of the law viewed as a whole, as in the expression *constitutional jurisprudence,* or *first-amendment jurisprudence.* Second, judges are often said to practice jurisprudence when they determine and apply legal rules or principles to concrete cases. And third, a few textbooks use *jurisprudence* as a convenient heading for all courses relating to the foundations of law.[7] Legal history, anthropology, and sociology are sometimes labeled jurisprudence, as are comparative law and systematic studies of legal process, reasoning, and rhetoric. The best way to be sure that the jurisprudence course you are interested in taking is a course in legal philosophy is to consult the instructor ahead of time.

Natural Law

Natural law is the oldest major legal philosophy. Its roots extend deep into classical Greek thought. A basic tenet of natural law theory is that nature, God, or reason sets the standard for human conduct and the law.[8] Natural law theories provide that a community may judge the justice or injustice of its laws by appeal to recognizably objective standards.

While natural law theories predate the birth of Christ, they have special ties to Christianity. Indeed, it was St. Augustine, a fourth-century North African Neo-Platonist, who provided natural law with its famous slogan that "an unjust law is no law at all." According to St. Augustine, the justice of a law is measured against the premier rule of reason, the law of nature; consequently, human law that transgresses the law of nature is not law but a perversion of law.

The foremost exponent of the natural law doctrine was St. Thomas Aquinas, another Christian philosopher. In his heavily Aristotelian *Summa Theologicae,* this thirteenth-century Dominican defined law as "an ordinance of reason for the common good, promulgated by him who has the care of the community."⁹ Aquinas held that natural law consists of self-evident principles signifying to persons of wisdom and rationality what is good and what is evil. The basic precept of natural law is that "good is to be done and promoted, evil is to be avoided." Reason, characterized as the imprint of divine light, selects as good things rational humans naturally seek. Food, security, knowledge, and propagation are chief among human goods. Aquinas maintained that every rational being has a built-in capacity for practical reasoning whereby good conduct can be distinguished from evil.

According to Aquinas, some human laws are derived directly from the principles of natural law, such as statutes criminalizing murder. Others, of which local ordinances prescribing fines for parking violations are good modern examples, are merely consistent with natural law. Although Aquinas held that natural law has objective validity for all human beings, he believed that the "common principles of natural law cannot be applied to all men in the same way because of the great variety of human affairs." Human law is variable, and natural law itself is capable of change "since many things for the benefit of human life have been added over and above the natural law, both by the divine law and by human laws."

Traces of the Thomistic natural law perspective were still evident in the writings of the early modern philosophers Thomas Hobbes and John Locke. By the beginning of the nineteenth century, natural law had lost ground to positivism. Yet the rationalist enterprise of natural law was not, and has not been, entirely abandoned. The Thomistic stamp on one recent legal theorist is unmistakable.¹⁰

John Finnis argued that the principles of natural law require that authority be exercised in accordance with the rule of law and with due respect for human rights. He posited basic practical principles that indicate the basic forms of human flourishing as goods to be pursued and realized. He posited methodological requirements of practical reasonableness to distinguish sound from unsound practical thinking. From there he derived a set of general moral standards applicable to political action, judicial decision making, and the lives of ordinary citizens. Finnis's moral standards purportedly justify government authority and ground a strong conception of individual rights. According to Finnis, human rights embody the requirements of justice, and their protection is a component of the common good. The modern language of rights, Finnis said, is a "supple and potentially precise instrument for sorting out and expressing the demands of justice."

By grounding the existence of rights in the rational requirements of human good, natural rights theories offer an answer to the puzzling question, Where do rights come from? Natural law theories buttress the powerful intuition that individuals in discriminatory nations such as Nazi Germany and South Africa have legal rights whether authorities recognize them or not. Defenders praise natural law theories for making reasonableness in the law a moral constraint that justifies procedural fairness and due process. Theories of natural law suggest an account of the sense in which reasonable judges deciding controversial cases not clearly governed by a rule can decide them justly.

Nonetheless, natural law theories have drawn harsh, even dismissive, criticism. A common complaint is that they commit the elementary blunder of conflating the concepts of law and morals. Secular critics ridicule theistic versions of natural law as infantile, abrogating human responsibility to a celestial parent. Empiricists reject secular versions of natural law on the grounds that it is unscientific or implausible moral realism. Recent critics have argued that natural law theories inevitably treat liberal market values and male hegemony as fixed verities. Ronald Dworkin and other recent critics argue that natural law ignores the rich institutional and political character of law. The law is not simply a matter of natural principles and their logical entailments.

In a series of important books, Ronald Dworkin has drawn attention to the adjudication of "hard" cases to illustrate his thesis that one party may have a right to win a lawsuit even when no settled rule disposes of the case. Dworkin's thesis has led some commentators to describe him as a proponent of a natural law theory. Dworkin rejects that description and in *Law's Empire* characterizes his legal theory as "law as integrity."[11] Law as integrity "holds that people have as legal rights whatever rights are sponsored by the principles that provide the best justification of legal practice as a whole." To reach the best justification, judges must interpret not only particular rules of law and precedent but the law as a whole. To the extent possible, Dworkin's ideal judge assumes that the law is a coherent set of principles about justice, fairness, and procedural due process.

One common thread running between natural law and law as integrity is the claim that determining legal rights is an exercise of rational moral judgment. Furthermore, both give a central role in the theory of justice to individual rights grounded on principle. Yet Dworkin's attempts to distance himself from natural law theory may be more significant in the final analysis than the tenuous similarities between his theory and natural law. Dworkin broke new ground when he sought to discredit the semantic understanding of law embraced by traditional natural lawyers, positivists, and realists, all of whom assume that what the law is can be pinned down without interpretation. Dworkin's emphasis on the importance of positive rules and other past political acts as interpretative constraints disables any straightforward equation of his theory with natural law.

Positivism

The British utilitarian John Austin is credited as the first full-fledged legal positivist. In *Lectures on Jurisprudence* he elaborated the "command theory" of law first suggested by the writings of Thomas Hobbes. Austin's lectures had two goals. The first was to define the scope of jurisprudence as a field of inquiry. The second, related goal was to provide a theory of positive law. Positive law, Austin said, is the law which exists "by position" as a social fact open to empirical investigation. As such, positive law may be just or unjust. While Austin did not deny the existence of a moral standard emanating from God, he argued that human knowledge of the metaphysical is too imperfect to be of concern to a scientific jurisprudence.

Published in 1651, Hobbes's *Leviathan* characterized the law as rules commanded by a commonwealth, establishing civil rights and wrongs. Austin's nineteenth-century version of the command theory conceived of laws as rules of a special type. Laws are the general commands of a sovereign, backed by force and obligating obedience. Austin gave the concept of legal obligation a psychological tilt. Subjects are obliged by their own fear of sanction to obey their sovereign's commands. The form and the content of Austin's theory have had a major impact on European and American legal philosophy. John Chipman Gray and Hans Kelsen are two of the notable twentieth-century theorists Austin influenced. Kelsen similarly stressed the coercive character of law and its purity as a system of positive norms distinct from morality.[12]

The most distinguished twentieth-century positivist to date is British philosopher H. L. A. Hart, author of *The Concept of Law*. Rejecting Austin's analysis of rules as general commands of a sovereign, Hart defined law as the union of primary and secondary rules. Primary rules of obligation require that individuals perform some actions and not others. Secondary rules of recognition, adjudication, and change extend rule-related powers. As Hart described them, secondary rules are rules about rules. They permit public or private parties to introduce new primary rules and to rescind or amend existing rules. The acceptance by a community of an "ultimate" rule of recognition gives law its obligatory force. Normally, courts decide cases in accordance with rules accepted by the community. But faced with a difficult case and a gap in the law or an ambiguous rule, secondary rules permit judges to balance interests and establish new law.

For Hart, legal rights are the mirror images of legal obligations established through primary and secondary rules. Rights-claimants are entitled to prevail if, pursuant to rules of law, they are designated beneficiaries of correlative legal obligations. In practical terms, contested legal rights are what judges ostensibly acting in accordance with rules say they are.

In Hart's hands, positivism offered the theoretical community a sophisticated, explanatory alternative to the scholastic vagaries of natural law. But even Hart's version of positivism has problems. Hart's theory has been criticized for failing to explain what makes a system of rules valid as law. Critics say that the mere fact that people accept rules or obey general commands out of fear does not make them valid as law. The rules of chess are not law. Muggers who exact compliance are not on equal legal footing with the Internal Revenue Service. Although law is not an arbitrary system of requirements accepted like the demands of a mugger or the rules of a board game, positivism cannot explain why.

Despite these criticisms, positivism nevertheless remains a popular theory. The idea that law is a system of rules is intuitively appealing for its seeming simplicity and consistency with the liberal democratic ideal of the rule of law. The natural lawyer's concept of law as the ordinance of reason lacks a comparable aura of simplicity. Parents expect even small children to ascertain the existence and application of rules. The rules of the regulatory state are admittedly complex, but the public's analogous expectation is that learned judges will find and uphold the law. Another dimension of positivism's popular appeal is that it purports to be a descriptive theory grounded in fact. Positivists acknowledge that the content of morality and law often overlap but insist that moral values do not limit—and therefore cloud the determination of—what counts as valid law.

One of positivism's apparent virtues may also be its core vice. It is simple, but too simple, according to its critics. Natural lawyers say the law is more complex than positivism would have us believe. It includes background principles of human rights and justice that limit the validity of positive rules. Denying this dimension of law entails that even Hitler's heinous laws were valid as laws. Dworkin's critique of positivism is that it misunderstands and understates the organic relationship between moral theory and legal interpretation. Dworkin argues that positivism cannot explain from an internal perspective the process of adjudication in hard cases. According to Dworkin, judges are not compelled to make up new rules when faced with cases not governed by existing rules, as the positivists say. They can and do formulate arguments of principle based on their interpretative understandings of the multifaceted requirements of their role. Legal realists also object to positivism but on the ground that it wrongly implies that legal reasoning is a logical, rule-governed process when in fact external social and political factors truly explain the law.

Realism

Legal realism was a major force in the United States in the 1920s and '30s. Realists subscribed to Oliver Wendell Holmes's famous dictum that "The life of the law has not been logic: it has been experience." Rather than as a search for workable solutions to the problems of the real world, legal reasoning in Holmes's day was often depicted as the scientific application of deductive and inductive methods to novel facts. Nineteenth-century formalists theorized that judges deduce the right outcomes for the cases brought before them from rules of positive (or natural) law; where rules are in doubt, judges induce covering norms from the evidence of past judicial decisions. To a great extent the nineteenth-century model presupposed logical consistency and denied the law's instrumental character. Reacting to this mechanical model of jurisprudence, Holmes suggested that the predictions of the conduct of the "bad man" are a better guide to the content of the law than the syllogisms of the philosopher.

In an article published in 1931 in the *Harvard Law Review,* Karl Llewellyn characterized realism as a technology rather than a philosophy. The technology of realism treats law as an instrument, as a means to an end rather than an end in itself. A society must therefore evaluate its laws on the basis of how well they serve worthy ends.

What ends are worthy? Llewellyn believed the realist programmatic included no "program in the normative aspect" by which to evaluate the effects of law. Yet Llewellyn himself noted the tendency of realist thought to approach most legal problems as opportunities to further a policy of risk allocation and reduction. Realism's pragmatic instrumentalism implicitly evoked the utilitarian norms of promoting human welfare and maximizing resources. It is no accident that the pervasiveness of economic cost-benefit analysis and "interest balancing" as techniques of resolving legal controversies has been attributed to the influence of legal realism. While the concept of interest balancing is opaque, the mandate to balance interests can be understood as the requirement that the preferences of all parties to a controversy be treated as equal, victory going to litigants discovered to represent the weightier set of

interests. Reliance upon economic cost-benefit analysis and interest balancing would appear to presuppose that the aim of maximizing human wealth or satisfaction is an aim worthy of the law.

Effective use of law as an instrument requires a detailed knowledge of how human individuals, groups, and institutions behave.
The realists emphasized the importance of empirical studies in the
fields of sociology, psychology, economics, and history. Because
societies change, the realists expected that the kinds of laws required by societies would change. Hence realism entailed skeptical
distrust of traditional legal rules and categories as the solutions to
problems of bygone ages.

The realists rejected natural law as lacking an empirical foundation. As for positivism, the realists found its empiricism congenial
but condemned its exclusive focus on the analysis of rules. Attacks
on the realist strands in contemporary law have come from positivist critics fearful of the antimajoritarian implications of aggres-
sively instrumental policy analysis by unelected judges. Attacks on
realism have also flowed from committed rights theorists, who
understand that realism regards rights enshrined in the common
law and the liberal philosophy of the Enlightenment as mere
interests to be balanced against others.

Law and Economics

The economic analysis of law was an important facet of the realist
turn in American legal thought. However, it took Ronald Coase
and Guido Calabresi to spark the law and economics movement.
In 1960, Coase published an article challenging the influential
theory of leading twentieth-century economist A. C. Pigou.[13] According to Pigou, economic efficiency requires rules of liability
creating rational incentives for commercial producers to internalize
the social costs (externalities) of their enterprises. Coase questioned the necessity of regulation to achieve an efficient market,
arguing that in the absence of transaction costs, efficiency will be
achieved through private bargaining without regard to liabilities
imposed by legal rules.

The economic analysis of law has not been altogether limited to microeconomics or the imaginary world of zero-transaction costs and perfectly rational utility maximizers. Today economic analysts address all areas of the law, adding realistic assumptions where possible and applying public-choice theory and game-theoretic concepts. Economic analysts have undertaken both descriptive and normative theories of law. Descriptive theories maintain that the workings of the law can be understood as an implicit effort to regulate human conduct in accordance with a principle of efficiency. Normative theories maintain that law ought to be instrumental, and take the efficient regulation of human conduct as its goal.

Among the best-known economic theories of law is the comprehensive theory of Richard Posner, a prolific scholar appointed to the United States Court of Appeals by former President Reagan. Judge Posner defines as efficient a social outcome that maximizes human satisfaction, measured by aggregate consumer willingness to pay for goods and services. His central descriptive argument is that much of the common law can be viewed as a set of principles, adherence to which over the long run tends toward economic efficiency. His central normative claim is that courts do, and should, seek further efficiency.

Judge Posner defends the goal of wealth maximization as an overarching moral goal for a society dedicated to the protection of "natural liberty." In fact, he defends his morality of wealth maximization as superior to leading philosophical moralities premised on Kantian principles of respect for persons and utilitarian principles of promoting happiness. Thus Judge Posner's negative criticisms of developments in constitutional, procedural, and regulatory law typically have a double point: Such law is inefficient and unjust.

Thanks to the contributions of Guido Calabresi, tort law has been one of the areas of the common law on which the economic analysis has often focussed.[14] The rules of tort law reallocate wealth, shifting the financial burden of physical or emotional injury from victims to wrongdoers. In *The Cost of Accidents,* Calabresi argued that the reallocative effect of tort law is justified, where justified, by the priority of the goal of reducing the economic and other social costs of accidents. His guiding premise was that the purpose of liability in tort law should be to reduce the costs of accidents.

While specific deterrence, that is, prohibiting risky activities, is an effective means of eliminating the costs of accidents, Calabresi argued that general deterrence, imposing liabilities when risky activities result in injury, is preferable. Calabresi reasoned that general deterrence respects free choice and individual preferences. It allows conduct on the condition that persons are willing and able fully to pay for its adverse consequences. Calabresi proposed to reduce accident costs through general deterrence by imposing liability on the "cheapest cost avoider"; avoiding the externalization of costs; and allocating costs to the "best briber"—the person who can enter into potentially cost-saving transactions most cheaply. In determining who is the cheapest cost avoider and best briber, Calabresi recommended that policymakers take into account differential transaction costs and the administrative costs of alternative reallocations of liability.

Some economic analysts do not claim that wealth maximization should be the goal of the law, and indeed shy away from normative analysis. They make the more modest claim that economic analysis potentially illuminates the interworking of the law and provides information to policymakers interested in the economic impact of competing policy options. Still, law and economics has been rejected on the grounds that it presupposes that wealth is a value, and that law is an infinitely flexible instrument in the service of wealth. For example, Ronald Dworkin has argued that wealth is not a value, as Judge Posner assumes, and that the economic principle of wealth maximization is not the basis of the best interpretation of Anglo-American legal traditions.

Law and economics has also been criticized as a thinly veiled utilitarian theory that is inconsistent with a vigorous theory of individual rights. Critics have charged that law and economics presupposes the impossible and obnoxious ideal of the perfectly rational, self-interested consumer. Against its claims of objectivity and neutrality, critics say the modes of policy analysis the movement presupposes are steeped in conservative political bias. Because economic analysis does not force its practitioners to question the justice of initial distributions of resources and because, as the saying goes, "It takes money to make money," law and economics has been criticized as systematically favoring certain groups. Notwithstanding Judge Posner's proposals for an experimental free market in white babies, critics say that certain human relationships are not amenable to analysis as market transactions.

Critical Legal Studies

Like law and economics, critical legal studies (CLS) is often referred to as a "movement." The spirit of the movement is embodied in its unofficial motto that "Law is politics." While some participants view CLS as an intellectually appealing set of philosophical tenets, others view it principally as a pragmatic framework for radical political reform. Indeed, students may first encounter CLS as a political force within their law schools' faculties for reshaping legal education and practice.

A direct outgrowth of legal realism, CLS is much more than a realist revival. From its earliest manifestation in the late 1960s and '70s, CLS has stressed the respects in which material and ideological realities shape the law and the potential of law as an instrument of change. Roberto Unger's eloquent *Knowledge and Politics* emphasized the possibility of change despite the false sense of necessity that pervades social life.[15] That legal values are products of human agency rather than metaphysical necessity is now an axiom of CLS.

Influenced by the seminal writings of Duncan Kennedy in the 1970s, CLS adherents describe legal rules as "indeterminate."[16] According to the indeterminacy thesis, legal rules seldom (if ever) dictate outcomes in particular cases. When judges purport to be applying rules of law with neutrality and objectivity to the facts before them, they are actually rationalizing mainstream cultural preferences. Proponents of CLS assert that the central substantive doctrines of the Anglo-American common law are "incoherent" and "self-contradictory."[17] Critical legal scholars employ a technique they call "deconstruction" to reveal irreconcilable assumptions and illogic in the law. Deconstruction is also employed to show that deciding cases in courts of law is a process of "legitimation" rather than logic. Lacking indefeasible foundations, mainstream law nonetheless presents itself as legitimating existing social conditions, the presumed rational path to liberal freedom.

The CLS critique of liberalism and individual rights are important aspects of the movement. Some CLS adherents describe themselves as political radicals, progressives, or Marxists. They associate liberalism, whether "left" or "conservative" or "libertarian," with traditional social hierarchies of class, race, and gender. Toward explaining liberalism's powerful grip as the dominant ideology, CLS has sought to deconstruct the concept and fix its origins in a distant era. CLS rejects liberal philosophies, in keeping with its rejection of all claims that nature, God, or reason establishes a set of knowable norms that stand or ought to stand as guideposts for just law. It rejects claims of justice and rights based on rational or immutable principles of conduct.

CLS thus represents the charge that by virtue of the indeterminacy of legal rules, and the incoherence and self-contradiction inherent in traditional law and theory, only culture and politics are left to explain legal phenomena. To back these difficult claims, proponents of CLS have relied upon continental philosophy and social theory, in addition to close exegesis of legal texts. Ironically Michel Foucault and Jacques Derrida, two exceedingly difficult philosophers, appear to have had a major role in the CLS effort to "demystify" the law. Opponents sometimes accuse CLS of elitism and self-serving or confused reliance upon ideas buried in European philosophy and social theory. Because he views the goal of legal philosophy as providing the best interpretation of legal institutions and practices, Ronald Dworkin is puzzled by the CLS posture of standing skeptically outside of the law and showing it in its worst light, as incoherent; rather than its best light, as principled.

The loss of faith in the ability to justify human action and institutions, at all or by appeal to norms of general application, has led to the characterization of CLS as nihilistic. But proponents of CLS do not typically view their claim that the legal system lacks its putative justificatory basis as a cause for despair. Some argue that deconstruction facilitates efforts by the committed to restructure society through the reinterpretation of the substance and purpose of law. And according to Joseph Singer, once it is understood that shared values and cultures rather than fixed norms hold society together, we may come to appreciate common ties and the creative potential for shaping alternative social arrangements.[18]

Feminism and Race Theory

The civil rights and women's movements of the 1960s helped to establish principles of equal employment opportunity. White women and people of color began to enter law teaching in significant numbers in the 1970s and '80s. The scholarship of these nontraditional law teachers has often focused on theoretical aspects of a long list of issues of special importance to historically subordinate groups: employment, education, affirmative action, voting rights, housing, capital punishment, emigration, reparations, reproductive rights, domestic violence, and pornography. Traditional scholars have addressed these issues as well, but typically without close analysis of the respects in which legal theory and practice center on the perspectives and interests of white males to the detriment of others.

Feminist scholars, most of whom are women, have brought fresh perspectives to legal theory. Minority race scholars representing African-American, Hispanic, Native American, and Asian-American cultures have also introduced new visions of the law. United by a commitment to egalitarian justice, these scholars reject legal institutions and practices that serve the interests of dominant groups at the expense of women of all races, men of color, and the poor. The egalitarian conceptions of justice advanced by feminist jurisprudes and critical race scholars depart dramatically from the liberal norm. Feminists have argued that the care-oriented values of women reflect alternative conceptions of egalitarian justice. Mari Matsuda has proposed that John Rawls's "veil of ignorance" approach to understanding the requirements of justice—built around hypothetical deliberations of self-interested, rational persons deprived of self-identifying information—be replaced by a "bottoms-up" perspective that treats the actual narrative experiences of the least advantaged members of our society as the sources of principles of justice.

To problems of race and gender, feminists and race scholars have applied insights drawn from leftist political theory, continental philosophy, and literature, in combination with legal realism and CLS. For example, Catherine A. MacKinnon relied upon structural analogies to Marxism in her critiques of the law's treatment of women and sexuality. Kimberle Crenshaw relied upon leftist theory and CLS when she attacked liberals and those within the CLS camp who fail to recognize a continuing role for legal rights in the political struggles of historically excluded peoples.[19]

Feminists and race theorists add new dimensions to conventional scholarly formats. Personal narratives in law journal articles are testing the assumption that only impersonal abstractions illuminate legal phenomena. The early realists sought to contextualize law through social science. Minority scholars, including Mari Matsuda, Richard Delgado, Patricia Williams, and Derrick Bell, today seek to contextualize the law through their own experiences and imagination. Bell's fiction is an arresting vehicle for messages about the real-world practice of sacrificing black interests to further the welfare, security, and status of whites.[20]

Personalization, voice, and context are major themes in the work of feminist theorists. In this connection, the developmental research of Carol Gilligan and like-minded psychologists has been remarkably influential. Gilligan's *In a Different Voice* presented evidence that women typically experience themselves as connected to others, embedded in a social context of responsibility. Women incline toward an ethic of care and communitarian conceptions of justice. By contrast, men experience themselves as separate and autonomous. They incline toward an ethic of rights and individualistic conceptions of justice.

In her legal theory Robin West makes a sweeping claim for female difference.[21] West alleges that both liberal theory and critical legal studies are grounded in a conception of separate, autonomous personhood, which implies the nonhumanity of women. Women, posits West, are not in fact separate but are linked to others through menstruation, pregnancy, breast feeding, and heterosexual intercourse. Of course, not all feminists agree with West that women are essentially different by virtue of these experiences.

Even some feminists who agree that women are different along the lines West and Gilligan suggest do not agree that laws should be premised on such differences. According to "sameness" feminists, equality requires laws that treat men and women alike. They caution that efforts to take differences into account in the past subjected women to detrimental legal paternalism. "Difference" feminists argue that equality requires laws that sometimes treat men and women differently, to take cultural and biological differences fully into account. Opposing "sameness" and "difference" perspectives on equality have already been a factor in debates over employee pregnancy leaves and paternal child custody.[22]

Carol Gilligan's influence can be seen in the arguments of numerous feminist lawyers that legal doctrine and practice ought to incorporate "female" conceptions of justice, styles of lawyering, and models of adjudication. For example, Leslie Bender has argued that a "male" conception of justice explains the longevity of the "reasonable man" standard within tort law and the failure of the common law to incorporate a Good Samaritan rule.[23] Judith Resnik has questioned whether judicial acumen stems from rationality and impartiality, rather than an appreciation of facts and circumstances viewed through the empathetic eyes of experience.[24] Finally, reflecting on constitutional law, Martha Minow has argued that courts must learn to recognize the limitations of their own viewpoints. Only then can they increase their potential to talk across differences of race, gender, and culture.[25]

RECOMMENDED READINGS

I. General Textbooks

Christie, George C., *Jurisprudence: Text and Readings on the Philosophy of Law* (St. Paul, Minn.: West Publishing, 1973).

Golding, M.P., ed., *The Nature of Law* (New York: Random House, 1966).

Murphy, Jeffrie and Jules Coleman, *The Philosophy of Law: An Introduction to Jurisprudence* (Totowa, New Jersey: Rowman and Allanheld 1984).

Schuchman, Philip, *Readings in Jurisprudence and Legal Philosophy* (Boston: Little, Brown and Company, 1979).

Sinha, Surya, *What Is Law?* (New York: Paragon House, 1989).

II. Natural Law and Legal Reasoning

Finnis, John, *Natural Law and Natural Rights* (Oxford: Clarendon Press, 1980).

Weinreb, Lloyd, *Natural Law and Justice* (Cambridge: Harvard University Press, 1987).

Dworkin, Ronald, *Law's Empire* (Cambridge: Harvard University Press, 1986).

Dworkin, Ronald, *Taking Rights Seriously* (Cambridge: Harvard University Press, 1977).

Greenawalt, *Conflicts of Law and Morality* (Oxford: Clarendon Press, 1987).

III. Positivism

Hart, H. L. A, *The Concept of Law* (London: Oxford University Press, 1961).

Raz, Joseph, *The Authority of Law: Essays on Law and Morality* (Oxford: Clarendon Press, 1979)

Soper, Philip, *A Theory of Law* (Harvard University Press, 1984).

IV. Realism

Cohen, Felix, "Transcendental Nonsense and the Functional Approach, 35 *Columbia Law Review* 1 (1935).

Holmes, Oliver Wendell, "The Path of the Law," 10 *Harvard Law Review* 61 (1897).

Grey, T., "Langdell's Orthodoxy," 45 *University of Pittsburgh Law Review* 1 (1983).

Llewellyn, Karl, "Some Realism About Realism—Responding to Dean Pound," 44 *Harvard Law Review* 1222 (1934).

V. Law and Economics

Calabresi, Guido, *The Cost of Accidents: A Legal and Economic Analysis* (New Haven: Yale University Press, 1970).

Kuperberg, Mark and Charles Beitz, ed., *Law, Economics and Philosophy* (Totowa, New Jersey: Rowman and Allanheld, 1983).

Polinsky, A. Mitchell, *An Introduction to Law and Economics* (Boston: Little, Brown and Company, 1983).

Posner, Richard, *The Economics of Justice* (Cambridge: Harvard University Press, 1961).

White, Barbara, "Coase and the Courts: Economics for the Common Man," 72 *Iowa Law Review* 577 (1987).

V. Critical Legal Studies

Gordon, Robert, "Unfreezing Legal Reality: Critical Approaches to Law," 15 *Florida State University Law Review* 1987.

Kairys, David, ed., *The Politics of Law: A Progressive Critique* (New York: Pantheon Books, 1982).

Kelman, Mark, *A Guide to Critical Legal Studies* (Cambridge: Harvard University Press, 1987).

VI. Feminist Jurisprudence

MacKinnon, "Feminism, Marxism, Method and the State: Toward Feminist Jurisprudence," 8 *Signs* 635 (1983).

Scales, Ann, "The Emergence of Feminist Jurisprudence: An Essay," 95 *Yale Law Journal* 1373 (1986).

"Women in Legal Education, Pedagogy, Law Theory and Practice," *Journal of Legal Education,* (March/June 1988).

West, Robin, "Jurisprudence and Gender," 55 *University of Chicago Law Review* 1 (1988).

VII. Critical Race Theory

Bell, Derrick, *Race, Racism and American Law,* 2d ed. (Boston: Little Brown, 1980).

Crenshaw, Kimberle, "Race, Reform and Retrenchment: Transformation and Legitimation in Antidiscrimination Law," 101 *Harvard Law Review* 1331 (1981).

Delgado, Richard, "The Imperial Scholar: Reflections on a Review of Civil Rights Literature," 132 *University of Pennsylvania Law Review* 561 (1984).

Matsuda, Mari, "Looking to the Bottom: Critical Legal Studies and Reparations," 22 *Harvard Civil Rights–Civil Liberties Law Review* 323 (1987).

"Minority Critiques of the Critical Legal Studies Movement," 22 *Harvard Civil Rights–Civil Liberties Law Review* 1 (1987)

Williams, Patricia, "Spirit Murdering the Messenger: the Discourse of Finger-Pointing as the Law's Response to Racism," 42 *University of Miami Law Review* 127 (1987).

NOTES

1. R. Pound, *Introduction to the Philosophy of Law* (New Haven: Yale University Press, 1922).

2. *Cf.* M. D. Bayles, *Principles of Law* (Boston: D. Reidel Publishing Company, 1987). Bayles attempts to schematize the norms implicit in the common law.

3. Joel Feinberg has published four studies of the moral foundations of the criminal law with Oxford University Press. They are *Harm to Others* (1984), *Harm to Self* (1986), *Offense to Others* (1985), *Harmless Wrongdoing* (1988).

4. *Cf.* A. White, *Grounds of Liability: An Introduction to the Philosophy of Law* (Oxford: Clarendon Press, 1985); R. Epstein, *Takings: Private Property and the Power of Eminent Domain* (Cambridge: Harvard University Press, 1985). These books treat philosophical questions relating to tort and property law, respectively.

5. *Cf.* P. S. Atiyah, *Promises, Morals and the Law* (Oxford: Clarendon Press, 1981). Atiyah argues that promissory obligation is not the moral or legal basis of contract law.

6. J. Rawls, *Theory of Justice* (Cambridge: Harvard University Press, 1971).

7. *See, e.g.,* P. Schuchman, *Readings in Jurisprudence and Legal Philosophy* (Boston: Little, Brown and Company, 1979).

8. L. Weinreb, *Natural Law and Justice* (Cambridge: Harvard University Press, 1987).

9. Excerpts from *Summa Theologicae* relating to the nature of law are reproduced in M. P. Golding, ed., *The Nature of Law* (New York: Random House, 1966) 9–24.

10. J. Finnis, *Natural Law and Natural Rights* (Oxford: Clarendon Press, 1980).

11. R. Dworkin, *Law's Empire* (Cambridge: Harvard University Press, 1986), 223–275.

12. H. Kelsen, *Pure Theory of Law* (Berkeley: University of California, 1967).

13. Coase, "The Problem of Social Cost," 3 *Journal of Law and Economics* 1 (1960).

14. G. Calabresi, *The Cost of Accidents: A Legal and Economic Analysis* (New Haven: Yale University Press, 1970).

15. R. Unger, *Knowledge and Politics* (New York: Free Press, 1975). While very difficult for the uninitiated, Unger's *The Critical Legal Studies Movement* is also well worth reading.

16. *See, e.g.,* Kennedy, "Form and Substance in Private Law Adjudication," 89 *Harvard Law Review* 1685 (1976).

17. *See, e.g.,* Kennedy, "The Structure of Blackstone's Commentaries," 28 *Buffalo Law Review* 205 (1979).

18. Singer, "The Player and the Cards: Nihilism and Legal Theory," 94 *Yale Law Journal* 1, 64–5 (1984).

19. Crenshaw, "Race, Reform and Retrenchment: Transformation and Legitimation in Antidiscrimination Law," 101 Harvard Law Review 1331 (1981).

20. For examples and a theoretical account of Bell's principle of sacrifice, see his *And We Are Not Saved: The Illusive Search for Racial Justice* (New York: Basic Books, 1987) and his treatise *Race, Racism and American Law,* 2d ed. (Boston: Little Brown, 1980) 7–8, 29–30.

21. West, "Jurisprudence and Gender," 55 *University of Chicago Law Review* 1 (1988).

22. Williams, "The Equality Crisis: Some Reflections on Culture, Courts and Feminism," 7 *Women's Rights Reporter* 175 (1982).

23. Bender, "A Lawyer's Primer on Feminist Theory and Tort," 38 *Journal of Legal Education* 3 (1988).

24. Resnik, "On the Bias: Feminist Reconsiderations of the Aspirations for Our Judges," 61 *Southern California Law Review* 1877 (1988).

25. Minow, "Foreword: Justice Engendered," 101 *Harvard Law Review* 1 (1987).

ABOUT THE CONTRIBUTORS

Anita L. Allen. Professor of Law, Georgetown University Law Center. Holds Ph.D. in philosophy in addition to law degree. Author of *Uneasy Access: Privacy for Women in a Free Society* (Rowman & Littlefield, 1988) and articles on varied constitutional and common-law topics.

Robert L. Bard. Professor, University of Connecticut Law School. Contributor (contracts) *American Bar Foundation Study of Teaching Materials in American Law Schools.*

Gary Bellow. Professor of Law, Harvard University; attorney and clinical instructor, Legal Services Institute, Jamaica Plain, Massachusetts. Author (with B. Moulton), *The Lawyering Process* (Foundation Press, 1978), and other books.

Paul Bender. Dean, College of Law, Arizona State University. Prior to becoming Dean at ASU in 1984, he taught constitutional law at University of Pennsylvania Law School. He is active in civil-rights litigation and a co-author of *Political and Civil Rights in the United States* (4th ed., Little, Brown, 1976, 1978).

Curtis J. Berger. Lawrence A. Wien Professor of Law, Columbia University. Author, *Land Ownership and Use* (3d ed., Little, Brown, 1982). Member, Advisory Committee, American Law Institute, Restatement, Third, Servitudes.

David L. Chambers, Professor of Law, University of Michigan Law School. Author in the fields of law and mental health and child support and child custody. President, Board of Governors, Society of American Law Teachers, 1977–79.

Bernard L. Diamond, M.D. Emeritus Professor of Law, University of California, Berkeley, and Clinical Professor of Psychiatry, University of California, San Francisco.

Norman Dorsen. Stokes Professor of Law, New York University School of Law. President, American Civil Liberties Union. First President of the Society of American Law Teachers, author and editor of several books, including *Political and Civil Rights in the United States* (Little, Brown, 1976), and *Our Endangered Rights* (Pantheon, 1984).

Robert L. Eblin. Second-year law student at Ohio State University College of Law; A.B. 1985, Harvard College. Mr. Eblin is treasurer of the National Lesbian and Gay Law Students Association, a trustee of the Ohio Human Rights Bar Association, chair of the OSU Gay and Lesbian Law Caucus, and a staff member of the *Ohio State Law Journal.*

Stephen Gillers. Professor of Law, New York University School of Law and a nationally recognized expert on legal ethics. Coauthor of *Regulation of Lawyers: Problems of Law and Ethics* (2nd ed. Little, Brown, 1989), a leading casebook in the area.

Carole E. Goldberg-Ambrose. Professor of Law, University of California at Los Angeles. Editor and coauthor, *Felix Cohen's Handbook of Federal Indian Law* (1982). Developer of courses in women and the law, rape law, and educational equity for women. Formerly Associate Dean of UCLA School of Law.

Robert A. Gorman. Kenneth W. Gemmill Professor of Law, University of Pennsylvania School of Law. Formerly Associate Dean responsible for curriculum reform. Former President, American Association of University Professors, and President-elect, Association of American Law Schools. Author of articles on legal education and books on labor law and copyright law.

Geoffrey C. Hazard, Jr. Sterling Professor of Law, Yale University. Director, American Law Institute. Reporter, American Bar Association Special Commission on Evaluation of Professional Standards. Author, *Ethics in the Practice of Law* (Yale University Press, 1978).

John R. Kramer. Dean, Tulane University School of Law. Chair from 1981–1986 of the Joint Task Force on Federal Financial Assistance for Law Students of the Association of American Law Schools, the American Bar Association Section of Legal Education, and the Law School Admissions Council.

Sylvia A. Law. Professor of Law and codirector of the Arthur Garfield Hays Program, New York University School of Law. Author, litigant, and teacher in the areas of health, welfare, equality, and reproductive freedom. In 1983 she was awarded the MacArthur Prize Fellowship.

Charles R. Lawrence III. Professor, Stanford University School of Law. Coauthor, *The Bakke Case: The Politics of Inequality* (Harcourt Brace Jovanovich, 1979). Member, Board of Governors, Society of American Law Teachers.

Jeffrey O'Connell. John Allan Love Professor of Law, University of Virginia. Coauthor of the principal work that proposed no-fault auto insurance.

Judith Resnik. Orrin B. Evans Professor of Law, University of Southern California Law Center. Author (with Robert Cover and Owen Fiss) of *Procedure* (Foundation Press, 1988). Chair, Section on Women in Legal Education, American Association of Law Schools; Member, Board of Governors, Society of American Law Teachers.

Rhonda R. Rivera. Professor of Law, The Ohio State University College of Law; B.A. 1959, Douglass College; M.P.A. 1960, Syracuse University; J.D. 1967, Wayne State University. President of the Ohio Human Rights Bar Association and adviser to the OSU Gay and Lesbian Law Caucus. She has written extensively on sexual orientation and AIDS law, including "Lawyers, Clients, and AIDS: Some Notes from the Trenches," 49 *Ohio St. Law Journal* 883 (1989).

Lloyd L. Weinreb. Professor of Law, Harvard Law School. Author, *Natural Law and Justice* (Harvard University Press, 1987), *Denial of Justice* (Free Press, 1977), *Criminal Process* (4th ed., Foundation Press, 1987), *Criminal Law* (4th ed., Foundation Press, 1986), *Leading Constitutional Cases on Criminal Justice* (annual ed., Foundation Press, 1989).

James Boyd White. Hart Wright Professor of Law, Professor of English, Adjunct Professor of Classical Studies, The University of Michigan. Author, *The Legal Imagination* (1973), *When Words Lose Their Meaning* (1984),

Heracles' Bow (1986), and *Justice as Translation* (1990). Coauthor (with Scarboro) *Constitutional Criminal Procedure* (1976).

Gerald Lee Wilson, Ph.D. Senior Associate Dean, Trinity College of Arts and Sciences, Duke University, and prelaw adviser for the past twenty years. Served as Chair of PLANC (Pre-Law Advisors National Council) from 1984–1989.